AF690605

Cybersecurity in Banking

Other related titles:

You may also like

- PBSE027 | Ullah | Explainable Artificial Intelligence (XAI) for Next Generation Cybersecurity | 2025
- PBSE022 | Merz | Phishing for Answers: Risk identification and mitigation strategies | 2024
- PBPC060 | Grima | Intelligent Multimedia Technologies for Financial Risk Management: Trends, tools and applications | 2023
- PBSE020 | Abd El-Latif | Artificial Intelligence for Biometrics and Cybersecurity: Technology and applications | 2023

We also publish a wide range of books on the following topics:
Computing and Networks
Control, Robotics and Sensors
Electrical Regulations
Electromagnetics and Radar
Energy Engineering
Healthcare Technologies
History and Management of Technology
IET Codes and Guidance
Materials, Circuits and Devices
Model Forms
Nanomaterials and Nanotechnologies
Optics, Photonics and Lasers
Production, Design and Manufacturing
Security
Telecommunications
Transportation

All books are available in print via https://shop.theiet.org or as eBooks via our Digital Library https://digital-library.theiet.org.

IET Security 280

Cybersecurity in Banking

Shriram K. Vasudevan, Sini Raj Pulari, T.S. Murugesh and Subashri Vasudevan

The Institution of Engineering and Technology

About the IET

This book is published by the Institution of Engineering and Technology (The IET).

We inspire, inform, and influence the global engineering community to engineer a better world. As a diverse home across engineering and technology, we share knowledge that helps make better sense of the world, accelerate innovation, and solve the global challenges that matter.

The IET is a not-for-profit organisation. The surplus we make from our books is used to support activities and products for the engineering community and promote the positive role of science, engineering and technology in the world. This includes education resources and outreach, scholarships and awards, events and courses, publications, professional development and mentoring, and advocacy to governments.

To discover more about the IET, please visit https://www.theiet.org/.

About IET books

The IET publishes books across many engineering and technology disciplines. Our authors and editors offer fresh perspectives from universities and industry. Within our subject areas, we have several book series steered by editorial boards made up of leading subject experts.

We peer review each book at the proposal stage to ensure the quality and relevance of our publications.

Get involved

If you are interested in becoming an author, editor, series advisor, or peer reviewer, please visit https://www.theiet.org/publishing/publishing-with-iet-books/ or contact author_support@theiet.org.

Discovering our electronic content

All of our books are available online via the IET's Digital Library. Our Digital Library is the home of technical documents, eBooks, conference publications, real-life case studies and journal articles. To find out more, please visit https://digital-library.theiet.org.

In collaboration with the United Nations and the International Publishers Association, the IET is a Signatory member of the SDG Publishers Compact. The Compact aims to accelerate progress to achieve the Sustainable Development Goals (SDGs) by 2030. Signatories aspire to develop sustainable practices and act as champions of the SDGs during the Decade of Action (2020–30), publishing books and journals that will help inform, develop, and inspire action in that direction.

In line with our sustainable goals, our UK printing partner has FSC accreditation, which is reducing our environmental impact to the planet. We use a print-on-demand model to further reduce our carbon footprint.

The Institution of Engineering and Technology (the "**Publisher**") is registered as a Charity in England & Wales (no. 211014) and Scotland (no. SC038698).

Copyright © The Institution of Engineering and Technology and its licensors 2026

First published: 2025

All intellectual property rights (including copyright) in and to this publication are owned by the Publisher and/or its licensors. All such rights are hereby reserved by their owners and are protected under the Copyright, Designs and Patents Act 1988 ("**CDPA**"), the Berne Convention and the Universal Copyright Convention.

With the exception of:

(i) any use of the publication solely to the extent as permitted under:

  a. the CDPA (including fair dealing for the purposes of research, private study, criticism or review); or
  b. the terms of a licence granted by the Copyright Licensing Agency ("**CLA**") (only applicable where the publication is represented by the CLA); and/or

(ii) any use of those parts of the publication which are identified within this publication as being reproduced by the Publisher under a Creative Commons licence, Open Government Licence or other open source licence (if any) in accordance with the terms of such licence, no part of this publication, including any article, illustration, trade mark or other content whatsoever, may be used, reproduced, stored in a retrieval system, distributed or transmitted in any form or by any means (including electronically) without the prior permission in writing of the Publisher and/or its licensors (as applicable).

The commission of any unauthorised activity may give rise to civil or criminal liability. Please visit https://digital-library.theiet.org/copyrights-and-permissions for information regarding seeking permission to reuse material from this and/or other publications published by the Publisher. Enquiries relating to the use, including any distribution, of this publication (or any part thereof) should be sent to the Publisher at the address below:

The Institution of Engineering and Technology
Futures Place,
Kings Way, Stevenage,
Herts, SG1 2UA,
United Kingdom

www.theiet.org

Whilst the Publisher and/or its licensors believe that the information and guidance given in this publication is correct, an individual must rely upon their own skill and judgement when performing any action or omitting to perform any action as a result of any statement, opinion or view expressed in the publication and neither the Publisher nor its licensors assume and hereby expressly disclaim any and all liability to anyone for any loss or damage caused by any action or omission of an action made in reliance on the publication and/or any error or omission in the publication, whether or not such an error or omission is the result of negligence or any other cause. Without limiting or otherwise affecting the generality of this statement and the disclaimer, whilst all URLs cited in the publication are correct at the time of press, the Publisher has no responsibility for the persistence or accuracy of URLs for external or third-party internet websites and does not guarantee that any content on such websites is, or will remain, accurate or appropriate.

Whilst every reasonable effort has been undertaken by the Publisher and its licensors to acknowledge copyright on material reproduced, if there has been an oversight, please contact the Publisher and we will endeavour to correct this upon a reprint.

Trade mark notice: Product or corporate names referred to within this publication may be trade marks or registered trade marks and are used only for identification and explanation without intent to infringe.

Where an author and/or contributor is identified in this publication by name, such author and/or contributor asserts their moral right under the CDPA to be identified as the author and/or contributor of this work.

British Library Cataloguing in Publication Data
A catalogue record for this product is available from the British Library

ISBN 978-1-83724-092-0 (hardback)
ISBN 978-1-83724-093-7 (PDF)

Typeset in India by MPS Limited

Cover image credit: Cover image: gahsoon/E+ via Getty Images

Contents

About the authors

Shriram K. Vasudevan is a distinguished technology leader and educator with over 18 years of experience spanning industry and academia. He currently serves as Senior Manager – Industrial AI at Accenture, driving innovation at the intersection of AI, data, and digital transformation. Previously, Dr. Shriram was a Technology Leader at Intel Corporation, where he led initiatives in AI, Generative AI, and Embedded Systems, shaping developer ecosystems and advancing applied research across the Asia Pacific and Japan Region. Holding a Doctorate in Embedded Systems, his expertise and passion for innovation are evident in his prolific contributions – 54 authored books published by Taylor & Francis, Wiley, and Oxford University Press, 14 granted patents, and over 150 research publications. A Fellow of IEI and IETE and Senior Member of IEEE, he has received prestigious recognitions from Harvard University, Google, and several international governments for his outstanding work in technology and education. Beyond his research, Dr. Shriram is a passionate advocate of hands-on, experiential learning. As an Intel oneAPI Certified Instructor and hackathon enthusiast, he has inspired thousands of learners globally. His remarkable contributions to the technology ecosystem have earned him a place in the Limca Book of Records. A TEDx Speaker, ACM Distinguished Speaker, and Top AI Evangelist, Dr. Shriram continues to empower global audiences through his talks, research, and thought leadership. He also engages an ever-growing community of 52,000+ YouTube subscribers, sharing practical insights that bridge academia, industry, and innovation. Shriram is also an internationally acclaimed AI advisor and delivers talks across the globe.

Sini Raj Pulari is a professor and tutor in the Faculty of EDICT (School of Creative Media) at Bahrain Polytechnic in the Kingdom of Bahrain. She has 16 years of computer science engineering research and professional experience at reputed Indian universities and in industry. She is an active member of the board of curriculum development for various universities and has also developed and guided around 40+ UG and PG projects. Her research interests include cybercrime analysis, cybersecurity, banking fraud detection, information retrieval, deep learning and machine learning, natural language processing, and recommender systems. She has authored 20+ Scopus-indexed publications and co-authored "Deep Learning: A Comprehensive Guide." She has delivered 40+ invited lectures on the applications, research advances, and emerging trends of disruptive technologies. She holds a master's degree in computer science engineering from Anna University, India.

T.S. Murugesh is an associate professor in the Department of Electronics and Communication Engineering at Government College of Engineering Srirangam, Tamil Nadu, India. He has 26 years of academic and industry experience, including 19+ years at Annamalai University. He has earned numerous certifications, including Intel oneAPI Innovator, Digital Productivity and AI Fluency, Innovation Mentor—StartupTN, (AICTE—NITTTR) Mentor—National Initiative for Technical Teachers Training, and Microsoft Educator Academy Professional. He has delivered 4 invited lectures at the international level and over 50 at the national level, including NIT Trichy, SASTRA University, etc. He is a reviewer for IEEE, Taylor and Francis, Inderscience, and Springer Nature. Other notable contributions include acting as an NTA Representative for the Conduct of NEET Exams, Evaluator for the Government of India's Toycathon, Smart India Hackathon, The Kavach, MentorTN, AICTE Reviewer, Chairman for Central Valuation, Master Assessor for the Naan Mudalvan Program, Mentor in MIT Art, Design and Technology University, Rajbaug, Loni Kalbhor, Pune, Chief Superintendent for Anna University Theory Examinations, and Subject Matter Expert (SME) for TCS iON. He has organized courses, including ATAL, as well as other national-level workshops. He holds the examinership of the Board of Studies Subject Expert, the Doctoral Committee Panel member in the Centre for Research, Anna University, etc. He is a hackathon enthusiast with around 40 international/national event participations, with multiple podium finishes as a three-time winner and two-time runner-up. He has been granted funding of Rs. 15 Lakhs for idea development for the incubation component under MSME, GoI. He has also been granted ₹30.975 lakh funding from Government of Tamil Nadu, Department of Higher Education, Directorate of Technical Education (DoTE), under Chief Minister's Research Grant, CMRG 2025-26 with Proposal ID: CMRG250966. He has more than 60 peer-reviewed publications and has published 10+ books, including with CRC Press, Taylor & Francis Group, and Nova Science Publishers USA. He holds three UK patent grants, seven Indian design patent grants, and five more Indian patents under development. He is a member of the Institution of Engineers (India).

Subashri Vasudevan is an Assistant Vice President at Bank of America with over a decade of experience in data engineering, ETL development, and financial technology solutions. She specializes in Azure Data Factory, Synapse Analytics, SSIS, SQL Server, and enterprise data warehousing, leading offshore development initiatives and driving efficiency improvements in banking systems. A patent holder and hackathon winner, Subashri has co-authored 20+ technical books across international publishers and is recognized as a Microsoft Community Champion, Google Women Techmaker, and Intel Software Innovator. She is passionate about technology enablement, knowledge sharing, and building scalable, secure data platforms in the banking domain.

Chapter 1
Cybersecurity—an introductory discussion

Learning objectives

After reading this chapter, the reader will gain a clear understanding of

(a) The need for cybersecurity in banking?
(b) Cybersecurity vs. information security
(c) The information security components
(d) Most made human errors
(e) Phishing—What is this?
(f) The best practices—Do not get victimized
(g) The risk mitigation measures

One thing all of us will agree on is that the world is becoming completely digitized. Like it or not, one must accept and go with this digital wave. Everything is digitized; it has many benefits. However, it also brings many challenges that need to be addressed. Adoption increases when there is no alternative. Digitization brought everything to fingertips and made things much easier than they had been earlier. Going to shops to buy what you want has been completely reduced with the advent of online shopping and purchasing options. Comfort at your fingertips. Does it come with all the safety for you and your money? Debatable. Let us now consider another example. A decade ago, if you wanted to transfer money to someone, you had to visit the bank, fill in the forms, get that submitted to the cashier, and the credit may not happen for many hours. Is this condition a prevailing one? Launch the application from the smartphone, click buttons on the touch screen, authorize the transaction, and send money. The recipient gets it in a whisker. Everything is real-time, and yes, in real time. Therefore, what is this point? Simply, convenience comes with a cost, which is in the form of cyber threats. The pros side is very bright, whereas the cons side remains gloomy.

This book is aimed at creating the necessary awareness of cyber threats related to banking. With case studies and easy-to-understand explanations, readers can gain more knowledge on how to safeguard their personal details, credentials, and money. There is a saying: "the money you saved is as good as the money earned." Now, there has been a slight change in this statement. Money you protected from attackers and cyber threats is the money you have earned. These days, it is very important not just to earn money and wealth, but it is more important to protect them without them being wiped out by the attackers. This book is intended to create awareness among readers about the cyber threats and challenges surrounding us, particularly in the banking sector. It is not just interesting to know; it is important to know, and one should be cautious without falling prey to the digital traps.

1.1 Introduction

One could ask a question: why now? The answer is, it is now or never. The digital revolution has been at its peak for the past few years, and it is expected to grow further and stronger. Hence, it is the apt time for all of us to know the cyber threats around us and the methods/techniques to keep us safe and away from the attacks. The first step in the prevention is understanding the threat landscape. It really helps. This book is aimed at establishing a clear understanding of the threat landscape with respect to banking.

Cybersecurity becomes super important in banking for various reasons. It is not just the financial aspect of it. It is even more than that.

The reasons are listed as follows:

- Protection of financial assets: So many financial transactions happen day in and day out. Cybersecurity measures certainly safeguard these transactions from unauthorized, non-permitted access and prevent financial theft.
- The data aspect: Banks have a huge volume of customer data, and needless to say, they are sensitive. If the data is lost or compromised, the trust that customers possess toward the bank is lost, and that is a huge, irreplaceable loss. Next to trust is the compliance and the regulations to be followed. To follow and adhere to compliance efficiently, cybersecurity initiatives help.
- Attacks and fraud prevention: The cybersecurity measures stand tall in terms of preventing attacks like phishing, etc. It protects the customers from losing valuable sensitive information and money from being stolen by attackers. The saying *prevention is better than cure* goes better with the banking domain than any other domain.
- Compliance saga: Any financial institution must follow a lot of compliance rules and standards. There are some standards like PCI DSS (Payment Card Industry Data Security Standard), the famous and well-known GDPR (Global Data Protection Regulation), etc., that must be adhered to properly. While adhering to these regulations, it becomes easier for the organizations to protect the customer and avoid any later consequences. It is important as a customer to know these regulations.
- The integrity perspective: All the financial institutions are almost digitized, and they have no option left. Cybersecurity measures and initiatives help organizations protect their digital assets and data from any disruptions or attacks, thereby maintaining the integrity of the services being offered to customers. The cybersecurity measures also suggest how to handle the risks. If there is an attack, how to proceed further, etc., shall be well handled with strong cybersecurity measures.

This book shall be a handbook for the readers who can enhance their understanding of cybersecurity and its connection with banking. Let us jump into the ocean of cybersecurity learning.

1.2 Cybersecurity vs. information security

It is logical to begin the learning process with a **clear definition of cybersecurity**, since much of today's banking and financial ecosystem operates in a digital environment.

Cybersecurity is both **proactive** and **reactive** in nature. It involves anticipating and preventing attacks while also providing mechanisms for rapid detection, containment, and recovery if an incident occurs. In practice, cybersecurity refers to the **protection of digital systems, networks, data, software, mobile devices, and online services** against threats that seek to disrupt operations, steal information, or cause financial and reputational damage.

The three fundamental principles that underpin cybersecurity are known as the **CIA triad**.

- **Confidentiality:** Ensuring that sensitive information (such as account credentials, financial transactions, or personal data) is accessible only to authorized users.
- **Integrity:** Guaranteeing that data remains accurate, consistent, and unaltered during storage or transmission. For example, ensuring that a customer's payment instruction is not tampered with en route to the bank.
- **Availability:** Ensuring that digital systems and services are accessible whenever needed. In banking, this means Automated Teller Machines (ATMs), internet banking, and mobile apps must be available 24×7 without interruption.

Cybersecurity also emphasizes **incident response and resilience**. It not only deploys protective measures like firewalls, intrusion detection systems, and multifactor authentication but also ensures **response mechanisms**, such as backup recovery, forensic investigation, and reporting, to reduce the impact of any successful breach. In short, *cybersecurity is not optional in modern banking; it is a mandate.*

Information security (Infosec)

While cybersecurity focuses on the **digital realm**, **information security (infosec)** is a **broader discipline** that encompasses the protection of **all forms of information**, whether in digital, physical, or even verbal formats. Infosec includes cybersecurity but extends its scope to cover **paper records, printed reports, physical files, and even conversations that may contain sensitive information**. The objective of information security, like cybersecurity, is to uphold the CIA triad: confidentiality, integrity, and availability. However, it does so across **all mediums of information storage and transfer**.

For example

- A customer's printed loan agreement (physical form) must be stored securely in filing systems with restricted access.
- A bank's digital transaction records (electronic form) must be encrypted and monitored for unauthorized changes.
- A strategic discussion between executives (verbal form) must be protected from eavesdropping or leaks.

Key distinction

- Cybersecurity is a **subset** of information security, limited to protecting digital assets and systems.
- Information security is **holistic**, aiming to secure both digital and non-digital information assets.

Thus, while cybersecurity focuses on defending online banking apps from malware or phishing, information security ensures that a **customer's entire information lifecycle**, from the data center to a printed receipt, is protected.

The major components of the infosec are provided in Figure 1.1.

It is important to know the infosec components. Let's discuss that one after another.

- Access control: Sensitive information should be protected from any form of attack or theft. Access control facilitates this through user roles, privileges, and strict authentication. E.g., giving access to sales data for grades above managers only. Whoever should know will know.
- Data encryption: It is a simple, age-old technique. Through this technique, information is encoded, making it unreadable and difficult for unauthorized persons to read, thereby ensuring confidentiality.
- Data integrity: Information goes through the lifecycle. This information should remain accurate, consistent, unaltered, and reliable throughout the life cycle.

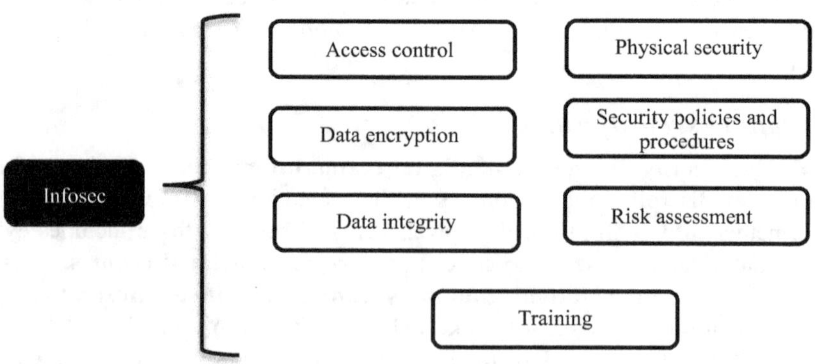

Figure 1.1 The Infosec components

- Physical security: While the age is digital, servers and data centers still hold and process all information and data. Protecting these physical assets is of paramount importance. Assets should be protected from theft, damage, or unauthorized access.
- Security policies and procedures: Guidelines, protocols, and procedures must be established with respect to storing, accessing, transmitting, or disposing of the information. This should be followed carefully.
- Risk management: Risk should be identified over time. Identifying, assessing, and mitigating them through proper action is essential. In this manner, information can be protected from all types of threats and vulnerabilities.
- Training: Educating employees and stakeholders is the best way to fight threats and vulnerabilities. Culture itself should be security-conscious.

Well, readers by now would have understood the differences between cybersecurity and information security. One can watch this quick video to understand the concepts discussed above crisply—https://youtu.be/qEO5_fjpsJw. It is time to quickly navigate to the next topic.

1.3 Most common human errors

One of the top banks in India, the State Bank of India, quoted in the cybersecurity booklet that they released, that 19 of 20 security breaches would not have happened if human errors were eliminated. That is scary. Yes, most problems arise because of human errors. Who can eliminate that? Only us. Therefore, users should be conscious and careful. When it comes to banking applications, users should be fully aware of the consequences of their actions.

What are the most common human errors? Can we list that and understand the same? The list is provided in Figure 1.2. One can refer to the same to obtain a glimpse of the most common human errors.

The first and foremost is the choice of the password. Many a time, the passwords are very weak. Many of us have the habit of keeping passwords as the names of children or family members. Some of us use the date of birth, followed by the names of some family members. All of these are easily guessable, and it is not a task for the attackers.

The next common mistake we tend to make is sharing confidential information with others. It includes the OTP, card numbers, transaction passwords, AADHAAR, a 12-digit individual identification number issued by the Unique Identification Authority of India (UIDAI) on behalf of the Government of India, or any identifiable information. Sharing the same over any chat platform or mail is not advisable and is a super risk.

Many of us get excited when we find free Wi-Fi. That is a source for the attackers. When you connect to unverified Wi-Fi, you are already at risk. This must be avoided.

People have this habit of clicking yes to all the permission requests while installing an application on a smartphone or on a computer. It is very important to

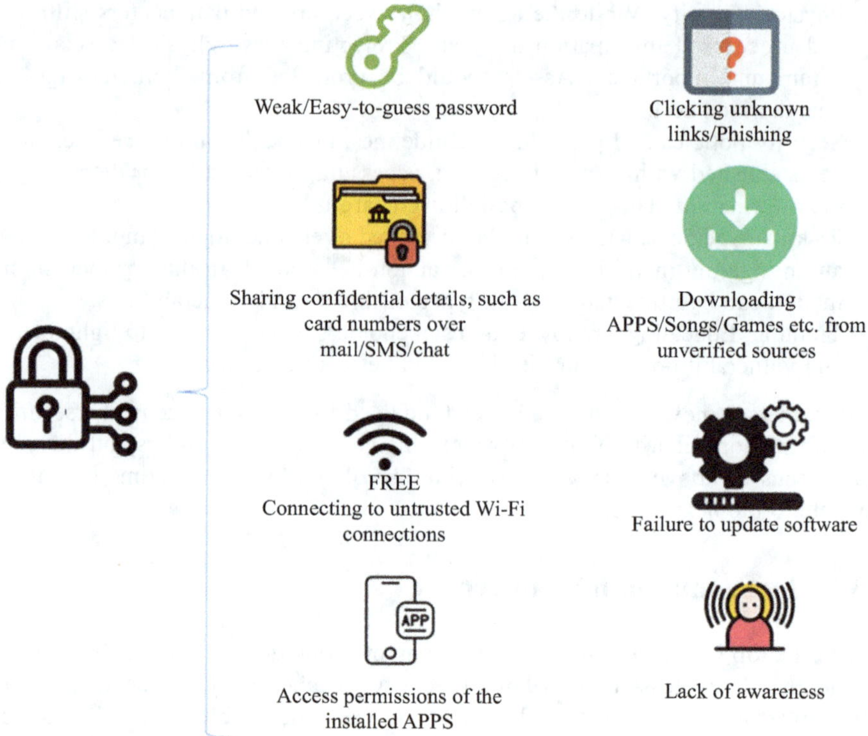

Figure 1.2 The most common human errors

understand what we are doing and why we do that. Giving access permissions to certain directories, call logs, or photos may end up in deep trouble.

Another way we get caught is through clicking on an unknown link from an unknown person who probably would be an attacker. If there is an email saying, "you have won 100000 USD, click the link to claim the prize," it should be moved to spam, and it is not prize money that comes. It is a phishing attack, which comes your way.

Downloading apps or songs from unverified, untrusted sources is very risky. It could also bring a bunch of malware for you. Hence, this is to be avoided.

We have seen this. People tend to ignore the software update requests. One should not ignore these kinds of updates, where some of the updates could be focused on the security aspects. Hence, it is very important to adhere to the update requests.

Above all these, interest and self-awareness are the most important aspects we lack. We should have awareness about all these attacks and protect ourselves and our assets too. One can have a look at the video—https://youtu.be/htmRjIz4grI?si=MbauvQaDp87wALBb to understand the most commonly made human errors.

1.4 The phishing—evergreen attack

The reader should understand the point about cyberattacks. An attacker always has three things in place. The first is a clear plan for an attack. The second is the path for the attack. Three, the target. The path is the route taken by the attacker to reach the target. Needless to say, the target is you and me. Finally, a mode of delivery is required to accomplish the attack mission. The primary mode of delivery chosen by attackers is email.

> Dear John,
>
> We regret to inform you that our security systems have detected suspicious activity on your account. In order to protect your account and prevent unauthorized access, we require your immediate attention.
>
> To secure your account, please click on the link below to verify your identity and update your password:
>
> [Link]
>
> Please note that failure to verify your identity within the next 24 hours may result in temporary suspension or permanent closure of your account. We urge you to act promptly to avoid any inconvenience.
>
> Thank you for your cooperation in maintaining the security of our platform.
>
> Best regards, Manager - XYZ Bank

Email has become immensely popular, and everyone has multiple accounts with different service providers. Most communication occurs via email. These days, even purchase receipts are sent online via email. Phishing is an attack that utilizes the popularity of emails.

It is time to define phishing. Phishing is the act of tricking a user into clicking on a website URL/link to provide sensitive personal information. The mail will be very much like a legitimate email. This would certainly provoke the user to click the link and provide all the information, and the attack starts. Sharp differences can be identified between a phishing email and a legitimate email. However, users' eyes should be widely open to identify these small differences.

A sample phishing email content is presented below:

One could see the sense of urgency that the mail is injecting into the user. On clicking the link, the user will be prompted to enter the confidential details, which could be account numbers, OTP, or passwords. This is phishing (refer to Figure 1.3).

While phishing prominently happens over email, it is also carried out through other platforms, including SMS, WhatsApp, etc.

Phishing is a social engineering attack that involves a lot of psychological manipulation, triggering emotions/sympathy, or even creating a panic situation, forcing the end user to give away the details at the earliest. The entire process will urge the user to give away details. So, one must be careful.

One common way of phishing involves sending mail, which is like the mail from banks. Readers should carefully understand this point. By looking at the email IDs, one can identify whether the email is fake or legitimate. For instance, the email ID can be xyz@citybank.com. Here is the catch. The bank's name is CITI Bank and

Dear John,

We regret to inform you that our security systems have detected suspicious activity on your account. In order to protect your account and prevent unauthorized access, we require your immediate attention.

To secure your account, please click on the link below to verify your identity and update your password:

[Link]

Please note that failure to verify your identity within the next 24 hours may result in temporary suspension or permanent closure of your account. We urge you to act promptly to avoid any inconvenience.

Thank you for your cooperation in maintaining the security of our platform.

Best regards, Manager - XYZ Bank

Figure 1.3 The phishing email sample

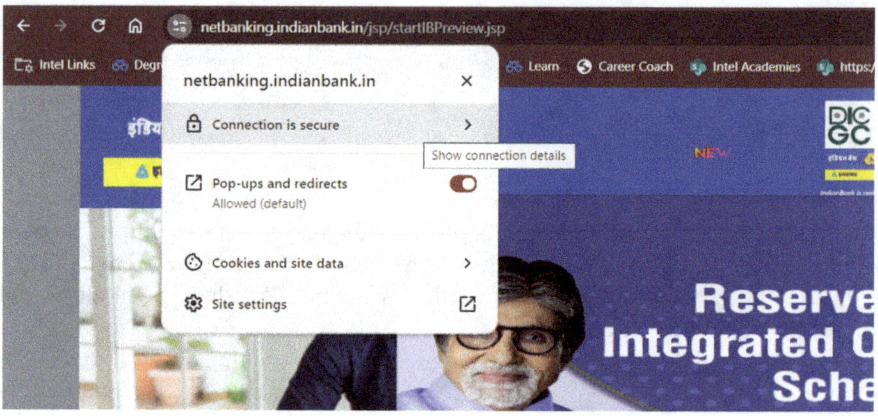

Figure 1.4 The secure connection

not CITY Bank. Thus, the mail ID is forged and fake, which needs to be ignored. This type of attack is called a typosquatting attack.

The takeaway here is that, if you are vigilant, no-one can attack or steal your data/information and assets.

What can be done to prevent phishing attacks? Do we have ways?

Yes, where there is a will, there is a way. This is also true for cybersecurity.

(a) Go through where the email has arrived. CITI Bank is not a CITY Bank.
(b) Reading through the entire email. The mail may be copyright@2019. We are in 2023. This indicates that it could have been a phishing email.
(c) The mail would not be addressed to a particular recipient in most phishing emails. However, this should be noted.
(d) Check whether your connection is secure. Figure 1.4 presents how someone can check whether the connection is secure. On any website where you transact money, it is always better to check if that connection is secure.

1.5 The best practice—easy to follow!

Readers must have read previous topics, where we highlighted the common mistakes that we all commit. If we avoid all these mistakes, they become best practices automatically. Isn't it? However, we list the best practices as follows.

1. The use of strong and complex passwords is preferred. Symbols can be added to passwords, such as Pa$$word@1. This is a complex combination, and not everyone can guess.
2. Do not download any apps or anything from a link sourced by an unknown person.
3. Do not click on links sent by unknown people. Moreover, do not share OTP or confidential details.
4. Use appropriate antivirus software for mobile devices and laptops.
5. Changing passwords frequently is a simple approach that can protect you from attacks.
6. Avoid using public Wi-Fi for financial transactions. This could be an expensive mistake.

The above six practices can help you avoid being attacked.

1.6 Risk mitigation measures

Cybersecurity is of great importance in the banking domain because of the amount of sensitive information involved and the financial risks associated. All the banks today are practicing the following risk mitigation measures:

- Use of firewalls and intrusion detection/prevention systems is one of the measures. Thus, the traffic can be monitored. Suspicious activities can be recognized, thereby preventing unauthorized access or malicious activities.
- MFA, expanded as multi-factor authentication, is in place for all banks to ensure safe/smooth digital transactions. In addition to passwords, an OTP will be sent to the registered mobile number or email ID. Thus, the double authentication ensures that the process is safe.
- Encryption, as described earlier, is a simple and widely used technique to protect sensitive data. Secure Socket Layer (SSL) and Transport Layer Security (TLS) are the commonly used protocols to implement encryption.
- Periodic audits and assessments of systems with proper testing are one of the most important mitigation measures that banks take.
- Grids behind credit/debit cards for online transactions are increasingly being used. For example, as shown in Figure 1.5, ICICI banks in India have begun using this feature. Before the transaction is authorized, codes for certain characters mentioned on the card are requested. The transaction is completed only when feeding it correctly.
- Despite having all the technology tools and infrastructure, if there is no awareness of the necessary training given to employees and stakeholders,

Figure 1.5 A sample grid for safer transactions

nothing can stop the attacks. It starts with the people who use the system and services.

- Regulations are already in place, which the financial organizations adhere to. The Payment Card Industry Data Security Standard (PCI DSS), the Gramm-Leach-Bliley Act (GLBA), and the General Data Protection Regulation (GDPR) are the major acts/regulations financial institutions adhere to.
- Risks can also come from the vendors/third parties. Yes, it is a major factor to be considered, too. Hence, assessing the vendors frequently for cybersecurity risks is mandatory. An evaluation must be carried out of the security practices that the vendors follow.

With all the above practices, risks can be largely mitigated. Yet, the awareness and training are seen to be the most effective approach. Learning will get better in the subsequent chapters.

Key points to remember

1. Digitization has transformed everyday banking and finance. The digital revolution has placed almost every financial service at the customer's fingertips, enabling instant access to payments, fund transfers, investments, and loan services. What once required visiting a physical branch is now available through secure mobile or internet platforms.
2. Securing digital money is as critical as earning it. In today's cyber-risk landscape, protecting funds from phishing, credential theft, and malware is essential. As the saying goes, *"the money you protect from attackers is the money you have truly earned."*
3. The digital revolution is ongoing and intensifying. Over the last decade, digital adoption in banking has surged due to smartphones, fintech innovations, and government initiatives. This growth is expected to accelerate further, making security an even more important foundation.
4. Understanding threats is the first step toward prevention. Awareness of risks such as phishing, social engineering, weak authentication, and insecure networks allows both banks and customers to prepare defenses. Without knowledge of the threat landscape, protective measures often fall short.

5. Cybersecurity involves protecting all layers of digital operations. It is the practice of safeguarding systems, networks, data, applications, and devices against digital attacks or damage. In banking, this includes securing core systems, mobile banking apps, customer data, and online transaction channels.
6. Information security extends beyond digital data. Infosec focuses on protecting all forms of information, whether physical (documents, records) or digital (databases, online accounts). For banks, this means protecting customer records, transaction details, and internal policies across every medium.
7. Human error remains the leading cause of breaches. The State Bank of India, in its cybersecurity booklet, reported that 19 out of 20 security breaches could have been prevented if human mistakes were eliminated. This emphasizes the importance of training employees and educating customers about safe practices.
8. Weak password practices must be avoided. Many users rely on predictable passwords such as family names, birthdays, or simple numeric sequences. Such choices make accounts vulnerable to brute-force or social engineering attacks. Banks recommend complex, unique passwords combined with multi-factor authentication.
9. Unverified Wi-Fi connections pose serious risks. Public or unprotected Wi-Fi networks expose users to man-in-the-middle (MITM) attacks, data interception, and credential theft. Customers must be educated to avoid online banking over unsecured networks.
10. Phishing remains one of the most dangerous threats. It involves tricking users into clicking on malicious links or entering sensitive data on fraudulent websites. Since phishing exploits human trust, awareness, and vigilance are the most effective defenses.
11. Firewalls and intrusion detection/prevention systems are baseline defenses. Every financial institution implements firewalls, IDS (Intrusion Detection Systems), and IPS (Intrusion Prevention Systems) systems to monitor network traffic, block unauthorized access, and detect malicious activities. However, these technical safeguards must be complemented by strong policies and human vigilance.

Questions (Try answering them yourself)

1. Explain why cybersecurity has become a necessity, not an option, for the banking sector in a fully digitized economy.
2. Differentiate between cybersecurity and information security with suitable examples from banking operations.
3. Describe the CIA triad (Confidentiality, Integrity, Availability) in the context of online banking services.
4. Using Figure 1.1 (Infosec components) as a guide, discuss how access control, encryption, and security policies work together to protect customer data.

5. Analyze how digitization has changed the customer journey in banking and identify the new risk points introduced.
6. "Convenience comes with a cost." Discuss this statement with respect to real-time fund transfers and mobile banking.
7. SBI's observation that 19 out of 20 breaches stem from human error is striking. Evaluate the types of human errors most responsible for such breaches in banking.
8. Propose a password policy for a retail bank's customers and justify each element (length, complexity, rotation, reuse).
9. Explain why connecting to unverified/public Wi-Fi is risky for online banking, and outline safe alternatives for customers.
10. Define phishing and distinguish it from related attacks (smishing, vishing, and spear-phishing). Provide two banking-specific examples.
11. With reference to Figure 1.3 (Phishing email sample), list observable red flags and map them to corresponding defense practices.
12. What is typosquatting? Illustrate how it deceives users in banking contexts and propose mitigation steps for both banks and customers.
13. Discuss the role of user awareness and training in reducing cyber risk. How should a bank measure the effectiveness of such programs?
14. Critically evaluate the statement: "Technology alone (firewalls, IDS/IPS) cannot secure a bank without strong processes and culture."
15. Explain the difference between proactive and reactive cybersecurity measures in banking, giving concrete examples of each.
16. Using Figure 1.4 (Secure connection), explain how SSL/TLS protects online transactions and what indicators end-users should verify.
17. List the major risk mitigation measures used by banks (MFA, audits, encryption, IDS/IPS, vendor risk management) and explain how they interact as a layered defense.
18. Analyze the security value of grids behind credit/debit cards (Figure 1.5). What threats do they address, and what are their limitations?
19. From a compliance perspective, discuss why frameworks such as PCI DSS and GDPR are critical for banks and how they influence day-to-day operations.
20. Develop a brief incident response playbook for a suspected phishing compromise in a bank: immediate actions, containment, customer communication, and lessons learned.

Objective questions

1. Why is cybersecurity especially important in banking?
   (a) To reduce paperwork
   (b) To secure financial transactions and sensitive data
   (c) To speed up internet connections
   (d) To increase marketing reach

2. Which of the following best describes cybersecurity?
   (a) Protecting physical assets only
   (b) Protecting systems, networks, and data from digital attacks
   (c) Restricting internet usage
   (d) Creating strong passwords alone
3. Which three principles form the foundation of cybersecurity?
   (a) Confidentiality, Integrity, Availability
   (b) Speed, Flexibility, Accuracy
   (c) Trust, Cost, Performance
   (d) Encryption, Firewalls, VPN (Virtual Private Network)
4. Information Security (infosec) is broader than cybersecurity because it:
   (a) Deals only with digital attacks
   (b) Protects information in both digital and physical forms
   (c) Focuses on antivirus software
   (d) Avoids compliance rules
5. Which of the following is an infosec component?
   (a) Access control
   (b) Password reuse
   (c) Ignoring software updates
   (d) Using public Wi-Fi
6. What does PCI DSS stand for?
   (a) Personal Cyber Information Data Security Standard
   (b) Payment Card Industry Data Security Standard
   (c) Private Cybersecurity Information Defense Standard
   (d) Public Cybersecurity International Data Secure System
7. According to SBI, how many of the 20 breaches could be avoided by removing human errors?
   (a) 5
   (b) 10
   (c) 15
   (d) 19
8. Which of the following is a common human error in banking security?
   (a) Using complex, unique passwords
   (b) Ignoring software update requests
   (c) Avoiding public Wi-Fi
   (d) Using verified apps only
9. What is phishing primarily delivered through?
   (a) Postal mail
   (b) Email
   (c) Printed leaflets
   (d) Phone books

10. Phishing emails often exploit which weakness?
    (a) User trust and urgency
    (b) Server bandwidth
    (c) Cloud storage limits
    (d) Encryption strength

11. Which attack involves fake domains such as CITYbank instead of CITIBank?
    (a) Typosquatting
    (b) Spoofing
    (c) Keylogging
    (d) Backdooring

12. Which protocol is commonly used to secure data through encryption in banking?
    (a) HTTP (Hypertext Transfer Protocol)
    (b) FTP (File Transfer Protocol)
    (c) SSL/TLS
    (d) POP3 (Post Office Protocol version 3)

13. Which one is a strong password example?
    (a) 123456
    (b) John1990
    (c) Pa$$word@1
    (d) abc123

14. Which of the following should NOT be shared with others?
    (a) OTP
    (b) Transaction password
    (c) Aadhaar number
    (d) All of the above

15. Which of these is considered a good cybersecurity best practice?
    (a) Using public Wi-Fi for fund transfer
    (b) Downloading apps from unknown links
    (c) Frequently changing passwords
    (d) Ignoring antivirus software

16. Which measure helps monitor and block suspicious network activities?
    (a) Risk ignorance
    (b) Firewalls and Intrusion Detection Systems
    (c) Weak password policies
    (d) Free Wi-Fi usage

17. Which method adds extra security beyond passwords?
    (a) Password recycling
    (b) Multi-factor authentication (MFA)
    (c) Public Wi-Fi authentication
    (d) Weak encryption

18. Which European regulation ensures the protection of personal data?
    (a) GDPR
    (b) GLBA
    (c) HIPAA (Health Insurance Portability and Accountability Act)
    (d) ISO (International Organization for Standardization)
19. What is the primary benefit of smart grids behind debit/credit cards?
    (a) Faster internet speed
    (b) Safer online transactions
    (c) More stylish design
    (d) Reduced card size
20. What is the most effective way to prevent cyberattacks in banks despite technology?
    (a) Training and awareness
    (b) Installing more hardware
    (c) Ignoring compliance
    (d) Reducing employees

Answer key

1. *b*
2. *b*
3. *a*
4. *b*
5. *a*
6. *b*
7. *d*
8. *b*
9. *b*
10. *a*
11. *a*
12. *c*
13. *c*
14. *d*
15. *c*
16. *b*
17. *b*
18. *a*
19. *b*
20. *a*

Further reading

[1] Basel Committee on Banking Supervision. *Risk Management Principles for Electronic Banking*. Bank for International Settlements; 2003.

[2] Reserve Bank of India. *Report of the Working Group on Information Security, Electronic Banking, Technology Risk Management and Cyber Frauds*. Mumbai: RBI; 2011.
[3] Reserve Bank of India. *Cyber Security Framework in Banks*. RBI Circular DBS.CO/CSITE/BC.11/33.01.001/2015-16; 2016.
[4] Federal Financial Institutions Examination Council (FFIEC). *Authentication in an Internet Banking Environment*. Washington, DC: FFIEC; 2005.
[5] European Central Bank. *Recommendations for the Security of Internet Payments*. Frankfurt: ECB; 2013.
[6] PCI Security Standards Council. *Payment Card Industry Data Security Standard (PCI DSS) v4.0*. PCI SSC; 2022.
[7] European Union. *Regulation (EU) 2016/679 of the European Parliament and of the Council (General Data Protection Regulation – GDPR)*. Official Journal of the European Union; 2016.
[8] National Institute of Standards and Technology (NIST). *Framework for Improving Critical Infrastructure Cybersecurity*. Gaithersburg, MD: NIST; 2018.
[9] International Organization for Standardization. *ISO/IEC 27001: Information Security Management Systems, Requirements*. Geneva: ISO; 2022.
[10] Hadnagy C. *Social Engineering: The Science of Human Hacking*. 2nd ed. Hoboken, NJ: Wiley; 2018.
[11] Mitnick KD, and Simon WL. *The Art of Deception: Controlling the Human Element of Security*. Hoboken, NJ: Wiley; 2002.
[12] Verizon. 2023 Data Breach Investigations Report. Verizon; 2023.
[13] World Economic Forum. *Global Cybersecurity Outlook 2023*. Geneva: WEF; 2023.
[14] Indian Computer Emergency Response Team (CERT-In). *Advisories and Guidelines*. Ministry of Electronics and IT, Government of India; 2023.
[15] Internet Crime Complaint Center (IC3). *2022 Internet Crime Report*. Washington, DC: FBI; 2023.
[16] Proofpoint. *The Human Factor 2022: People-Centric Cybersecurity*. Proofpoint; 2022.
[17] SANS Institute. *Security Awareness Report: Managing Human Risk*. Bethesda, MD: SANS; 2022.
[18] Symantec Corporation. *Internet Security Threat Report 2020*. Mountain View, CA: Symantec; 2020.
[19] International Monetary Fund (IMF). *Cybersecurity Risk Supervision*. Washington, DC: IMF; 2020.
[20] World Bank. *Cybersecurity in Financial Sector Development*. Washington, DC: World Bank; 2021.

Chapter 2

Malware, security, vulnerabilities, and more

Learning objectives

After going through the chapter, the reader will gain a clear understanding of

(a) What is a malware? How impactful is it?
(b) Types of malware and the respective protection measures.
(c) Vulnerabilities connected to passwords.
(d) Firewalls and the role of firewalls.
(e) Denial of Service attacks.
(f) How to improve network security?
(g) What is wireless security, and how can it be safer?

It is important to understand some key terms in cybersecurity. Malware is a term that requires attention. This chapter is phrased with complete details on malware as the first part, followed by ransomware. Let us begin with the definition of malware.

2.1 Malware first, then the types

Malware is an abbreviation of malicious software. They are designed to disrupt, trouble, damage, or gain unauthorized access to digital assets, networks, or data.

Many of us may fail to interpret "malware" as encompassing a wide range of malicious software, including viruses, Trojan horses, spyware, adware, and even ransomware. All of these are classified as malware or malicious. Malware can even lock your computer and demand money from you to unlock it.

The malware is waiting for the entry. Yes, once entered, it will do what it is destined for. Malware can be distributed in several ways. It can be sent to you via simple email as an attachment. Even on the websites you visit, if infected, malware can be injected into the machine. Removable storage devices, including pen drives and hard drives, are also a source of malware injection. Once injected, malware can perform a plethora of harmful actions. It can steal sensitive information such as passwords, banking information, and credentials. It can also corrupt files/data. To be concise, this can disrupt the system. Malware can also open doors to further attacks.

As everyone can easily predict, the main motive behind a malware injection is to milk money from the victim. Creating chaos is the easiest way to make money, and malware is good at that task. Therefore, it is very important to protect the system and oneself from malware.

Malware attacks various devices and machines. For instance, malware can attack Windows or Linux machines. Even mobile phones and smartwatches cannot escape. However, malware can never function independently. In other words, it needs someone to trigger it. Therefore, technically, someone must activate malware. It would require someone to download, click, and enable it to be injected. If users are careful, malware can be avoided, and they can easily protect themselves and their systems from this painful chaos.

As already conveyed, it needs someone to trigger it. In addition, malware is normally bundled and packed with free offerings such as the MP3 cutter, ringtone maker, video editor, Word to PDF converter, etc. The moment someone downloads, the non-invited guest also comes in and starts the task.

2.2 Malware types

Well, it is important to understand the different types of malware we have all around us.

Figure. 2.1 presents the malware types in a nutshell.

Let us understand what each of these means.

(A) Trojan, often referred to as a Trojan horse, is a well-known malware that presents itself as legitimate software and tricks or provokes users to install it

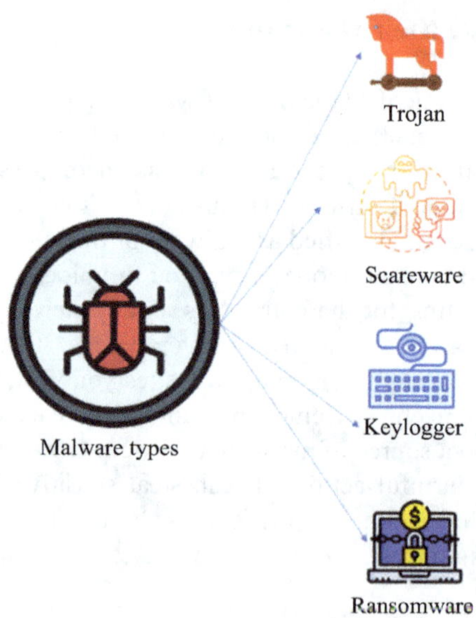

Figure 2.1 Malware types

on their respective devices. This is the beginning of the end. It can now perform all potentially harmful actions, including stealing sensitive data and information, corrupting data, and even spying on user activities. Trojans can perform various tasks, including:

- ✓ Data theft—Trojans can steal banking information, passwords, credit card details, and more. They can also steal documents.
- ✓ Remote access—Some harmful Trojans have doors open for remote attackers. When doors are open, the attackers never remain calm. They are strong and do all the chaotic things for the users.
- ✓ Spamming—Trojans can control the infected entities and trigger spam emails or even initiate a DDoS attack (Distributed Denial of Service Attack).
- ✓ Setting modification—Trojans can modify the settings of the system. The most important configuration files can be deleted or altered. This can also render the device unusable.

The only way one can protect against the Trojans is by having extra caution when prompted to download the files or click on the links. Also, keeping the devices with proper antivirus software installed helps.

(B) Scareware is a very common type of malware. Readers would have come across this kind of malware. The pop-up message on the screen says, "Your computer has been infected with a virus, click here to clean the computer." If the user clicks that link, the user turns out to be a victim. The most common scareware techniques include:

- ✓ Pop-up alerts—Warning messages that have a sense of urgency, being presented like "Your data under threat or your system is attacked by virus," etc.—are the most common scareware. One such instance is presented in Figure 2.2.

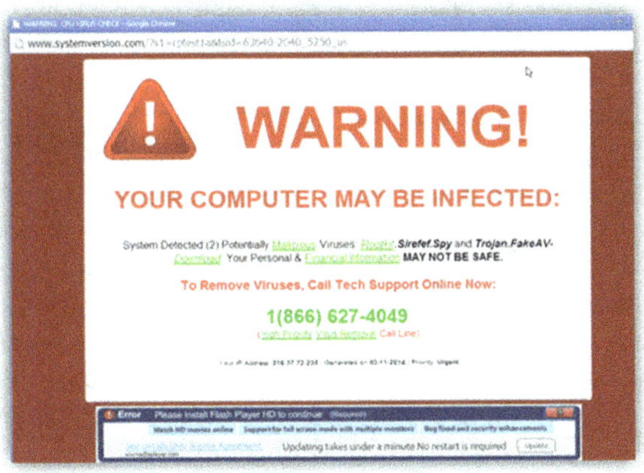

Figure 2.2 The scareware

- ✓ The pressure game—The scareware shall pressure the user to act immediately. It can pressurize the user to purchase antivirus software or to click a link immediately. Once clicked, it is the end and the road to hell.
- ✓ Highly deceptive content—Scareware may push the users to some deceptive websites, which look extremely real and legitimate. This way, the users are convinced that the fake websites are real and become victims.

  The best way to get protection from scareware is through a sense of caution. Users should never respond to pop-up messages of this sort. In addition, one should not click the links that are not from reliable sources. Usage of the antivirus and keeping the OS and software applications all updated with proper security patches is always helpful. Postponing updates is harmful and will open the door for further troubles.

(C) Keylogger—This is a type of malware that captures the user's keystrokes without their knowledge and sends them to an attacker over the Internet. Keystrokes can serve as passwords or confidential information. It is interesting to note that the keylogger can be software or hardware. Sometimes, keyloggers are used for stalking purposes, which is unethical and dangerous. With a keylogger, attackers can monitor the victim's online activities.

(D) Ransomware—Ransomware is a type of malware that locks the files in the computer where it gets in. Alternatively, it can even encrypt the files and demand Bitcoins to decrypt them. The process is very interesting, and it is very important to know the process; we should be cautious about ransomware.

- ✓ First, it begins with an infection. Ransomware infects a computer through simple phishing emails or attachments. Once malware is activated, it starts to encrypt the files. Encryption algorithms are very strong, and they may not be easily broken. Decryption keys are inevitable.
- ✓ The infection may not stop locally in a machine. If connected to a network, it could also spread to the entire network, and all the files could be encrypted. The damage could be bigger and more severe for an organization to face.
- ✓ Now comes the important stage. The ransom note shall be displayed on the victim's screen. The note contains information about the files being encrypted and details on how to pay the ransom. The ransom is mostly bitcoin. The ransom note carries information on how to reach the attackers and receive the decryption key. A deadline is connected to the payment of the ransom. If not paid by the deadline, the decryption key may be destroyed, or the attackers will increase the ransom amount.
- ✓ Once the victim is prepared to pay the ransom and completes the payment, they can receive the decryption key. In other words, there is no guarantee that the decryption key will work fine and obtain all the decrypted files. The victim may even be victimized by not obtaining the correct decryption key.

Again, it comes down to the individuals to be careful. The organizations must have proper cybersecurity training and policies in place. Antivirus software plays a major role, too. At the end of the day, if the individuals are careful, the majority of these attacks can be curtailed.

2.3 Vulnerabilities connected to passwords

Readers may think, “is it so important to have a distinct topic on passwords and related vulnerabilities?” Yes, is the loud answer. The following points should be considered when setting the passwords. Passwords are crucial in banking applications.

Experts say that a strong password is the first step that users should take toward a safer digital experience. In addition, people say it this way—a password is like a signature, and hence, it must be unique.

The following are the guidelines that one can follow to set strong passwords. In addition to banking applications, these guidelines are suitable for any application that requires a password (refer to Figure 2.3).

- The password must have at least eight characters comprising one uppercase, one lowercase, one number, and one special character. This makes the password stronger and more difficult to predict. One example password where all the above-mentioned combinations are used can be Pa$$w0rd@1.

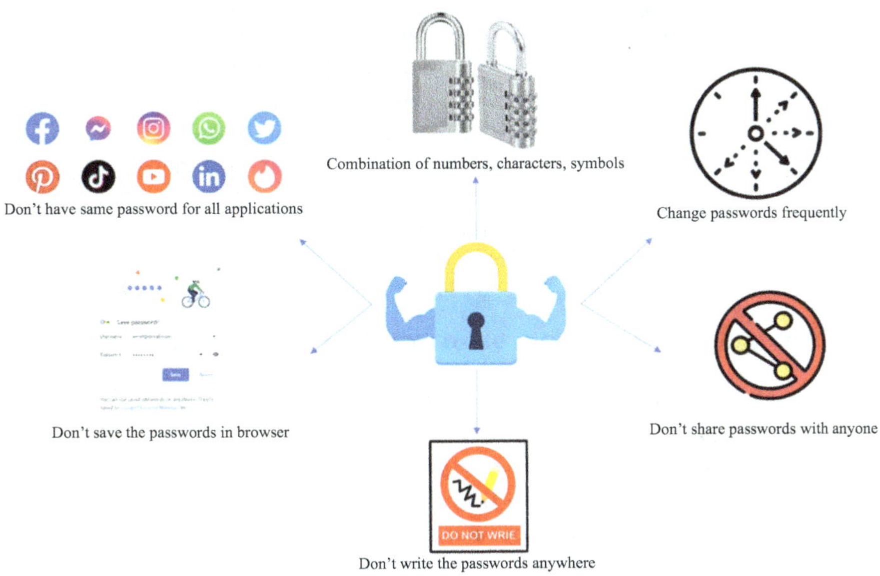

Figure 2.3 The password saga

- Avoid frequently used dictionary words. People set passwords such as "umbrella," "monkey," "princess," etc., which are very easy to try and crack. Users should avoid these easily guessable passwords.
- People setting passwords as QWERTY or ASDFGH are highly vulnerable and easy to guess. In addition, people even use "secret1" or "secretnumber1" kind of passwords. All of these are very susceptible to the attack and are also risky.
- One should never share a password with anyone. Be it friends, family members, or anyone. Passwords are passwords that should remain confidential with one person. When the moment password is shared, it cannot qualify as a password. Banking passwords should never be shared with anyone, including banking officials.
- Changing the password at frequent intervals. Maintaining the same password for a longer duration is generally not preferred.
- Do not write a password in a notebook or elsewhere. It is very risky, and instead of memorizing the passwords.
- Do not have the same password for all applications. Different passwords for different applications have been strongly suggested.
- Do not ever use the save password option with the browsers.
- In addition, if there is an option for multi-factor authentication, commonly regarded as MFA, enabling it can help.

An attack is called a brute-force attack, to which weak passwords are highly vulnerable. A brute-force attack uses automated tools to algorithmically try various combinations of characters until the correct password is identified. In this way, attackers gain access to banking applications and can access all malicious items.

Attackers are always one step ahead of users. They use a dictionary of prebuilt passwords or guess passwords through publicly available information about users. For these types of attackers, it is easy to guess weak passwords.

Most importantly, weak passwords pave the way for insiders to easily exploit that and attack the system for their personal gain.

Above all points, if carefully followed with respect to the passwords, it will be a safer digital experience and can avoid any sort of attack because passwords are vulnerable. Readers are encouraged to watch https://youtu.be/rllEJiVLV-U to understand the concepts discussed in an easier way.

2.4 Firewalls and the role of firewalls in secure banking

A firewall, as the name indicates, is a protection for your digital device, like a computer. In other words, it is a security guard to protect the computer from unauthorized access. A firewall, in simple terms, is a barrier between the computer and the Internet, which controls the flow of data in and out with utmost care. One must stop the spread of fire if it occurs, and a physical firewall will play a role. Similarly, when it comes to computers, the digital firewall carefully blocks all unauthorized access and unwanted data from entering the computer while seamlessly allowing safe data to pass through. With the firewall in place, one can obtain

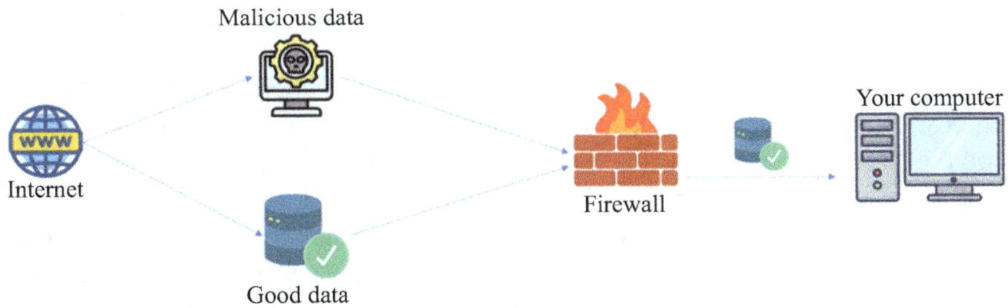

Figure 2.4 The firewall

computers protected from cyberattacks through a set of predefined rules to monitor the traffic flow. (Refer to Figure 2.4)

Considering the amount of financial and confidential information connected to the banking systems, firewalls play a major role in ensuring safe transactions.

Assuming that you are doing your online banking transactions, the firewall shall ensure that your financial information and personal details remain safe from the hands of attackers. It protects all of your information and transactions from cyber threats. Firewalls block all unauthorized access from hackers. In this way, financial fraud, identity theft-related attacks, or unauthorized suspicious transactions are completely blocked, thereby keeping the money and sensitive data always safe.

Banks cannot relax and remain free after setting up firewalls. Firewalls and similar security initiatives are not set-it-and-forget-it solutions. These solutions help. However, banks must continuously monitor their systems and networks for suspicious activities. They should always have an eye to identify potential breaches. Banks are expected to be proactive, rather than reactive. They have to prevent these kinds of breaches and attacks to ensure their customers receive a seamless and secure digital experience.

Banks must also comply with regulations related to data security and privacy. GDPR and HIPAA are strong regulations followed in Europe and the United States, respectively, and must be followed by banks to protect customer data and financial information.

Note: GDPR stands for General Data Protection Regulation, and HIPAA stands for Health Insurance Portability and Accountability Act.

2.5 Distributed Denial of Service (DDoS) attacks—a quick walk-through

Before diving into the Distributed Denial of Service attack, it is important to know what a Denial of Service attack is.

It is a form of cyberattack aimed at making digital resources unavailable to the intended users through some mode of disruption. This can be a temporary disruption or an indefinite one due to the flooding of excessive requests. When excessive requests for a particular resource occur, it would certainly exhaust all resources, including bandwidth, computing, or memory. Hence, these resources are not available to the intended users. The point to be clearly understood here is that in a Denial of Service (DoS) attack, it is a single attacker or a single source that will flood the target with a huge volume of malicious traffic, thereby troubling the target and making it inaccessible to the most needed one.

A simple example is shown in Figure 2.5. Assume that you are ready for a party organized at your house. Many of your friends have already come in, and you are about to start. During that time, a naughty boy keeps ringing the bell, and you have to run to see who it is. You are needed at the party hall, but you keep running to see who is ringing the bell, as it is continuously being done. This scenario is comparable to that of a DoS attack.

It is time for readers to understand what a DDoS attack is all about and how it is different from a DoS attack. Multiple compromised devices have come into play. These are technically referred to as bots or zombies. These bots, or zombies, flood the target system with considerable traffic simultaneously, making the target system or even the network unusable for the intended users. Remote attackers can even control the infected bots. DDoS is technically very difficult to control or mitigate, as the amount of traffic generated is large compared to a normal DoS attack. It also becomes very difficult for someone to classify traffic as legitimate or malicious when using the DDoS.

Let us consider the same example of the party-hall scenario presented in Figure 2.5. You are preparing for the party with your friends, and everything is ready for the start. Now, a group of naughty boys plays with your doorbell (Figure 2.6). They keep ringing the bell continuously as a group, which is certainly annoying for you. You cannot concentrate on the party or cater to guests who have come to attend the party. This scenario is comparable to that of the DDoS attacks.

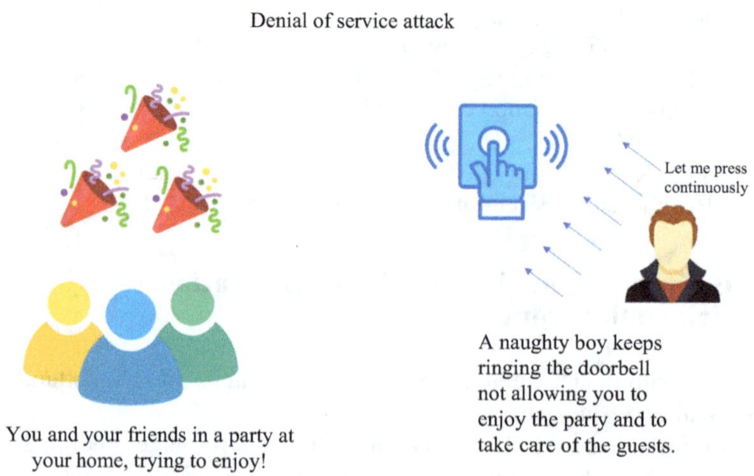

Figure 2.5 Denial of Service attack

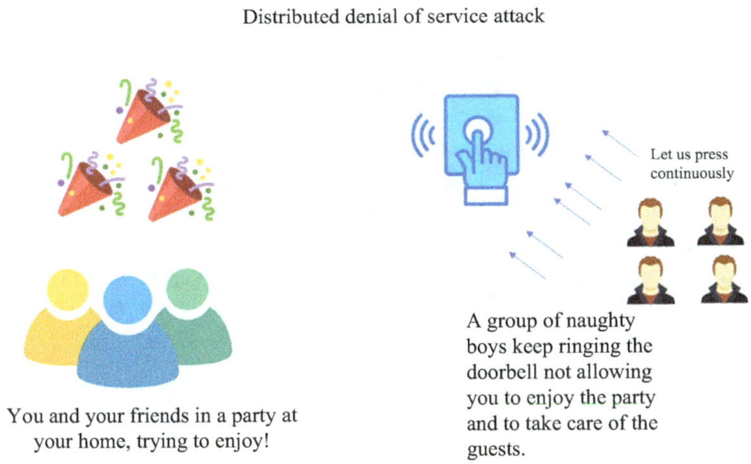

Figure 2.6 Distributed Denial of Service attack

How to mitigate these attacks? Do we not have a way to do it?

The good news is we have ways. Let us discuss that now. The financial organizations can follow the below inputs to avoid these kinds of tragic attacks.

DoS mitigation

1. Bandwidth management: The financial and banking organizations should be capable of handling spikes in traffic. In addition, they can implement mechanisms to prioritize legitimate traffic over malicious traffic.
2. Filtering techniques: There are techniques, such as ingress and egress filtering, that can be deployed to reduce DoS attacks.
3. Rate limiting: This is one of the preferred techniques where the restriction of incoming traffic from individual IP addresses is carried out, and thereby, one can control the traffic being flooded from a single source.
4. Load balancing: This technique is being followed by all organizations these days, where the incoming traffic is properly distributed and shared across multiple servers. Thus, the load is distributed, and DoS attacks can be minimized.
5. Firewalls and Intrusion Prevention Systems (IPS): This is a traditional approach in which firewalls and intrusion prevention systems are deployed. This approach is beneficial to a very good extent.

Similarly, there are some mitigation techniques available for the DDoS attack. Readers shall be introduced to the same in the section below.

DDoS mitigation

1. Traffic scrubbing services: Going ahead with the third-party, market-proven services is the best choice. These scrubbing services use highly sophisticated traffic analysis techniques to block malicious traffic in advance to protect the network.

2. Anomaly detection systems: Organizations can employ anomaly detection systems to understand the deviations of network traffic. In this way, one can find the attacks and take preventive measures against sudden spikes in traffic.
3. IP reputation blocking: It is preferable to obtain a list of malicious IP addresses and block the traffic from these addresses.
4. Cloud-based protection: This approach, although slightly expensive, is becoming popular. Cloud-based DDoS protection can be utilized, and this would be appropriate for a distributed environment.
5. Network segmentation: Isolating the most critical services is a simple yet effective technique. Even if there is an attack, this approach helps to protect critical resources.

One can watch https://youtu.be/cN3s1VCZkJM to understand the DoS and DDoS attacks in a crisp manner.

2.6 Improving the network security

Along with other security measures, it is important to improve network security. What is network security? Simple! It is a set of guidelines, measures, or practices that enable the protection of the network infrastructure, which includes every component in it and the data transmitted over the network, from any sort of unauthorized access or misuse. Network security also protects everything from cyber threats, attacks, and disruptions. With proper network security measures in place, one can ensure the confidentiality, integrity, and availability of information, as required.

Thus, network security cannot be ignored. It is necessary to safeguard the assets and ensure the smooth running of the business. In addition, this enables customers to repose faith in the organization against all modern-day cyberattacks.

In banking and financial applications, network security is even more crucial, as the data handled is highly sensitive in nature. Organizations can take the following measures to enhance network security:

1. Improved authentication: Organizations can implement and enforce MFA (multi-factor authentication) to access applications. This additional layer of security measures will ensure that users are required to go through layers of authentication, and only on proper validation will they be given access. In addition to passwords, there can be biometrics, OTP, etc., as the second level of security measures.
2. Encryption: Organizations can utilize encryption standards and protocols, such as SSL/TLS, to safely encrypt the data transmitted from clients and servers. Generally, encrypting records is a good approach to protect them from the wrong hands.
3. Improved network architecture: If there is a secure design, then the architecture will be sufficiently strong to combat attacks. While designing the architecture, one should include Intrusion Detection and Prevention Systems (IDPS), Virtual Private Networks (VPN), and firewall systems in place.

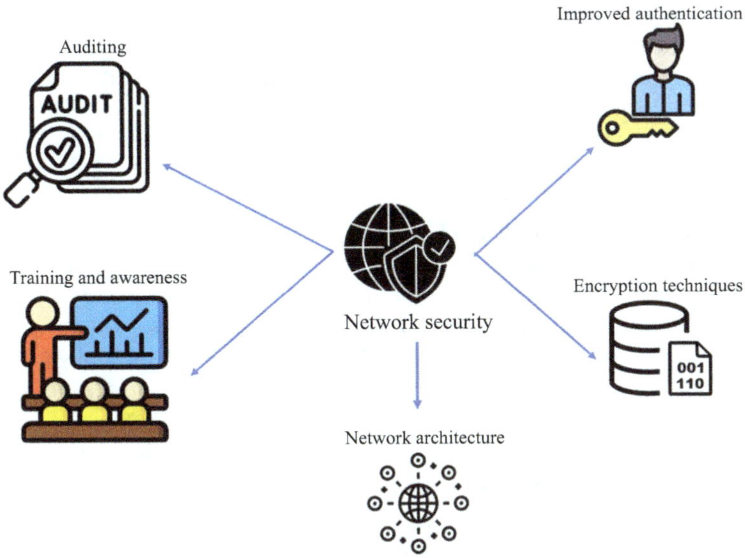

Figure 2.7 Improved network security

4. Consistent auditing and penetration testing: Conducting regular security audits is one of the easiest ways to identify weaknesses in a network. Penetration testing is another method of exposing vulnerabilities. Organizations can follow these approaches to expose vulnerabilities and take immediate action to combat any type of attack.
5. Employee training: Although so many systems and techniques are in place, at the end of the day, if employees are not educated about cybersecurity best practices, every other measure will be of no use. Employees should be educated about phishing, methods of handling sensitive data, and understanding security policies.
6. Regular software updates: Organizations should ensure that they keep all the network devices and software (including OS) up to date with the latest security patches and updates, which play a major role in mitigating all cyber risks.

All the above are not just one-time attempts; they are to be followed consistently. With consistency comes good results. (Refer to Figure 2.7)

2.7 Improving the web security

Web security is an important area of research. Web security ensures that websites and web applications remain safe from any sort of vulnerability or attack. Web security includes measures to prevent malicious activities, unauthorized access attempts, and data breach attempts, which can influence the confidentiality and integrity of the data. Web security fundamentally aims to provide resilience against all types of attacks and to ensure a safe and secure web experience for users.

The measures to be taken by financial organizations remain the same as those of network security measures.

Key points to remember

1. ***Malware*** *(short for malicious software) is a general term for programs created with harmful intent. These can disrupt operations, steal sensitive data, damage systems, or gain unauthorized access to networks and devices.*
2. *Malware can take many forms, including viruses, worms, spyware, Trojans, and ransomware, each exploiting different vulnerabilities. Regardless of type, its objective remains the same: compromise the confidentiality, integrity, or availability of digital assets.*
3. ***Ransomware*** *is a specific type of malware that either locks files or encrypts them, rendering them inaccessible until the victim pays a ransom, usually demanded in cryptocurrencies like Bitcoin. It has caused massive disruptions in the banking and healthcare sectors.*
4. ***Trojans (Trojan horses)*** *disguise themselves as legitimate applications or files but carry hidden malicious payloads. Once installed, they allow attackers to gain backdoor access, steal data, or install additional malware.*
5. ***Keyloggers*** *are malware programs that secretly record every keystroke made by a user. This data, often containing passwords, credit card details, and sensitive information, is sent to attackers, enabling credential theft and fraud.*
6. ***Password hygiene*** *is a fundamental defense. Experts emphasize that strong, unique passwords combining letters, numbers, and special characters act as the first layer of protection against cyberattacks.*
7. ***Brute-force attacks*** *rely on automated tools that attempt thousands or millions of password combinations until the correct one is found. Weak or short passwords are especially vulnerable to such attacks.*
8. ***Firewalls*** *act as barriers between a private computer/network and the Internet. They monitor and control incoming and outgoing traffic based on predefined security rules, preventing unauthorized access while allowing legitimate communication.*
9. ***Denial of Service (DoS) attacks*** *overwhelm a system or network with excessive requests, rendering resources unavailable to intended users. For example, a bank's online portal could be flooded with traffic, disrupting services.*
10. ***Distributed Denial of Service (DDoS) attacks*** *are a more advanced version of DoS, where multiple compromised systems (botnets) simultaneously flood a target. Due to the massive traffic volumes, distinguishing between genuine and malicious requests becomes extremely difficult.*
11. ***In banking and financial applications****, network security is paramount. Banks deal with highly sensitive financial transactions and personal data, making them prime targets for attackers. Even small lapses can result in large-scale financial losses and reputational damage.*

12. ***Web security*** *focuses on safeguarding websites and online applications against threats such as SQL (Structured Query Language) injection, cross-site scripting (XSS), and phishing. Strong web security ensures customers can safely access digital banking services without risk of data theft or manipulation.*

Objective questions

1. What best defines malware?
   (a) Helpful utility software
   (b) Software designed to harm or gain unauthorized access
   (c) A network-monitoring tool
   (d) An operating system feature
2. Which is not a malware type?
   (a) Trojan
   (b) Keylogger
   (c) Ransomware
   (d) VPN
3. A Trojan primarily...
   (a) Self-replicates across networks
   (b) Disguises as legitimate software to trick users
   (c) Encrypts files and demands payment
   (d) Blocks web traffic with filters
4. Scareware commonly uses...
   (a) Slow bandwidth
   (b) Pop-ups that create urgency to click or buy
   (c) Air-gapped media
   (d) Hardware tokens
5. Keyloggers are dangerous because they...
   (a) Delete backups automatically
   (b) Capture keystrokes like passwords secretly
   (c) Disable firewalls
   (d) Jam Wi-Fi channels
6. First step in a typical ransomware incident is...
   (a) Payment confirmation
   (b) File decryption
   (c) Initial infection via phishing/attachment
   (d) Legal notification
7. Strong defense against Trojans includes...
   (a) Blindly installing freeware
   (b) Clicking on unknown links
   (c) Updated AV + cautious downloads
   (d) Using public Wi-Fi

8. Which password is strongest?
   (a) qwerty123
   (b) Pa$$w0rd@1
   (c) birthday1990
   (d) secret1
9. A brute-force attack...
   (a) Sends phishing emails
   (b) Tries many password combinations automatically
   (c) Alters firewall rules
   (d) Disables MFA
10. Best practice for passwords includes...
   (a) Same password for all sites
   (b) Writing passwords in a notebook
   (c) Changing them periodically and using MFA
   (d) Saving passwords in any browser by default
11. Firewalls mainly...
   (a) Speed up CPUs
   (b) Monitor/allow/deny traffic by rules
   (c) Generate encryption keys
   (d) Replace antivirus tools
12. DoS vs DDoS: the distinct trait of DDoS is...
   (a) Targets only routers
   (b) Uses multiple compromised devices (botnet)
   (c) Requires physical access
   (d) Only affects Wi-Fi
13. Effective DoS mitigation includes...
   (a) Rate limiting and load balancing
   (b) Sharing admin passwords
   (c) Disabling logs
   (d) Ignoring traffic spikes
14. One DDoS mitigation method is...
   (a) IP reputation blocking/scrubbing services
   (b) Removing all firewalls
   (c) Turning off SSL/TLS
   (d) Using weak passwords
15. A core network security improvement will...
   (a) Skip audits to save time
   (b) Do regular patching and security updates
   (c) Allow default credentials
   (d) Disable encryption to reduce overhead

16. Which helps secure data in transit for banking apps?
    (a) HTTP
    (b) SSL/TLS
    (c) Telnet
    (d) FTP
17. A sound architecture measure is to...
    (a) Avoid VPNs and IDPS
    (b) Include firewalls, VPN, and IDPS
    (c) Expose admin ports to the Internet
    (d) Use flat networks only
18. Key human-centric control for network/web security is...
    (a) Employee training on phishing and data handling
    (b) Longer maintenance windows
    (c) Disabling MFA
    (d) Public Wi-Fi mandates
19. Safer wireless security generally recommends...
    (a) Open networks without passwords
    (b) WEP (Wired Equivalent Privacy) because it is older
    (c) WPA3 (Wi-Fi Protected Access 3) with strong passphrases and hidden SSIDs
    (d) Using default router credentials
20. Web security primarily aims to prevent...
    (a) Spreadsheet formatting errors
    (b) SQLi (SQL injection)/XSS and unauthorized access to web apps
    (c) Hardware overheating
    (d) Image compression issues

Answer key

1. *b*
2. *d*
3. *b*
4. *b*
5. *b*
6. *c*
7. *c*
8. *b*
9. *b*
10. *c*
11. *b*
12. *b*
13. *a*
14. *a*

15. *b*
16. *b*
17. *b*
18. *a*
19. *c*
20. *b*

Questions (Try answering them yourself)

1. Define *malware*. How does it affect digital systems, and why is it a major concern in banking?
2. Differentiate between viruses, Trojans, spyware, adware, and ransomware with suitable examples.
3. Explain how ransomware works step by step. Why is paying ransom not always a guaranteed solution?
4. What are scareware attacks? Illustrate how they trick users with examples of common pop-ups.
5. Discuss the role of keyloggers (both hardware and software) in cyberattacks. How can they be detected and prevented?
6. Why is human action often necessary to trigger malware? Provide examples where user negligence leads to infections.
7. Suggest best practices to protect against Trojan horse malware.
8. What are the vulnerabilities associated with weak passwords? Provide examples of weak and strong password practices.
9. Explain a brute-force attack. Why are dictionary-based attacks considered dangerous?
10. Write guidelines for creating strong and secure passwords. How does MFA enhance password security?
11. What is a firewall? Describe its role in protecting banking systems from cyber threats.
12. Explain how firewalls are not "set and forget" tools. Why do banks need continuous monitoring even after firewall deployment?
13. Differentiate between DoS and DDoS attacks with real-world examples.
14. Using the "party and doorbell" analogy, explain the working of DoS and DDoS attacks.
15. List and describe three DoS as well as DDoS mitigation techniques.
16. What is network security? Why is it more critical in banking applications compared to other domains?
17. How can improved authentication mechanisms like MFA and biometrics improve network security in banks?
18. Discuss the role of encryption (SSL/TLS) in securing financial transactions. Why is it necessary?
19. Why are regular security audits and penetration tests essential for financial organizations?
20. Explain what web security means. How does it protect against attacks like SQL injection and cross-site scripting (XSS)?

Further reading

[1] Shehab R, Alismail A-S, Almaiah MA, Alkhdour T, AlWadi B, and Alrawad M. Assessment of cybersecurity risks and threats on banking and financial services. *J Internet Serv Inf Secur*. 2024;14(3):167–190.

[2] Kshetri N, Rahman MM, Sayeed SA, and Sultana I. cryptoRAN: A review on cryptojacking and ransomware attacks w.r.t. banking industry—threats, challenges & problems. *2024 2nd International Conference on Advancement in Computation & Computer Technologies (InCACCT)*, Gharuan, India, 2024, pp. 523–528.

[3] Beaman C. Ransomware: Recent advances, analysis, challenges and future research directions. *J Cybersecur Digit Forensics*. 2021;111:102490.

[4] Jimmy F. Understanding Ransomware attacks: Trends and prevention strategies. *J Knowl Learn Sci Technol*. 2024;2(1):180–210.

[5] Cremer F, Sheehan B, Fortmann M, *et al*. Cyber risk and cybersecurity: A systematic review of data breach studies and implications. *J Cybersecur*. 2022;47(3):698–736.

[6] Waliullah M, Hossain George Z, Hasan MT, Alam K, Munira MSK, and Siddiqui NA. Assessing the influence of cybersecurity threats and risks on the adoption and growth of digital banking: A systematic literature review. *arXiv preprint*. 2025 Mar 23.

[7] Gulyás O and Kiss G. Impact of cyber-attacks on the financial institutions. *Procedia Comput Sci*. 2023;219:84–90.

[8] Ravichandran N. DDoS, Ransomware, and Trojan Horse Attacks: Detection, effects, and prevention. *Preprints.org*. 2024.

[9] TechTarget. *What Is Ransomware? Definition and Complete Guide*. 2025 Apr 23.

[10] Black P, Gondal I, and Layton R. A survey of similarities in banking malware behaviours. *Comput Secur*. 2018;77:756–772.

[11] Wikipedia contributors. Dridex. *Wikipedia*. 2025 Sep.

[12] Wikipedia contributors. Ransomware. *Wikipedia*. 2025 Sep.

[13] Wikipedia contributors. Zeus (malware). *Wikipedia*. 2025 Sep.

[14] Wikipedia contributors. Tiny Banker Trojan. *Wikipedia*. 2025 Sep.

[15] Wikipedia contributors. Clampi (trojan). *Wikipedia*. 2025 Sep.

[16] Tom's Guide. *Dangerous Android Banking Trojan Found Lurking in Malicious Apps with 19 Million Installs*. 2025 Aug 25.

[17] TechRadar. *Criminals Are Targeting Hundreds of Legitimate Banking & Crypto Apps Using Advanced Virtualization*. 2025 July.

[18] Wired. *Automated Sextortion Spyware Takes Webcam Pics of Victims Watching Porn*. 2025 Sep 3.

[19] Shehab R, Alismail A-S, Almaiah MA, Alkhdour T, AlWadi B, and Alrawad M. Assessment of cybersecurity risks and threats to banking and financial services. *J Internet Serv Inf Secur*. 2024;14(3):167–190.

Chapter 3
Internet banking

Learning objectives

After reading the chapter, the reader will gain a clear understanding of

(a) The concept of Internet banking and its significance in modern financial services.
(b) Differentiation between various authentication practices and evaluation of their effectiveness in securing online transactions.
(c) Identifying key virtualization technologies in banking and analyzing the challenges and risks they introduce.
(d) Assess common security issues in virtualization and propose mitigation strategies.
(e) Cloud computing adoption in banking, highlighting regulatory, compliance, and security concerns.
(f) Applying knowledge of Internet banking in real-world application scenarios, including retail, corporate, mobile, and international banking.
(g) Case studies evaluation to understand practical threats, best practices, and lessons learned in securing Internet banking systems.

3.1 Introduction

Internet banking, also referred to as "e-banking" or "online banking," has fundamentally transformed the way customers interact with financial institutions. Traditionally, customers depended on physical branches for routine tasks such as balance inquiries, fund transfers, and bill payments. Today, these services are delivered seamlessly through secure digital channels, empowering users to access account information, transfer funds, apply for loans, and even invest in financial products anytime and anywhere. This transformation has not only improved customer convenience but also reshaped the banking industry's operational models, forcing institutions to embrace digital-first strategies.

At its core, Internet banking represents the digitization of financial services, where physical processes are replaced by secure online platforms accessible via web browsers, mobile applications, or Application Programming Interfaces (APIs) integrated into third-party services. Customers expect speed, transparency, and ease of use, while regulators demand resilience, compliance, and strict controls. Meeting these diverse expectations requires banks to invest heavily in technology, cybersecurity, and customer education.

Growth and adoption

The adoption of Internet banking has accelerated due to factors such as:

- Smartphone penetration and mobile apps providing 24×7 banking on the go.
- Government initiatives and Fintech innovations are driving digital payments, particularly in developing markets such as India, with systems like Unified Payments Interface (UPI).
- Pandemic-driven digital transformation has reduced reliance on branch-based services and accelerated trust in digital transactions.

According to multiple global reports, more than 70% of retail banking transactions worldwide are now initiated through digital channels, a figure that continues to rise annually. This statistic reflects not just customer demand but also a broader shift in the financial ecosystem toward cloud-based operations, digital wallets, and integrated payment platforms.

Security as a central concern

While the benefits are evident, the growth of Internet banking has created a complex landscape of risks. Unlike traditional banking, where threats were largely physical (e.g., branch robberies or fraudulent checks), Internet banking threats are largely cyber-driven. Attackers exploit weaknesses in:

- Authentication systems, targeting customers with phishing, credential theft, and social engineering.
- Virtualized infrastructure, where multiple banking systems share the same physical resources, makes hypervisors and misconfigured virtual machines attractive targets.
- Cloud environments, which, although agile and cost-efficient, introduce concerns around data sovereignty, compliance, insider threats, and vendor lock-in.

Banks must therefore balance innovation with security, ensuring that digital services remain trustworthy while still delivering speed and convenience.

Scope of the chapter

This chapter examines the **foundational elements of Internet banking security**. The following themes are explored in depth:

1. Authentication practices and types—Analyzing the evolution from simple passwords and PINs to modern methods such as biometrics, behavioral analysis, and multi-factor authentication.
2. Virtualization and allied challenges—Highlighting how virtualization supports scalability and efficiency in banking IT but introduces risks such as hypervisor attacks, VM (Virtual Machine) sprawl, and insider misuse.

3. Addressing security issues in virtualization—Presenting key mitigation strategies, including hypervisor hardening, VM lifecycle management, and zero-trust access.
4. Cloud computing and related concerns—Discussing IaaS (Infrastructure as a Service), PaaS (Platform as a Service), and SaaS (Software as a Service) adoption in banking, the shared responsibility model, compliance obligations, and associated risks.
5. Application scenarios of Internet banking—Illustrating how services span retail, corporate, mobile/UPI, and international banking, with case studies showing both opportunities and vulnerabilities.
6. Case studies and future trends—Examining real-world examples such as the rise of UPI, incidents like ESXi ransomware, and evolving technologies like AI-powered fraud detection.

3.2 Authentication practices and types

Authentication forms the first line of defense in safeguarding Internet banking systems. Its effectiveness determines whether unauthorized access is prevented.

3.2.1 Fundamentals of authentication

Authentication is the process of verifying that a user or system is truly who they claim to be. In the banking sector, where highly sensitive financial data is managed, robust authentication plays a vital role in preventing fraud and safeguarding customer trust. Common methods used include passwords, Personal Identification Number (PINs), security tokens, biometric identifiers such as fingerprints or facial recognition, and advanced multi-factor authentication systems that combine two or more of these approaches for stronger security.

Figure 3.1 depicts the authentication flow in Internet banking, where the user verifies identity through credentials, OTP (One-Time Password), or biometrics before gaining access to the banking application via the authentication server.

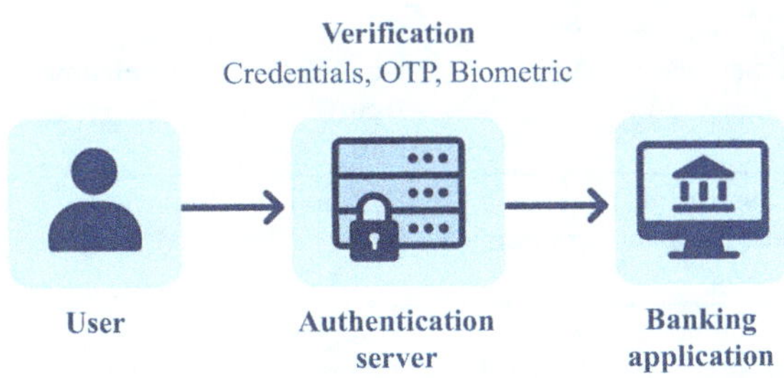

Figure 3.1 Internet banking authentication flow

3.2.2 Types of authentication

Before diving into the specifics, it is important to recognize that authentication in Internet banking is not a one-size-fits-all mechanism. Different banks, regions, and customer segments adopt varied approaches depending on factors such as usability, regulatory requirements, cost, and perceived risks. While traditional methods like passwords and PINs still dominate, newer techniques such as biometrics and multifactor authentication (MFA) have gained momentum due to their enhanced security. Each method offers unique advantages and limitations, making it critical for banking institutions to strike a balance between security strength and user convenience. Table 3.1 below summarizes the most widely used authentication practices, outlining their description, strengths, weaknesses, and real-world applications in Internet banking.

3.2.3 Emerging trends in authentication

As cybercriminals grow more sophisticated, traditional authentication mechanisms like static passwords or PINs are no longer sufficient to safeguard online banking transactions. Banks and financial institutions are increasingly adopting next-generation authentication methods that are adaptive, user-centric, and resistant to common attack vectors. Three major innovations shaping the future of Internet banking authentication are behavioral biometrics, Risk-Based Authentication (RBA), and FIDO2 (Fast Identity Online)/passwordless banking.

Table 3.1 Authentication types in internet banking

Authentication type	Description	Strengths	Weaknesses	Example in banking
Password/PIN	User enters secret text string	Simple, inexpensive	Vulnerable to brute force, phishing	Net Banking login
OTP (One-Time Password)	Time-based/dynamic password sent via Short Message Service (SMS)/ email/app	Easy to deploy, dynamic	SIM-swap fraud, phishing	OTP for fund transfer
Hardware tokens	Physical device generates codes	Strong, isolated from Internet	Expensive, cumbersome	RSA SecurID
Biometric	Fingerprint, iris, voice, and facial recognition	Difficult to forge	Spoofing, privacy issues	FaceID login in mobile app
Multi-Factor Authentication (MFA)	Combines two or more factors (e.g., password + OTP)	Strongest defense	Usability concerns	UPI + PIN + OTP

Behavioral biometrics

Unlike static biometrics (fingerprints, iris, or facial scans), **behavioral biometrics** analyze unique patterns in how a user interacts with a device.

Examples of measurable traits

- Typing speed, keypress intervals, and pressure (keystroke dynamics).
- Mouse movements and click behavior.
- Gait recognition on mobile devices via accelerometer/gyroscope.
- Swipe patterns and screen pressure on smartphones.

Strengths

- Continuous authentication rather than one-time verification.
- Difficult for attackers to replicate since behaviors are dynamic.
- Nonintrusive, happens in the background without interrupting the user.

Limitations

- Accuracy can be affected by physical changes (injury, stress, fatigue).
- Requires large datasets and machine learning for effective profiling.
- Privacy concerns, as behavioral data can reveal sensitive personal patterns.

Real banking application example: Several banks and payment providers, including Barclays and NatWest in the UK, have piloted behavioral biometrics for fraud detection, monitoring how customers type and navigate banking portals to flag unusual behavior.

Risk-Based Authentication (RBA)

Risk-Based Authentication adapts its level of scrutiny depending on the **context of the transaction**. Instead of applying the same security check for every action, the system evaluates the **risk profile** in real time.

Factors considered in RBA

- Device recognition (familiar vs. new device).
- IP address, geolocation, and network reputation.
- Time of day and frequency of login attempts.
- Size and type of transaction (e.g., ₹500 vs. ₹50,000 transfer).

Workflow

- Low-risk activity (e.g., logging in from the user's home device with a known IP address) → Allow access with basic authentication.
- High-risk activity (e.g., unusual foreign login + large fund transfer) → Trigger additional verification such as OTP, biometric, or knowledge-based questions.

Advantages

- Balances **user experience and security** by only challenging suspicious activity.
- Reduces customer friction compared to blanket MFA for every action.

Limitations

- Relies heavily on accurate profiling and risk models.
- Can generate false positives, frustrating legitimate users.

Real banking application example: The European Union's PSD2 (Payment Services Directive 2) requires Strong Customer Authentication (SCA), and many European banks now employ RBA to determine when step-up authentication is necessary, aligning with regulatory exemptions.

FIDO2 and passwordless banking

The **FIDO2 standard**, developed by the **FIDO (Fast Identity Online) Alliance** and the **World Wide Web Consortium (W3C)**, enables passwordless authentication using public-key cryptography.

How does it work?

- During registration, the device creates a unique cryptographic key pair.
- The **private key** remains on the user's device, secured in a hardware module such as TPM (Trusted Platform Module), Secure Enclave, or security key.
- The **public key** is registered with the bank's server.
- Authentication is performed using biometrics (e.g., fingerprint), a PIN tied to the device, or a physical security key (e.g., YubiKey).

Advantages

- Resistant to phishing; no passwords transmitted or stored.
- Eliminates risks of credential stuffing and brute force.
- Improves user convenience with fast login.

Limitations

- Requires hardware and ecosystem support (browsers, operating systems).
- Initial rollout costs for banks can be high.
- Customers may resist change if unfamiliar with passwordless methods.

Real banking application example: In 2019, Microsoft enabled FIDO2 passwordless authentication across its platforms, and banks leveraging Azure AD (Active Directory) services adopted it. In Asia, the Development Bank of Singapore Limited (DBS Bank—Singapore) piloted passwordless login for corporate banking portals.

Case study 3.1: Weakness in biometric-only authentication (HSBC, 2016)

In 2016, **HSBC launched voice recognition authentication** for its UK telephone banking service, marketing it as a secure and convenient alternative to passwords and PINs. Customers enrolled by recording a voiceprint, which the system would later match during login or verification calls.

- **Incident:** In a widely reported BBC investigation, a journalist demonstrated that his nonidentical twin brother was able to mimic his voice and gain access to the HSBC account. Despite some differences in tone and accent, the biometric system accepted the impostor.

- **Impact:** This raised significant concerns about the reliability of voice biometrics when used as the sole authentication factor, especially in scenarios involving close relatives or high-quality voice spoofing.
- **Lessons learned**
  - Biometrics should **never be the only factor**; they must be paired with additional security, such as OTPs or device recognition.
  - Attackers may exploit **voice synthesis/deepfakes** to trick systems.
  - Banks began reinforcing biometric deployments with multi-factor or risk-based checks after the incident.

Key takeaway: Emerging technologies like biometrics, behavioral analysis, and passwordless systems improve convenience, but they must be deployed as part of a **layered security strategy** rather than in isolation.

3.3 Virtualization and allied challenges

Virtualization enables banks to maximize infrastructure efficiency by running multiple systems on shared physical resources. While it improves scalability and cost savings, it introduces unique security, management, and compliance challenges.

3.3.1 Virtualization in banking IT infrastructure

Virtualization has become a cornerstone of modern banking IT environments, enabling institutions to optimize resources and streamline operations. By allowing multiple virtual machines (VMs) to run on a single physical server, banks can efficiently support **core banking systems, data storage platforms, and customer-facing applications** without the need for dedicated hardware for each function. This flexibility not only reduces infrastructure costs but also enables the **rapid deployment of new services**, such as digital wallets or mobile apps, in response to market demands. Furthermore, virtualization enhances **business continuity and resilience** by simplifying disaster recovery strategies; VMs can be quickly replicated or restored in alternate data centers while also supporting **load balancing** during high-traffic periods, such as salary credits or festive-season transactions. In essence, virtualization provides the scalability, agility, and reliability that are essential for today's digital-first banking operations.

3.3.2 Challenges in virtualization

While virtualization delivers undeniable benefits in terms of flexibility, cost efficiency, and scalability, it also introduces a unique set of **security and operational risks** that cannot be overlooked. Because multiple virtual machines share the same underlying infrastructure, any weakness in configuration, governance, or access control can amplify the impact of an attack. Issues such as **hypervisor vulnerabilities,**

Table 3.2 Virtualization challenges in banking

Challenge	Explanation	Banking example
Hypervisor attacks	If compromised, all hosted VMs are exposed	Attack on VMware ESXi leading to mass data leaks
VM sprawl	Too many VMs without proper oversight	Banks running hundreds of test VMs without patching
Resource contention	Performance bottlenecks due to shared hardware	High-traffic spikes during salary credit dates
Compliance issues	Auditors demand strict isolation	Basel III compliance for sensitive workloads
Insider threats	Admins misuse privileged access	Unauthorized VM snapshots leaked to outsiders

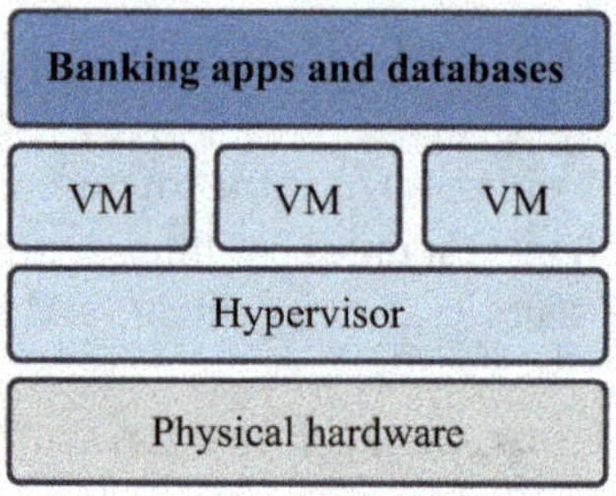

Figure 3.2 Virtualized banking environment

unchecked VM growth, resource competition, and compliance constraints pose real threats to banking environments where data integrity and availability are critical. In addition, the human element, particularly privileged administrators, remains a significant risk if proper oversight mechanisms are not in place. The following table highlights the most pressing challenges associated with virtualization in banking, along with real-world scenarios that illustrate how these risks manifest (Table 3.2).

Figure 3.2 illustrates the layered structure of a virtualized banking environment, showing how physical hardware supports a hypervisor, multiple VMs, and finally the banking applications and databases.

3.4 Addressing security issues in virtualization

3.4.1 Key mitigation strategies

To address the unique risks posed by virtualization in banking, institutions must adopt layered security practices that safeguard both the infrastructure and the workloads running on it. The following strategies are widely recognized and implemented in the financial sector:

Hypervisor hardening

The hypervisor is the backbone of any virtualized environment, and if compromised, all hosted virtual machines (VMs) become vulnerable. Banks should ensure that the hypervisor is regularly patched with the latest vendor updates to fix security vulnerabilities. Unused services, drivers, and interfaces must be disabled to minimize the attack surface. Additionally, administrative access to the hypervisor should be tightly controlled and audited.

VM lifecycle management

Unmanaged or forgotten VMs, commonly referred to as "VM sprawl," increase security risks and waste resources. Financial institutions should adopt strict policies for VM provisioning, monitoring, and decommissioning. Regular reviews of active VMs, combined with automated tools for patching and updates, help reduce exposure to unpatched or redundant systems that attackers could exploit.

Segmentation

Logical and physical segmentation ensures that sensitive workloads are isolated from less critical or experimental environments. For example, core banking systems should be hosted on dedicated VMs or clusters, separated from test or development VMs. Micro-segmentation technologies can further restrict lateral movement between workloads, ensuring that an attacker cannot move easily across systems if one VM is compromised.

Monitoring and logging

Centralized monitoring provides visibility into the behavior of both hypervisors and VMs. Integrating logs into a Security Information and Event Management (SIEM) platform allows real-time detection of anomalies such as unauthorized VM creation, suspicious login attempts, or abnormal resource usage. Continuous monitoring ensures that any breach or misuse can be quickly identified and addressed, reducing the risk of undetected exploitation.

Zero-trust access control

In a zero-trust model, no user or process is implicitly trusted, even within the internal network. For virtualization, this means enforcing granular, role-based access controls (RBAC) for administrators and operators. Privileges should be limited strictly to what is necessary for a task. Multi-factor authentication (MFA) should be mandated for all administrative accounts, and privileged actions must be logged and reviewed periodically. This prevents insider threats and reduces the impact of credential compromise.

Key takeaway: By combining hypervisor security, disciplined VM management, workload isolation, continuous monitoring, and zero-trust principles, banks can significantly reduce the risks associated with virtualization while preserving their operational advantages.

3.4.2 Tools and technologies

In addition to sound governance and policies, specialized technologies can significantly strengthen the security of virtualized environments in the banking sector. Some notable solutions include:

VMware NSX for micro-segmentation

VMware NSX enables network micro-segmentation, where security policies are applied at the VM or application level rather than only at the network perimeter. This ensures that even if one virtual machine is compromised, attackers cannot freely move laterally to access other critical workloads. For banks, this is particularly valuable for protecting core banking applications, payment systems, and customer data repositories by segmenting them from less sensitive or development environments.

Citrix virtual apps with multi-layer authentication

Citrix Virtual Apps and Desktops provide centralized management of virtualized applications while incorporating multi-layer authentication mechanisms such as smart cards, MFA, and adaptive access controls. This combination allows financial institutions to deliver customer-facing and employee applications securely while ensuring only authorized users can access sensitive systems. By adding multiple checkpoints, Citrix reduces risks from credential theft and insider misuse.

Intel® TDX (Trusted Domain Extensions) for workload isolation

Intel Trusted Domain Extensions (TDX) is a hardware-based technology designed to provide confidential computing by isolating virtual machines at the CPU level. With TDX, workloads run inside trusted domains that are protected from both malicious software and potentially compromised system administrators. This helps banks host sensitive applications, such as real-time payment systems or risk analytics engines, in highly secure environments that are shielded from unauthorized access even within the same virtualized infrastructure.

Case study 3.2: ESXiArgs Ransomware, 2021

In 2021, the ESXiArgs ransomware campaign highlighted the dangers of unpatched and poorly secured virtualization environments. Attackers targeted VMware ESXi hypervisors, exploiting known vulnerabilities in systems that had not been updated with critical security patches. Once inside, the ransomware encrypted the configuration files of multiple virtual machines hosted on the compromised hypervisors.

- **Impact on financial institutions:** Several organizations, including banks and fintech providers, experienced downtime and data unavailability as their production VMs were rendered inaccessible. Since ESXi hypervisors often host dozens of mission-critical workloads, a single compromised hypervisor created a **cascade effect**, bringing multiple applications offline simultaneously.

- **Root cause:** Many affected systems had either outdated software or misconfigured management interfaces exposed to the Internet, making them easy entry points for attackers.
- **Lessons learned**
    - Regular patching and hypervisor hardening are essential.
    - Exposed management consoles must always be firewalled or restricted to internal networks.
    - Backup and recovery plans must include VM configuration files, not just data volumes, to enable rapid restoration.

Key takeaway: The ESXiArgs incident demonstrated that virtualization offers efficiency but also magnifies risks if foundational security practices are neglected. It reinforced the need for technology-assisted defense (like NSX, Citrix, and TDX) combined with disciplined patch management in financial institutions.

3.5 Cloud computing and related concerns

Cloud computing has become an integral part of digital transformation strategies in banking. By moving beyond traditional on-premises infrastructure, banks gain the ability to scale services rapidly, reduce capital expenditure, and deliver innovative customer experiences. Functions such as digital payment gateways, fraud detection systems, real-time analytics, and mobile banking platforms are increasingly hosted in the cloud to leverage its flexibility and resilience.

However, this adoption also introduces significant challenges. The regulatory environment for banking is strict, requiring compliance with standards such as PCI DSS (Payment Card Industry Data Security Standard), GDPR (General Data Protection Regulation), and RBI (Reserve Bank of India) data localization guidelines. The shared responsibility model in the cloud often creates confusion about which security controls lie with the provider and which are the bank's responsibility. Additionally, issues such as multi-tenancy risks, insider threats, and vendor lock-in highlight the need for careful planning before and during migration.

In short, while the cloud unlocks agility and cost efficiency, banks must balance these benefits with robust governance, continuous monitoring, and strict compliance practices to ensure security and trust in their digital services.

3.5.1 Cloud service models in banking

Cloud services are typically consumed through three primary models: Infrastructure as a Service (IaaS), Platform as a Service (PaaS), and Software as a Service (SaaS), each offering different benefits and risk considerations for banks.

Infrastructure as a Service (IaaS)

- Provides virtualized computing resources such as servers, storage, and networking.

- Banks use IaaS for hosting core banking applications, disaster recovery sites, and big data analytics platforms without investing in physical data centers.
- Example: An Indian bank using Microsoft Azure for high-availability disaster recovery, ensuring quick failover during outages.
- Risk concern: Misconfigured storage buckets or open ports in IaaS environments have previously led to customer data leaks, highlighting the importance of configuration management.

Platform as a Service (PaaS)

- Offers a ready-made environment for developers to build, test, and deploy applications without managing the underlying infrastructure.
- Enables Fintech innovation; APIs for payments, loan processing systems, and AI-driven chatbots can be quickly developed and scaled.
- Example: Banks leveraging Google Cloud's PaaS for machine learning models to detect fraudulent transactions in real time.
- Risk concern: If not properly governed, PaaS integrations can create vulnerabilities through third-party code or unverified APIs.

Software as a Service (SaaS)

- Provides fully managed software solutions delivered over the Internet.
- Widely adopted for CRM (Customer Relationship Management) platforms, fraud detection tools, compliance monitoring systems, and collaboration tools within banks.
- Example: A global bank using SaaS-based fraud analytics solutions to monitor transaction anomalies across millions of accounts.
- Risk Concern: SaaS applications may involve sensitive data hosted outside the bank's infrastructure, raising questions of data sovereignty, encryption standards, and vendor trustworthiness.

Figure 3.3 illustrates the three primary cloud service models in banking, showing IaaS at the base, PaaS in the middle, and SaaS at the top with their respective components and applications.

3.5.2 Security concerns in cloud banking

Although cloud computing offers banks scalability and cost efficiency, it also introduces critical risks that demand careful oversight. From regulatory obligations to operational dependencies, each area poses challenges that can directly impact data security, compliance, and customer trust. Issues such as data sovereignty, blurred responsibilities between providers and banks, insider misuse, vendor dependency, and stringent audit requirements are particularly relevant in the financial sector, where both regulators and customers expect the highest level of protection. Table 3.3 below summarizes the most pressing concerns associated with cloud adoption in banking, along with real-world examples of how these challenges manifest.

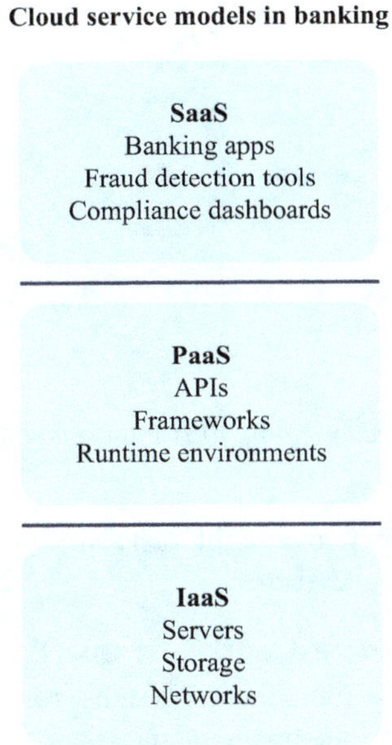

Figure 3.3 Cloud service models in banking

Table 3.3 Cloud concerns in banking

Concern	Explanation	Banking example
Data sovereignty	Regulations require data to reside in-country	RBI mandates data localization for payment data
Shared responsibility	Banks assume wrongly that providers secure everything	Misconfigured AWS S3 buckets leaking KYC (Know Your Customer) data
Insider threats	Cloud admins may access sensitive data	Cloud contractor misusing privileged accounts
Vendor lock-in	Difficult to migrate workloads across providers	Long-term contracts with limited flexibility
Compliance and audits	PCI DSS, GDPR, RBI guidelines	Noncompliance leads to heavy penalties

Figure 3.4 highlights the shared responsibility model in cloud banking, showing how infrastructure security lies with the provider while applications and data remain the bank's responsibility, with certain controls managed jointly.

3.5.3 Mitigation strategies

To address the risks associated with cloud adoption in banking, institutions must adopt a layered approach that combines technical safeguards, identity controls,

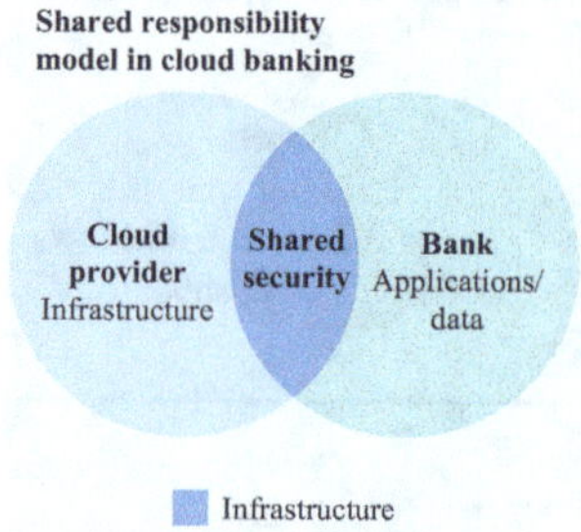

Figure 3.4 Shared responsibility model in cloud banking

visibility tools, and regulatory oversight. The following strategies are widely implemented across the financial sector.

Strong encryption (data at rest and in transit)

Encryption is one of the most fundamental defenses against unauthorized access. Banks must ensure that sensitive financial data is encrypted both at rest (while stored in databases, backups, or file systems) and in transit (while moving across networks). Industry standards such as AES-256 (Advanced Encryption Standard) for storage and TLS 1.2/1.3 (Transport Layer Security) for data transfer are widely adopted. This ensures that even if data is intercepted or stolen, it remains unintelligible without decryption keys. Key management practices, including Hardware Security Modules (HSMs), are also essential to safeguard encryption keys.

Multi-Factor Authentication (MFA) and Identity & Access Management (IAM)

Unauthorized access is one of the leading causes of cloud breaches. Enforcing MFA ensures that user authentication requires more than a single factor, combining something the user knows (password), something the user has (OTP, token), and/or something the user is (biometric). Alongside MFA, IAM frameworks allow banks to define granular access policies, implement the principle of least privilege, and segregate duties to minimize insider risks. Periodic reviews of IAM policies prevent privilege creep, where users accumulate unnecessary access rights over time.

Cloud Access Security Brokers (CASB) for visibility

CASBs act as intermediaries between users and cloud service providers, giving banks deep visibility into cloud usage and enforcing security policies. With CASBs, institutions can monitor data flows, detect shadow IT (unauthorized cloud apps), enforce data loss prevention (DLP) rules, and identify anomalous behavior such as bulk downloads or unusual logins. For example, if a user attempts to upload large amounts of customer data to an unapproved SaaS platform, the CASB can block the action or trigger alerts. This visibility is critical in highly regulated banking environments.

Periodic regulatory compliance audits

Banks operate under stringent regulations, and compliance is nonnegotiable. Conducting regular compliance audits ensures that cloud deployments align with frameworks such as PCI DSS (for payment card data), GDPR (for customer privacy), and RBI guidelines (for data localization and financial data protection in India). Audits not only validate technical configurations but also review access logs, incident response procedures, and vendor contracts. Proactive auditing helps identify gaps before regulators or attackers exploit them, safeguarding both compliance posture and institutional reputation.

Key takeaway: By combining encryption, robust identity management, visibility tools, and rigorous compliance practices, banks can mitigate the unique risks of cloud adoption while continuing to reap the benefits of agility and scalability.

3.6 Application scenarios of Internet banking

Internet banking today extends far beyond simple fund transfers. It has evolved into a comprehensive digital ecosystem that caters to both **individual customers and corporate clients**, enabling a wide range of financial services from basic account management to complex trade finance operations. By leveraging mobile platforms, cloud integration, and secure transaction frameworks, banks can provide **real-time, accessible, and scalable services** to millions of users simultaneously. The following subsections highlight the major application scenarios of Internet banking.

Figure 3.5 presents the Internet Banking Service Landscape, highlighting key services like fund transfers, bill payments, loan applications, investments, insurance, and mobile recharge in a circular model.

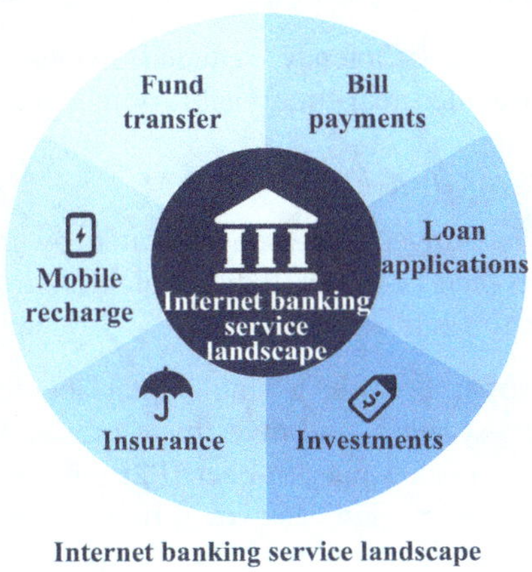

Figure 3.5 Internet banking service landscape

3.6.1 Retail banking

Retail Internet banking services are the foundation of digital banking adoption, designed to meet the needs of individual customers. Key services include:

- **Account management:** Customers can view account balances, transaction history, and digital statements on demand.
- **Fund transfers:** Facilities like NEFT (National Electronic Funds Transfer), RTGS (Real-Time Gross Settlement), IMPS (Immediate Payment Service), and UPI allow secure money transfers domestically in real time.
- **Bill payments:** Utility bills, credit card dues, and recurring payments can be automated via net banking portals.
- **Personal finance tools:** Customers can track spending patterns, set savings goals, and access personalized financial advice.

Value for customers: Convenience, 24×7 access, reduced need for physical branch visits, and improved transparency in account activity.

3.6.2 Corporate banking

Corporate Internet banking provides enterprises with advanced tools for managing large-scale financial operations. Key services include:

- **Bulk payments:** Companies can process payroll disbursements, vendor payments, and statutory dues through centralized online systems.
- **Trade finance:** Digital issuance of letters of credit, guarantees, and import/export documentation reduces paperwork and accelerates trade cycles.
- **Liquidity management:** Corporations can consolidate multiple accounts, track cash flow across subsidiaries, and optimize working capital through real-time dashboards.
- **Treasury operations:** Online platforms enable investments, hedging, and foreign exchange transactions with minimal delays.

Value for businesses: Efficiency reduced manual intervention, lowered operational costs, and provided real-time visibility into financial transactions.

3.6.3 Mobile banking and UPI

The growth of mobile banking has been accelerated by innovations such as the **Unified Payments Interface (UPI)** in India, which has redefined the speed and accessibility of digital payments.

- **Mobile banking apps:** Provide a single interface for fund transfers, loan applications, account services, and investment products.
- **UPI system:** Enables instant peer-to-peer (P2P) and peer-to-merchant (P2M) payments using mobile devices, requiring only a virtual payment address (VPA).
- **Features:** Interoperability across banks, real-time settlement, integration with QR (Quick Response) codes, and support for micro-payments.

- **Ecosystem expansion:** UPI is integrated into third-party apps like Google Pay, PhonePe, and Paytm, boosting adoption even among small businesses and individuals in rural areas.

Value for customers: 24×7 availability, zero/minimal transaction fees, and seamless integration with e-commerce and service platforms.

3.6.4 International banking

Global connectivity has made international Internet banking essential for both individuals and corporations. Services include:

- **Forex transfers:** Secure transfer of funds across borders using SWIFT and other remittance systems.
- **Remittances:** Migrant workers and global citizens can remit funds to their home countries directly via mobile or online platforms.
- **Digital trade platforms:** Banks offer online platforms for cross-border trade settlements, reducing dependency on paper-based processing.
- **Multi-currency accounts:** Customers can manage funds in multiple currencies with online conversion and hedging tools.

Value for users: Faster, more cost-effective global transactions, simplified compliance checks, and reduced reliance on physical intermediaries.

Case study 3.3: India's UPI revolution

India's **Unified Payments Interface (UPI)** has become a global benchmark for mobile-first banking innovation. In 2023, UPI processed **over 10 billion transactions in a single month**, demonstrating the scalability of digital payment systems when backed by strong infrastructure and regulatory support.

- **Background:** Launched by the National Payments Corporation of India (NPCI) in 2016, UPI was designed as a real-time payment system allowing users to link multiple bank accounts to a single mobile application.
- **Growth factors**
  - **Accessibility:** UPI works seamlessly across banks and third-party apps.
  - **Cost advantage:** Zero or minimal transaction fees have encouraged rapid adoption by merchants and consumers alike.
  - **Security:** Integration of **multi-factor authentication (MFA)** and transaction-level encryption ensured that large-scale adoption did not compromise trust.
  - **Government push:** Incentives for digital transactions, demonetization in 2016, and pandemic-driven digital adoption boosted growth.
- **Security measures**
  - **Two-factor authentication:** A combination of device binding and UPI PIN entry.
  - **Real-time fraud detection:** Banks and NPCI use machine learning models to flag anomalies such as unusual transaction patterns or geographic inconsistencies.

  - **Transaction limits:** Daily and per-transaction limits reduce systemic risks.

- **Impact**
  - Revolutionized **P2P and merchant payments**, including micro-transactions at local shops.
  - Empowered financial inclusion by enabling millions of unbanked and underbanked users to transact digitally.
  - Inspired international adoption, with countries like Singapore and the UAE exploring UPI linkages for cross-border payments.

Key lesson: The UPI case shows that **security, scalability, and inclusivity** can co-exist in mobile-first Internet banking when backed by robust authentication and continuous fraud monitoring.

Key points to remember

- Internet banking provides unmatched convenience but also brings new risks. Customers now have 24×7 access to banking services such as fund transfers, bill payments, and investments from anywhere in the world. However, this digital shift also exposes financial institutions to a broader attack surface, where threats may arise from weak authentication practices, misconfigured virtual machines, or insecure cloud deployments. Convenience must therefore always be balanced with robust cybersecurity measures.
- Authentication is the first line of defense, and its methods are evolving. Early systems relied solely on passwords and PINs, which are simple but vulnerable to brute force, phishing, and credential theft. Modern banking increasingly relies on Multi-Factor Authentication (MFA), combining knowledge (password), possession (OTP, hardware token), and inherence (biometric). Emerging trends such as behavioral biometrics (typing rhythm, mouse movement, and mobile swipe patterns) and FIDO2 passwordless systems are reducing reliance on static credentials. Still, each method has limitations, making layered authentication strategies essential.
- Virtualization enhances scalability and resource efficiency but comes with inherent risks. Banks use virtualization to run core banking applications, storage, and disaster recovery solutions on shared infrastructure, reducing costs and deployment time. However, weaknesses such as hypervisor attacks, VM sprawl, and resource contention create vulnerabilities. If the hypervisor is compromised, attackers can potentially access all hosted VMs. Proper VM lifecycle management, hypervisor hardening, and micro-segmentation are necessary to mitigate these risks.
- Cloud adoption in banking offers agility but demands strict compliance and governance. Cloud services, whether IaaS, PaaS, or SaaS, enable banks to innovate rapidly and scale operations. Yet, they also introduce concerns about data sovereignty (where customer data must reside within national borders), shared responsibility (dividing roles between provider and bank), and vendor

lock-in (difficulty in moving workloads between providers). Compliance frameworks such as PCI DSS, GDPR, and RBI guidelines must be adhered to, with regular audits and strong encryption practices ensuring customer trust.

- Case studies reinforce the importance of continuous monitoring, patching, and awareness. Real-world incidents such as the HSBC voice biometric bypass, the ESXiArgs ransomware campaign, and the UPI scaling success story illustrate that technology alone is not sufficient. Banks must implement continuous patching, proactive monitoring with SIEM and CASB tools, and user awareness programs to stay ahead of evolving threats. Customer education is equally important, as social engineering remains a leading cause of financial breaches.

Questions (try answering yourself)

1. Define Internet banking and explain how it has transformed customer interaction with financial institutions.
2. Discuss the role of authentication in Internet banking and compare different authentication methods used today.
3. What are the strengths and weaknesses of biometric authentication in banking systems?
4. Explain behavioral biometrics with examples and evaluate its effectiveness in Internet banking security.
5. What is risk-based authentication (RBA), and how does it balance user convenience with security?
6. Discuss the concept of passwordless authentication (FIDO2) and its relevance in modern banking.
7. Differentiate between social engineering-based attacks and authentication bypass in Internet banking.
8. Explain the concept of virtualization in banking IT infrastructure and its importance.
9. List and explain the major challenges associated with virtualization in banking environments.
10. How can hypervisor hardening and VM lifecycle management help mitigate virtualization risks?
11. Analyze the role of micro-segmentation and workload isolation in securing virtualized banking environments.
12. Explain the ESXiArgs ransomware case and discuss its implications for the banking sector.
13. Describe the different cloud service models (IaaS, PaaS, SaaS) and their applications in banking.
14. What are the major concerns banks face when adopting cloud computing? Provide relevant examples.
15. Explain the shared responsibility model in cloud banking with a suitable diagram.
16. Discuss the role of encryption, IAM, CASB, and compliance audits in mitigating cloud risks.

17. Evaluate the application of Internet banking in retail banking, corporate banking, and international banking.
18. Explain the role of UPI in transforming mobile banking in India, with supporting statistics.
19. Using suitable case studies, illustrate how weak security controls in Internet banking have been exploited.
20. Summarize the key lessons banks must learn from the adoption of Internet banking to balance innovation with security.

Objective questions

1. Internet banking is also known as:
   (a) E-banking
   (b) Mobile banking
   (c) ATM banking
   (d) Core banking

2. Which of the following is the weakest form of authentication?
   (a) Password
   (b) OTP
   (c) Biometric
   (d) Multi-factor authentication

3. True/False: Behavioral biometrics include typing rhythm, mouse movement, and touchscreen swipes.
4. Risk-Based Authentication adapts security checks based on:
   (a) Transaction context
   (b) Customer feedback
   (c) Bank policy only
   (d) Random chance

5. FIDO2 is primarily designed to enable:
   (a) Passwordless authentication
   (b) Faster Internet browsing
   (c) Secure VPN tunnels
   (d) Biometric data storage

6. Which incident exposed the weakness of voice-only authentication in banking?
   (a) Colonial Pipeline attack
   (b) HSBC Voice Recognition breach
   (c) ESXiArgs ransomware
   (d) Google invoice fraud

7. Virtualization allows multiple _______ to run on a single physical server.
   (a) Browsers
   (b) Virtual Machines

(c) Passwords
(d) Routers

8. The software layer that manages VMs in virtualization is called:
   (a) Kernel
   (b) Hypervisor
   (c) Container
   (d) Firewall
9. True/False: VM sprawl occurs when too many VMs are deployed without proper oversight.
10. Which of the following tools is used for micro-segmentation in banking virtualization?
    (a) Proofpoint
    (b) VMware NSX
    (c) Hoxhunt
    (d) Splunk
11. ESXiArgs ransomware exploited vulnerabilities in:
    (a) Citrix
    (b) Hyper-V
    (c) VMware ESXi
    (d) Oracle VirtualBox
12. In cloud banking, IaaS provides:
    (a) Ready-made applications
    (b) Virtualized infrastructure resources
    (c) AI-driven fraud detection tools
    (d) Identity verification services
13. PaaS in banking is primarily used for:
    (a) Developing and deploying Fintech solutions
    (b) Storing raw transaction data
    (c) Running ATMs
    (d) Auditing financial records
14. SaaS solutions in banking typically include:
    (a) Fraud detection tools
    (b) Branch networking
    (c) Currency printing systems
    (d) ATM card readers
15. True/False: In the shared responsibility model, banks are solely responsible for securing physical infrastructure.
16. Which of the following ensures data protection during transmission?
    (a) AES-256
    (b) TLS 1.3
    (c) RSA Token
    (d) VPN

17. A CASB tool helps banks with:
    (a) Fraudulent email detection
    (b) Cloud visibility and policy enforcement
    (c) ATM hardware monitoring
    (d) Employee performance evaluation
18. Which regulatory requirement mandates that payment data be stored within India?
    (a) GDPR
    (b) HIPAA
    (c) RBI Data Localization Guidelines
    (d) CCPA
19. The Unified Payments Interface (UPI) in India was launched by:
    (a) RBI
    (b) NPCI
    (c) SBI
    (d) SEBI
20. True/False: UPI transactions in India crossed 10 billion per month in 2023.

Answers for the objective questions

1. a) E-banking
2. a) Password
3. True
4. a) Transaction context
5. a) Passwordless authentication
6. b) HSBC Voice Recognition breach
7. b) Virtual Machines
8. b) Hypervisor
9. True
10. b) VMware NSX
11. c) VMware ESXi
12. b) Virtualized infrastructure resources
13. a) Developing and deploying Fintech solutions
14. a) Fraud detection tools
15. False (Providers secure infrastructure; banks secure apps and data)
16. b) TLS 1.3
17. b) Cloud visibility and policy enforcement
18. c) RBI Data Localization Guidelines
19. b) NPCI
20. True

Further reading

[1] Basel Committee on Banking Supervision. *Risk Management Principles for Electronic Banking*. Bank for International Settlements; 2003.

[2] Reserve Bank of India. *Report of the Working Group on Information Security, Electronic Banking, Technology Risk Management and Cyber Frauds*. RBI; 2011.

[3] National Payments Corporation of India. *UPI Product Statistics*. NPCI; 2023.

[4] European Central Bank. *Internet Payments Security Guidelines*. ECB; 2013.

[5] Federal Financial Institutions Examination Council (FFIEC). *Authentication in an Internet Banking Environment*. Washington, DC: FFIEC; 2005.

[6] Hadnagy C. *Social Engineering: The Science of Human Hacking*. 2nd ed. Wiley; 2018.

[7] Mitnick KD, and Simon WL. *The Art of Deception: Controlling the Human Element of Security*. Wiley; 2002.

[8] VMware. *VMware NSX Data Center Security Overview*. VMware Inc.; 2020.

[9] Citrix Systems. *Citrix Virtual Apps and Desktops Security Features*. Citrix; 2021.

[10] Intel Corporation. *Intel® Trust Domain Extensions (Intel® TDX) Architectural Specification*. Intel; 2022.

[11] CERT-In. *Advisory on Ransomware Targeting VMware ESXi Servers*. Indian Computer Emergency Response Team; 2023.

[12] FIDO Alliance. *FIDO2: Moving the World Beyond Passwords*. FIDO Alliance; 2019.

[13] European Union. *Directive (EU) 2015/2366 on Payment Services (PSD2)*. Official Journal of the European Union; 2015.

[14] Microsoft. *Azure Security and Compliance Blueprints*. Microsoft; 2021.

[15] Google Cloud. *Cloud Security for Financial Services: Whitepaper*. Google LLC; 2022.

[16] Proofpoint. *The Human Factor 2022: Threat Landscape Report*. Proofpoint; 2022.

[17] PCI Security Standards Council. *PCI DSS v4.0 Requirements and Security Assessment Procedures*. PCI SSC; 2022.

[18] World Bank. *Digital Financial Inclusion: Global Progress and Challenges*. Washington, DC: World Bank; 2020.

[19] Singh A, and Paliwal S. UPI: The architecture of India's digital payments revolution. *Communications of the ACM*. 2021;64(12): 74–80.

[20] SANS Institute. *Cloud Security Essentials for Financial Services*. SANS Whitepaper; 2022.

Chapter 4
Mobile banking

Learning objectives

After reading through the chapter, the reader will gain a clear understanding of

- The concept of mobile banking and its role in modern digital financial services.
- Identifying major security concerns associated with mobile banking, including malware, phishing, and device vulnerabilities.
- Password security practices and the importance of multi-factor authentication in safeguarding accounts.
- Unified Payments Interface (UPI) architecture analysis and security features that make it a trusted digital payment method in India.
- Recognizing best practices for ensuring mobile and UPI transaction safety from both customer and bank perspectives.
- Evaluating risk mitigation strategies adopted by banks, regulators, and customers to minimize fraud.
- Developing a holistic approach to mobile banking security through awareness, technology adoption, and responsible usage.

4.1 Introduction

The digital revolution has transformed the way people interact with financial institutions. At the forefront of this change is mobile banking, which allows customers to conduct transactions, monitor balances, transfer money, and even access advanced investment services directly from their smartphones. Unlike traditional banking, which required physical branch visits, mobile banking enables 24/7 convenience at the customer's fingertips.

Globally, mobile banking adoption has skyrocketed due to increasing smartphone penetration, cheaper internet access, and the growing preference for cashless transactions. In India, this trend has been accelerated by initiatives such as Unified Payments Interface (UPI), digital wallets, and government pushes toward financial inclusion. Mobile banking has moved beyond simple balance checks to a complete financial ecosystem, covering payments, insurance, investments, and credit.

However, with convenience comes risk. Mobile banking is a prime target for cybercriminals due to its widespread usage and the direct link to financial assets.

Threats such as malware, phishing apps, SIM swap fraud, and weak passwords expose users to significant vulnerabilities. This makes security awareness and risk mitigation essential for both banks and customers.

The shared responsibility model applies strongly here; banks must implement advanced security measures, regulators must enforce strong guidelines, and customers must practice safe digital habits. Only then can the promise of mobile banking be realized without undue risk.

4.2 Mobile banking security concerns

Mobile banking, while revolutionary in terms of accessibility and convenience, comes with a host of security concerns that cannot be overlooked. The very factors that make it popular—ease of use, instant access, and wide adoption—also make it a prime target for cybercriminals. Unlike traditional branch-based banking, where the physical infrastructure serves as a barrier, mobile banking depends entirely on the customer's device, the bank's application, and the network environment. This dependence creates a complex ecosystem of vulnerabilities at multiple levels.

One of the foremost concerns in mobile banking security is the growing menace of malware and rogue applications. Fraudsters design malicious software disguised as legitimate applications, often circulating them through third-party app stores, phishing links, or even infiltrating official app markets. Once installed, these apps gain access to sensitive functions on the phone, such as reading SMS messages containing one-time passwords (OTPs) or overlaying fake login screens to harvest credentials. Global incidents like the Anubis Trojan, which specifically targeted Android users, demonstrate how powerful such malware can be in silently capturing passwords, banking details, and even enabling remote control of the device. In India too, fake loan apps and counterfeit versions of popular banking apps have repeatedly surfaced, duping unsuspecting users into handing over their personal and financial information.

Closely linked to this is the rise of phishing and smishing (SMS phishing) attacks. These methods exploit human psychology rather than technical flaws. Fraudsters send emails or SMS messages that appear to be from trusted institutions, often using logos, formatting, and language that mimic official communication. Messages typically contain alarming statements such as, "Your account will be blocked unless you verify your details," or "Update your KYC immediately to avoid suspension." Victims who click on the provided links are redirected to fraudulent websites crafted to look identical to genuine banking portals. Once users enter their usernames, passwords, or card details, the information is immediately stolen. Several Indian banks have reported waves of such attacks, where customers unknowingly compromised their own accounts by trusting fraudulent communication. The effectiveness of phishing lies in its ability to trigger fear and urgency, two emotions that often override rational thinking.

Another significant threat comes from SIM swap fraud and identity theft. In these cases, criminals gather personal details about the victim through data leaks, social engineering, or phishing and then approach telecom operators with fake identification documents to request a duplicate SIM card. Once issued, the original SIM is deactivated, and all OTPs and alerts for banking transactions are routed directly to the fraudsters. Victims typically realize what has happened only when their phone loses network connectivity, by which time their accounts may already have been emptied. High-profile SIM swap cases reported in cities like Mumbai and Delhi underscore how vulnerable mobile banking systems become when telecom identity verification is lax.

Public Wi-Fi usage further amplifies mobile banking risks. Many customers access their banking apps while connected to free Wi-Fi networks in airports, cafes, or hotels. Such networks, while convenient, are often poorly secured and susceptible to man-in-the-middle attacks. Cybercriminals also set up rogue hotspots with names resembling legitimate ones, such as "Airport_FreeNet," to lure victims into connecting. Once connected, attackers can intercept the unencrypted traffic, capturing login credentials, card details, or session information. In such scenarios, the very act of logging into one's account in a public space can unknowingly hand over sensitive financial data to malicious actors.

Device-level vulnerabilities also form a critical layer of concern. Many users fail to update their smartphone operating systems or banking apps, leaving them exposed to known security flaws. Outdated devices, especially those running older versions of Android or iOS, miss out on crucial security patches, making them easy targets for attackers. The risks multiply when users deliberately root or jailbreak their devices to bypass restrictions, often in pursuit of customization or to install unauthorized apps. This process, however, strips away many of the built-in security controls designed to protect sensitive data, thereby weakening the device's ability to safeguard mobile banking transactions.

Weak authentication practices continue to be one of the simplest yet most devastating risks in mobile banking. Despite repeated awareness campaigns, many customers still use easily guessable passwords such as "123456," birthdates, or their own names. Even worse, password reuse across multiple platforms means that if credentials from a social media breach are leaked, they can be tested against banking platforms in what is called a credential-stuffing attack. Banks have introduced stronger mechanisms such as two-factor authentication and biometric logins, yet weak customer practices often undermine these protections. A single weak password can render even the most advanced security system ineffective.

Adding to these risks are social engineering attacks, where fraudsters impersonate bank representatives or customer support agents to trick users into revealing sensitive details. Customers are often told that their accounts will be suspended unless they share their credentials or that they need to provide OTPs to complete KYC verification. In reality, such calls are nothing more than manipulative schemes designed to extract information directly from the victim. Technology alone cannot defend against this, since the fraud succeeds not through hacking but through persuasion and deception.

App cloning represents another emerging threat. Fraudsters often publish counterfeit versions of legitimate banking applications on unofficial app stores, sometimes even sneaking them past the security checks of popular ones.

Customers, failing to verify the authenticity of the app, download and install these clones, unknowingly handing over their banking credentials to criminals. Repeated instances of fake State Bank of India (SBI) or ICICI banking apps appearing in app markets highlight how sophisticated and widespread this problem has become.

What ties all these concerns together is the growing sophistication of cybercriminals and the rapid adoption of mobile banking. As transaction volumes grow into the billions each month, especially in India with UPI, the incentive for fraudsters increases. User negligence, whether through weak passwords, outdated devices, or misplaced trust, amplifies risks. Organized crime networks are also leveraging systemic loopholes, creating well-coordinated fraud schemes that transcend borders and industries.

In conclusion, mobile banking security concerns are not confined to technology alone. They span human behavior, device vulnerabilities, communication clarity, and organizational preparedness. Addressing these concerns requires a comprehensive approach; banks must fortify their applications, regulators must enforce stringent guidelines, and customers must adopt safe digital practices. Only through shared vigilance can mobile banking continue to grow as a secure and reliable platform for the future of finance.

Figure 4.1 portrays the key threats, including malware, phishing, SIM swaps, insecure Wi-Fi, device vulnerabilities, weak authentication, social engineering, and

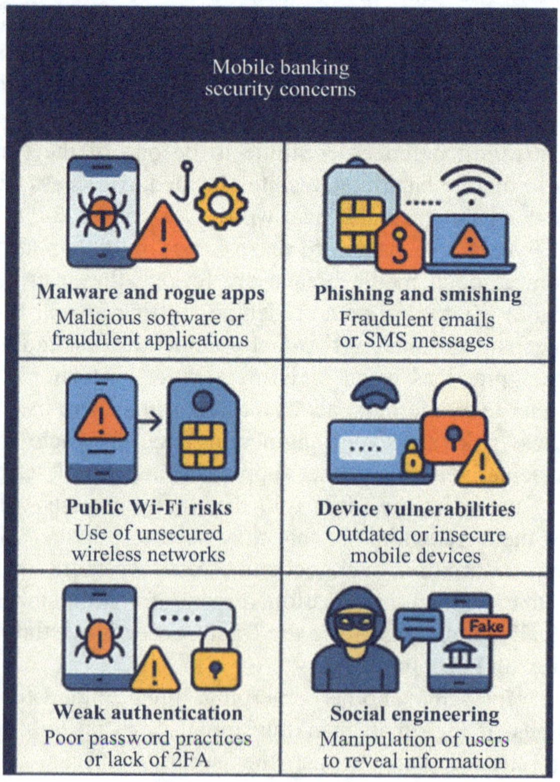

Figure 4.1 Mobile banking security concerns

app cloning. As depicted in Figure 4.1, mobile banking faces diverse security concerns ranging from malware and phishing to SIM swaps and fake applications.

4.3 Password security

Passwords remain one of the most fundamental yet fragile pillars of mobile banking security. Despite advances in biometric authentication, two-factor authentication (2FA), and token-based systems, the majority of customers still rely on passwords or PINs as their primary line of defense. The simplicity and familiarity of passwords make them convenient, but this convenience often comes at the cost of security. Weak, reused, or poorly managed passwords are consistently ranked among the leading causes of financial fraud in the digital era.

One of the major challenges is the continued reliance on weak or predictable passwords. Many users still choose easily guessable combinations such as "123456," birthdates, anniversaries, or their own names. Such passwords can be cracked almost instantly through brute-force or dictionary attacks. Credential-stuffing attacks, in which hackers test usernames and passwords leaked from unrelated platforms against banking portals, have also become alarmingly common. Since many people reuse the same password across multiple services, a breach in one domain (like social media) often leads directly to compromises in another (like mobile banking). This creates a dangerous chain reaction where a seemingly harmless password leak ends up exposing critical financial assets.

Another concern is the practice of storing passwords insecurely. Customers frequently jot them down in notebooks, save them in phone notes, or even share them with friends and family. In some cases, they rely on the browser's autofill feature or store them in unencrypted formats. Such practices expose passwords to theft if the device is lost, stolen, or compromised with malware. Banks have consistently warned against such practices, but the habit persists, often due to the human tendency to prioritize convenience over caution.

Mobile banking apps themselves, though increasingly sophisticated, are not immune to password-related vulnerabilities. Some older versions of banking apps lacked strict password complexity requirements, allowing customers to set short and weak passwords. Others did not enforce periodic password resets, leaving accounts vulnerable for years. Modern banking applications now enforce stricter rules, such as a minimum of eight to twelve characters, mandatory inclusion of numbers and special symbols, and limits on repeated characters. However, these measures are effective only if customers embrace them, rather than attempting to find shortcuts.

To counter these risks, multi-factor authentication has emerged as a critical safeguard. Beyond the password, customers are required to provide an additional layer of verification, typically in the form of OTPs delivered via SMS or email, app-based authenticators, or biometric checks like fingerprint and facial recognition. Multi-factor authentication (MFA) significantly reduces the chances of unauthorized access, since a stolen password alone is not enough to compromise an account. However, this too faces challenges, particularly with SIM swap frauds that divert OTPs or phishing campaigns that trick users into providing both their password and the OTP.

An emerging solution is the use of password managers, which generate and store complex, unique passwords for every service. These tools remove the burden of memorization while drastically reducing the risk of password reuse. Despite their benefits, adoption in mobile banking contexts has been slow, largely due to a lack of awareness and hesitation among less tech-savvy users. Similarly, biometric authentication (such as fingerprint scanning and Face ID) offers a convenient alternative, but it is not foolproof, as spoofing attempts and device vulnerabilities have occasionally been reported.

Ultimately, the effectiveness of password security rests not only on technological safeguards but also on customer behavior. Even the most secure system can be compromised if users ignore basic hygiene practices, such as regularly updating passwords, avoiding reuse, and never sharing credentials. Banks must therefore combine strict password policies with continuous customer education. Regular awareness campaigns, in-app reminders, and clear communication about the importance of strong authentication can go a long way in reducing risks.

In essence, password security represents the delicate balance between **user convenience and robust protection**. It is not enough for banks to mandate complex rules; they must also make compliance easy and intuitive. Similarly, customers must recognize that passwords are their first line of defense in mobile banking, and negligence here could mean the difference between safety and devastating financial loss.

As shown in Figure 4.2, adopting good password practices like uniqueness, complexity, and MFA significantly strengthens mobile banking security compared to weak or reused credentials.

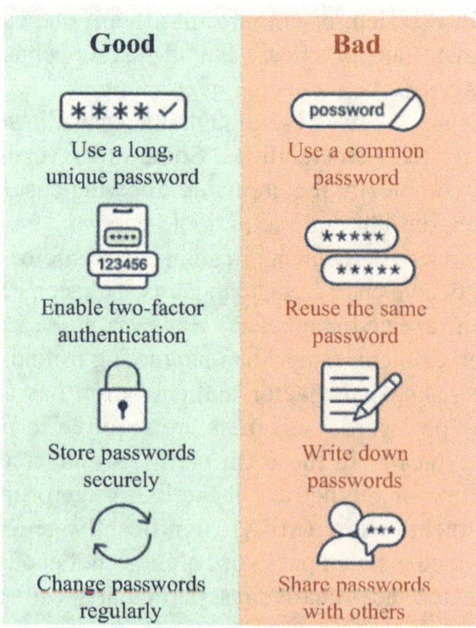

Figure 4.2 Good vs. bad password practices

4.4 UPI and security features

The Unified Payments Interface (UPI) has revolutionized digital payments in India, becoming one of the most widely adopted payment systems in the world. Developed by the National Payments Corporation of India (NPCI) and launched in 2016, UPI allows users to transfer money instantly between bank accounts using just a mobile device. Its design emphasizes simplicity, requiring only a Virtual Payment Address (VPA), mobile number, or QR code to initiate transactions, eliminating the need to enter lengthy account details or Indian Financial System Code (IFSC) codes. As of 2024, UPI has grown to process billions of transactions every month, reflecting its success as a secure, interoperable, and real-time payment platform.

At the core of UPI's success lies its security-first architecture. Every transaction is authenticated using a two-factor system mandated by the Reserve Bank of India (RBI). Customers must verify payments with both their mobile number (linked to their bank account) and a unique UPI PIN, which acts as a second layer of defense. Unlike traditional card-based systems, where card numbers and Card Verification Value (CVV) codes can be easily skimmed, UPI does not expose sensitive bank account details during transactions. This design reduces the surface area for fraud and enhances consumer confidence.

Another important security feature of UPI is end-to-end encryption. All transaction data transmitted between the customer, the app, and the bank is encrypted, ensuring that sensitive information cannot be intercepted by attackers. Furthermore, UPI is designed with real-time settlement capabilities, which means there is no prolonged "pending" window during which transactions could be manipulated or altered.

UPI also incorporates device binding, which ties the customer's account to a specific smartphone and SIM card. This prevents attackers from logging in from unauthorized devices even if they manage to obtain the user's credentials. When a new device is registered, the system requires fresh authentication using both the bank-linked mobile number and additional verification measures.

To further strengthen protection, UPI mandates the use of dynamic one-time passwords (OTPs) and alerts. For sensitive operations such as PIN resets or device changes, customers receive instant SMS or in-app notifications, enabling them to detect suspicious activities quickly. These proactive alerts play a crucial role in empowering customers to respond before fraudsters succeed.

Additionally, UPI platforms like Bharat Interface for Money (BHIM), Google Pay, PhonePe, and Paytm have introduced their own app-level security layers. These include biometric locks (fingerprint or facial recognition), app PINs, and AI-based fraud detection that can flag unusual patterns such as repeated failed transactions or transfers to suspicious accounts. Many apps now display explicit warnings reminding customers that entering a UPI PIN is required only for sending money, not for receiving it, a crucial safeguard against the rising wave of social engineering scams.

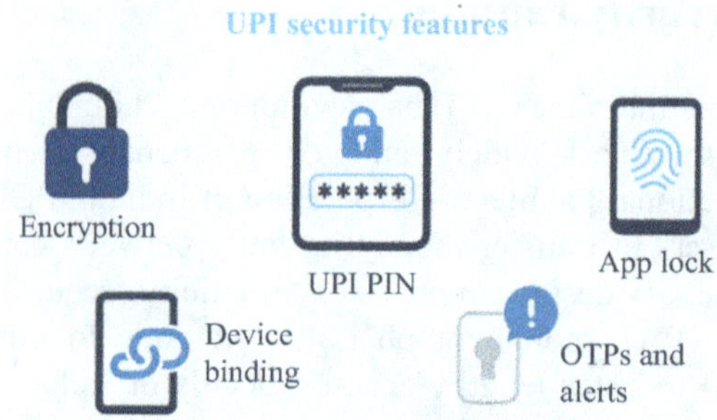

Figure 4.3 UPI security features

From a regulatory perspective, the RBI and NPCI continuously issue guidelines to enhance UPI safety. These include transaction limits, restrictions on failed authentication attempts, and stronger reporting frameworks for fraud. UPI apps are also required to provide easy in-app reporting tools, enabling customers to flag suspicious activity directly.

In short, UPI's rise as a trusted payment platform can be attributed not only to its convenience but also to its robust and evolving security framework. By combining encryption, device binding, two-factor authentication, and proactive alerts, UPI has set a benchmark for digital payment systems globally. However, its effectiveness ultimately depends on customer awareness, knowing when to enter a PIN, verifying payment requests, and reporting fraud promptly.

Encryption, UPI PIN, device binding, OTPs, alerts, and app locks together provide layered protection for safe digital transactions and are the key security features. As illustrated in Figure 4.3, UPI safeguards digital payments through layered security features like encryption, PINs, device binding, OTPs, and app-level protections.

4.5 Best practices for mobile and UPI security

The effectiveness of mobile and UPI banking systems does not rest solely on the technological defenses provided by banks and regulators. Customers themselves play a decisive role in ensuring safe transactions by adopting responsible practices. Cybercriminals often exploit human negligence more than system weaknesses, making user awareness and disciplined habits the cornerstone of secure mobile banking.

One of the most important practices is maintaining strong and unique authentication credentials. Customers must avoid predictable passwords and PINs such as birthdates, phone numbers, or simple sequences like *123456*. Instead, they should create complex combinations of letters, numbers, and special characters, ensuring that each service—banking, email, and e-commerce—has its own unique password. With credential-stuffing attacks on the rise, password reuse across platforms remains one of the easiest ways for fraudsters to compromise accounts. Equally critical is the confidentiality of UPI PINs, which should never be disclosed, written down, or shared, even with close family members.

Another essential best practice is keeping devices and applications regularly updated. Mobile operating systems and banking apps frequently release security patches to fix vulnerabilities. Delayed updates leave devices exposed to malware, spyware, and zero-day exploits. Customers should enable automatic updates wherever possible, ensuring their apps and systems always run the latest versions. Similarly, installing apps only from trusted sources such as Google Play or the Apple App Store reduces the risk of downloading cloned or malicious applications disguised as legitimate banking tools.

Safe connectivity habits also form a vital layer of protection. Customers must avoid accessing mobile banking services over unsecured public Wi-Fi networks found in airports, cafes, or hotels. Such networks are easily compromised, allowing attackers to intercept login details and financial data. Where access is unavoidable, the use of Virtual Private Networks (VPNs) can provide an additional security shield. Additionally, mobile devices should always be protected with screen locks, biometrics, or app-specific passwords to prevent misuse in case of loss or theft.

Equally important is awareness of red flags in digital communication. Fraudsters frequently send emails, SMS messages, or even WhatsApp texts pretending to be from banks or UPI platforms. These messages often carry a sense of urgency, such as "Update your KYC immediately" or "Your account will be blocked." Customers must recognize that banks never ask for sensitive details via links or calls. A simple practice of manually visiting the bank's app or website, instead of clicking on provided links, can prevent many phishing attempts. Similarly, UPI users must remember that entering a UPI PIN is required only while sending money, never while receiving it. Fraudsters often trick victims into authorizing debit transactions under the guise of incoming payments.

Another best practice involves monitoring accounts regularly and proactively. Customers should check transaction histories frequently, ensuring there are no unauthorized withdrawals or transfers. Many banks and UPI apps offer in-app notifications for every transaction; enabling these alerts ensures that any suspicious activity is noticed immediately. Prompt reporting to the bank's helpline or the National Cyber Crime Portal (cybercrime.gov.in in India) can often prevent further losses and even allow partial recovery of stolen funds.

Finally, building a habit of digital hygiene is crucial. This includes avoiding oversharing personal details on social media, not storing banking credentials in plain text, and being cautious of unsolicited calls or messages. Customers must treat their digital identities as carefully as they treat their physical wallets. Just as one would not hand over their ATM PIN to a stranger, UPI PINs and mobile banking passwords must be guarded zealously.

In conclusion, best practices for mobile and UPI security revolve around three principles: strong authentication, safe usage habits, and constant vigilance. Banks and regulators can only provide the framework; it is the customer's responsibility to implement secure behaviors consistently. When customers practice safe digital

Figure 4.4 Best practices for mobile and UPI security

habits alongside the security features built into banking platforms, the result is a resilient ecosystem where fraudsters have fewer opportunities to succeed.

The simple do's and don'ts as seen above highlight safe authentication, device protection, vigilance, and reporting habits for secure digital banking. As shown in Figure 4.4, following the clear do's and don'ts ensures safer mobile and UPI transactions by combining strong authentication, secure habits, and timely vigilance.

4.6 Risk mitigation

Risk mitigation in mobile banking is the combined effort of banks, regulators, and customers to reduce the likelihood and impact of fraud. While no system can be made entirely immune to threats, layered defenses and proactive strategies can significantly minimize losses. Risk mitigation does not rest solely on technology but also on governance, education, and human behavior.

At the organizational level, banks must implement advanced fraud detection systems capable of monitoring transactions in real time. Artificial Intelligence (AI) and Machine Learning (ML) models are increasingly used to flag unusual activity, such as rapid transfers to unfamiliar accounts or transactions originating from abnormal geographies. By analyzing patterns across millions of data points, banks can identify anomalies that human oversight might miss. Early warning systems not only prevent fraud but also preserve customer trust, which is critical for the adoption of mobile banking services.

Multi-layer authentication remains one of the most effective mitigation tools. Combining something the user knows (a PIN or password), something they have (a registered mobile device or token), and something they are (biometric identifiers such as fingerprints or facial recognition) drastically reduces the risk of unauthorized access. Even in cases where a password is compromised, attackers are stopped by additional barriers, such as OTPs or biometric checks. Regulators like the Reserve Bank of India (RBI) mandate two-factor authentication for mobile banking precisely because it balances convenience with security.

Regulatory frameworks form another crucial pillar of risk mitigation. RBI and NPCI have issued detailed guidelines on UPI transaction limits, authentication protocols, and customer grievance mechanisms. The mandated "*zero liability policy*" ensures that customers are not held responsible for losses if they promptly report unauthorized transactions. Such policies increase reporting rates and encourage vigilance. In addition, CERT-In (Computer Emergency Response Team – India) provides coordination during large-scale cyber incidents, enabling systemic responses rather than fragmented action.

From the customer perspective, self-protection habits form the first line of defense. Customers must be educated to recognize phishing messages, avoid oversharing personal data, and immediately report suspicious activities. Banks can enhance this by embedding in-app awareness tools, such as pop-ups reminding users that UPI PINs are never required for receiving money. Regular SMS and email advisories further reinforce awareness.

Data encryption and secure app design are equally important for risk mitigation. All mobile banking apps must encrypt sensitive data both in transit and at rest, ensuring that intercepted information cannot be exploited. Apps should undergo continuous security testing, penetration testing, and audits to ensure vulnerabilities are addressed before attackers can exploit them. Banks should also implement automatic session timeouts to minimize risks from unattended devices.

Another key mitigation approach is collaborative intelligence sharing. Fraudulent activities often span multiple banks and service providers, making isolated responses ineffective. By sharing intelligence on fraud trends and attack patterns, institutions can strengthen collective resilience. Cross-industry collaboration between telecom providers, payment platforms, and banks ensures that scams like SIM swaps or phishing campaigns are contained faster.

Finally, customer empowerment through easy reporting channels is central to mitigation. Quick access to helplines, in-app fraud reporting tools, and national cybercrime portals ensures that incidents are reported without delay. Time is critical in fraud prevention; rapid reporting often determines whether stolen funds can be frozen or traced. Educating customers about these channels, while ensuring that they are simple to use, greatly improves response efficiency.

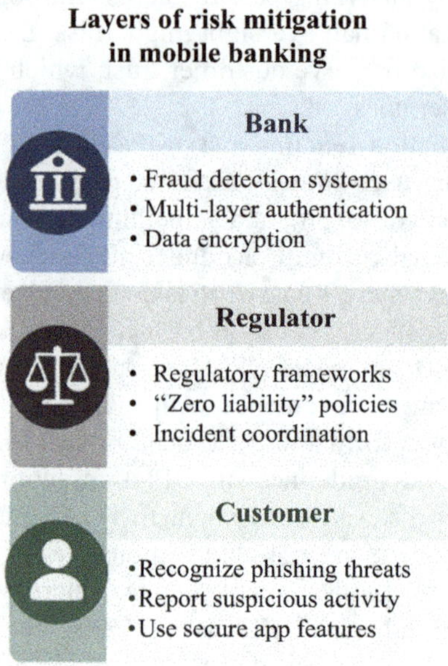

Figure 4.5 Layers of risk mitigation in mobile banking

In essence, risk mitigation in mobile and UPI banking is not about eliminating risk entirely but about reducing the window of opportunity for attackers. A robust ecosystem integrates advanced technology, regulatory oversight, and customer vigilance into a seamless shield. By doing so, the financial sector can ensure that mobile banking continues to deliver convenience and trust without being overshadowed by fraud and insecurity. Banks, regulators, and customers each play distinct yet interconnected roles in minimizing fraud risks.

As illustrated in Figure 4.5, risk mitigation in mobile banking relies on layered efforts from banks, regulators, and customers working together to reduce fraud.

Key points to remember

1. Mobile banking offers convenience but introduces new risks. Smartphones act as gateways to financial systems, making them attractive targets for fraudsters.
2. Malware and rogue apps are persistent threats. Fake apps can steal credentials, intercept OTPs, or even remotely control devices.
3. Phishing and smishing attacks exploit human psychology. Messages with urgency or fear are designed to trick users into revealing sensitive details.
4. SIM swap fraud compromises OTP-based security. Attackers use fake IDs to obtain duplicate SIMs, diverting all bank alerts and OTPs.
5. Public Wi-Fi poses serious risks for financial transactions. Unsecured or spoofed networks can enable attackers to intercept data in real time.

6. Device vulnerabilities increase exposure. Outdated operating systems or rooted/jailbroken devices weaken built-in protections.
7. Weak and reused passwords remain the frailest link. Credential-stuffing attacks exploit reused passwords across platforms.
8. Social engineering bypasses technology. Fraudsters impersonating bank officials often succeed when customers lack awareness.
9. App cloning remains a global issue. Fake banking apps continue to appear in app stores, tricking unsuspecting customers.
10. Password security is nonnegotiable. Strong, unique passwords combined with multi-factor authentication are essential.
11. Password managers and biometrics can ease security. These tools help balance strong authentication with customer convenience.
12. UPI's architecture emphasizes security. Two-factor authentication, encryption, and device binding are built into its design.
13. Dynamic alerts enhance user vigilance. SMS and in-app notifications allow quick detection of unauthorized activities.
14. App-level security adds another shield. Fingerprint locks, Face ID, and AI-based fraud detection complement UPI's protections.
15. Safe digital habits are the customer's responsibility. Avoiding public Wi-Fi, verifying links, and never entering UPI PINs for receiving money are key.
16. Monitoring accounts regularly prevents damage. Detecting anomalies early enables timely reporting and fund recovery.
17. Banks must implement advanced fraud detection. AI/ML-based monitoring of unusual transaction patterns is critical.
18. Regulatory frameworks protect customers. RBI and NPCI guidelines, zero liability policies, and transaction limits strengthen trust.
19. Collaboration between banks, telecoms, and regulators is vital. Fraud is cross-industry, requiring coordinated defenses.
20. Risk mitigation is a shared responsibility. When banks secure systems, regulators enforce standards, and customers stay vigilant, mobile banking becomes safer.

Questions (Try answering them yourself)

1. Why has mobile banking become both a convenience and a cybersecurity concern in the digital era?
2. Explain how malware and rogue applications compromise mobile banking security with real-world examples.
3. What makes phishing and smishing attacks particularly effective against mobile banking customers?
4. Discuss the process of SIM swap fraud. How does it bypass OTP-based authentication?
5. Why is using public Wi-Fi networks for mobile banking transactions considered risky?
6. How do outdated or rooted devices increase vulnerabilities in mobile banking?

7. Why are weak and reused passwords considered the weakest link in mobile banking security?
8. How can social engineering tactics succeed even when strong technical defenses are in place?
9. What risks do cloned or fake mobile banking apps pose to customers?
10. Explain the importance of multi-factor authentication in strengthening password security.
11. Compare the effectiveness of password managers and biometrics in mobile banking security.
12. Describe the architecture of UPI and the security features that make it robust.
13. How does device binding in UPI reduce fraud risks?
14. What role do alerts and notifications play in empowering customers against fraud?
15. How do app-level security features like fingerprint locks and AI fraud detection enhance protection?
16. What are the best practices customers should follow to ensure safe mobile and UPI banking?
17. Why is it important for customers to regularly monitor their bank accounts and transaction history?
18. Discuss the role of banks in implementing AI/ML-based fraud detection systems.
19. How do regulatory frameworks like RBI guidelines and the zero liability policy protect mobile banking users?
20. Explain the concept of shared responsibility in mobile banking security with examples.

Objective questions

1. Which of the following is a major threat in mobile banking?
   (a) Malware and rogue apps
   (b) Public libraries
   (c) Physical ATMs
   (d) Check books

2. Smishing refers to:
   (a) Malware hidden in QR codes
   (b) Phishing attacks via SMS
   (c) Fraudulent SIM swaps
   (d) App cloning

3. SIM swap fraud primarily compromises:
   (a) Device screen lock
   (b) Bank's internal server
   (c) OTP-based authentication
   (d) Internet speed

4. Public Wi-Fi networks are unsafe for banking because:
   (a) They are slow
   (b) They can enable man-in-the-middle attacks
   (c) They block SMS alerts
   (d) They cannot support UPI

5. Rooted or jailbroken devices are risky because:
   (a) They run faster
   (b) They bypass built-in security controls
   (c) They disable app icons
   (d) They improve encryption

6. The most common reason passwords fail as a security measure is:
   (a) They are too long
   (b) They are reused or weak
   (c) They require symbols
   (d) They expire often

7. Credential-stuffing attacks rely on:
   (a) Stolen SIM cards
   (b) Reusing leaked passwords across platforms
   (c) Fake banking apps
   (d) Malicious QR codes

8. In social engineering frauds, attackers usually:
   (a) Hack bank servers directly
   (b) Persuade users to share sensitive details
   (c) Infect devices with ransomware
   (d) Bypass encryption

9. Cloned mobile banking apps are dangerous because:
   (a) They delete original apps
   (b) They collect and misuse user credentials
   (c) They improve user experience
   (d) They block transactions

10. Multi-factor authentication works by combining:
   (a) Only passwords and OTPs
   (b) Something you know, something you have, something you are
   (c) Just biometrics
   (d) Only app-level PINs

11. Which of the following is a benefit of password managers?
   (a) Allowing password reuse
   (b) Auto-generating strong, unique passwords
   (c) Eliminating the need for banking PINs
   (d) Disabling biometrics

12. What makes UPI different from traditional card-based payments?
    (a) Use of CVV codes
    (b) No need to share account details, only VPA or QR code
    (c) Requires physical swiping
    (d) Operates only during business hours
13. Which UPI security feature ties accounts to a specific smartphone and SIM card?
    (a) OTP alerting
    (b) Device binding
    (c) Password reuse prevention
    (d) App PIN lock
14. UPI PIN must be entered:
    (a) Only when receiving money
    (b) Only when sending money
    (c) For both receiving and sending money
    (d) Never required
15. Which of the following is an app-level UPI security feature?
    (a) Fingerprint or Face ID lock
    (b) ATM withdrawal limits
    (c) Internet speed testing
    (d) Device recycling
16. What is the primary customer-side best practice for mobile banking?
    (a) Sharing PINs with family
    (b) Monitoring transactions regularly
    (c) Using unsecured Wi-Fi
    (d) Downloading apps from any source
17. Why are SMS and in-app alerts important?
    (a) They reduce internet usage
    (b) They allow quick detection of fraud
    (c) They stop device heating
    (d) They block app downloads
18. Which of the following is an RBI-mandated safeguard?
    (a) Free SIM swaps
    (b) Two-factor authentication
    (c) Unlimited UPI transaction attempts
    (d) Shared passwords
19. The “zero liability policy” ensures that:
    (a) Customers pay for all losses
    (b) Banks are not liable for frauds
    (c) Customers are not held responsible if they promptly report fraud
    (d) Telecom operators refund stolen funds

20. Risk mitigation in mobile banking works best when:
    (a) Only banks implement security
    (b) Only regulators enforce guidelines
    (c) Customers act independently
    (d) Banks, regulators, and customers share responsibility

Answer key

1. *a*
2. *b*
3. *c*
4. *b*
5. *b*
6. *b*
7. *b*
8. *b*
9. *b*
10. *b*
11. *b*
12. *b*
13. *b*
14. *b*
15. *a*
16. *b*
17. *b*
18. *b*
19. *c*
20. *d*

Further reading

[1] KPMG India. *Unified Payments Interface (UPI) Information Security Compliance Framework 2025*. New Delhi: KPMG; 2025.

[2] *Indian Computer Emergency Response Team (CERT-In). Advisory CIAD-2024-0050: Phishing Scams*. New Delhi: Ministry of Electronics and Information Technology; 2024.

[3] *Resecurity Inc. Digital Threat Report 2024 for India's BFSI Sector*. Mumbai: Resecurity; 2024.

[4] *Indian Computer Emergency Response Team (CERT-In). Advisory CIAD-2022-0014: Trojan masquerading as Banking App*. New Delhi: Ministry of Electronics and Information Technology; 2022.

[5] Malhotra T, and Kadyan S. Mobile banking security risks: An analysis. *J Inf Syst Eng Manage*. 2025;10(1): 1–12.

[6] ESYA Centre. *Mobile Security: An Assessment of Cybersecurity Threats in the Indian Ecosystem*. New Delhi: ESYA; 2023.

[7] Enkash. *How Unified Payments Interface Works: Security Framework and User Authentication*. Mumbai: Enkash; 2025.

[8] SSRana & Co. *Regulating the UPI Ecosystem: Ensuring Consumer Rights and Privacy*. New Delhi: SSRana; 2025.

[9] *Ministry of Financial Services, Government of India. Cyber Security & Fintech: Overview of the Financial Sector*. New Delhi: MoFS; 2024.

[10] Cyber Security Knowledge Centre (CSK). *Digital Threat Report 2024*. Bengaluru: CSK; 2024.

[11] Reserve Bank of India. *FAQs on Remittances and Mobile Banking Security Measures*. Mumbai: RBI; 2023.

[12] National Payments Corporation of India (NPCI). *UPI Procedural Guidelines and Security Features*. Mumbai: NPCI; 2024.

[13] Reserve Bank of India. *Circular: Strengthening Authentication for Card and Mobile Payments*. Mumbai: RBI; 2022.

[14] National Payments Corporation of India (NPCI). *UPI Chalega – Awareness and Security Campaign Report*. Mumbai: NPCI; 2021.

[15] Deloitte. *Securing Mobile Banking Channels: Risk Assessment in Indian BFSI*. Mumbai: Deloitte; 2023.

[16] PwC India. *Digital Banking Security Landscape Report*. New Delhi: PwC; 2022.

[17] SISA Information Security. *Emerging Threats in Mobile Banking Transactions*. Bengaluru: SISA; 2023.

[18] Indian Banks' Association (IBA). *Report on Digital Banking Security Concerns and Recommendations*. Mumbai: IBA; 2022.

[19] World Bank. *Cybersecurity Risks in Mobile Payments and Financial Inclusion*. Washington DC: World Bank; 2021.

[20] International Monetary Fund (IMF). *Financial Stability Report: Digital Banking and Cybersecurity Challenges*. Washington DC: IMF; 2022.

Chapter 5

Cybersecurity—an introductory discussion

Learning objectives

After reading through the chapter, the readers will gain a clear understanding of

- The concept of cyber fraud and why it poses a growing threat in the digital economy.
- Examining fraud risk management frameworks and their importance in reducing organizational vulnerabilities.
- Identifying key components of fraud management systems, including governance, controls, and technology.
- Methods to analyze fraud detection, such as data analytics, artificial intelligence (AI)/machine learning (ML) models, and anomaly monitoring.
- Evaluating the importance of customer awareness programs in reducing fraud success rates.
- Recognizing the role of employee training in building strong internal defenses against cyber fraud.
- Applying best practices for fraud prevention, integrating technology, policy, and human vigilance.

5.1 Introduction

In the digital age, fraud has evolved from traditional forgery and theft into far more sophisticated and technology-driven forms. The term "cyber fraud" refers to any fraudulent activity conducted through digital platforms, networks, or electronic devices with the intent to deceive, manipulate, or steal from individuals, businesses, or institutions. Unlike conventional crimes, cyber fraud exploits the anonymity, reach, and speed of technology, making it one of the fastest-growing threats in the global financial and commercial landscape.

The rise of online banking, mobile payments, e-commerce, and digital communication channels has created new avenues for both opportunity and exploitation. Fraudsters no longer need physical access to commit crimes; instead, they rely on malware, phishing campaigns, social engineering, and identity theft to achieve their goals. With billions of digital transactions processed daily, the scale of potential damage is immense. The financial sector, in particular, has been one of the prime targets, but no sector, whether healthcare, retail, telecom, or government, is immune.

Statistics highlight the urgency of addressing cyber fraud. The Reserve Bank of India (RBI) reported that frauds in the banking sector alone amounted to over ₹13,000 crore in 2023–2024, with a significant portion linked to digital transactions. Globally, reports from institutions such as the Association of Certified Fraud Examiners (ACFE) and PricewaterhouseCoopers (PwC) Global Economic Crime Survey reveal that cyber-enabled fraud has surpassed traditional fraud in frequency and impact. Common forms include phishing scams, payment fraud, ransomware-based extortion, synthetic identity fraud, and business email compromise (BEC).

A key reason cyber fraud thrives is the human factor. While technology is constantly advancing with stronger encryption, biometrics, and AI-powered detection systems, human behavior remains susceptible to manipulation. Customers can be deceived into sharing one-time passwords (OTPs), employees may inadvertently click malicious links, and insiders might abuse system privileges. Fraudsters capitalize on urgency, fear, and curiosity to bypass even the strongest technological defenses. This reality reinforces that cyber fraud is not just a technical challenge but also a psychological and cultural one.

Organizations face a dual challenge: on one hand, they must safeguard their systems and data from ever-evolving threats; on the other, they must foster a culture of awareness among employees and customers. Fraud has become increasingly cross-border and organized, often carried out by networks of criminals operating across multiple jurisdictions. The dark web has further enabled fraudsters by providing stolen credentials, hacking tools, and money laundering services. This interconnected ecosystem means that fraud incidents are rarely isolated; they often ripple across industries, geographies, and even national economies.

In this context, effective fraud risk management frameworks are indispensable. They provide organizations with structured approaches to identify, assess, detect, and respond to fraud risks. Equally important is the empowerment of customers and employees through awareness campaigns, training, and continuous engagement. Preventing fraud requires collaboration among all stakeholders: businesses, regulators, technology providers, and end-users.

This chapter delves into the world of cyber fraud by exploring the frameworks and tools that organizations can deploy, the components of fraud risk management, the technologies driving fraud detection, and the essential role of customer and employee awareness. It concludes with best practices for fraud prevention, emphasizing that fraud defense is not the sole responsibility of technology but rather a shared responsibility model involving systems, processes, and people.

In short, cyber fraud represents one of the greatest risks of our digital era, yet it can be mitigated through vigilance, collaboration, and the intelligent use of technology and awareness. The key aspects include types of fraud, anonymity enabled by technology, human factors, and prevention strategies.

As shown in Figure 5.1, cyber fraud is an emerging threat driven by digital platforms, human vulnerabilities, and organized crime, requiring robust prevention strategies.

Figure 5.1 Cyber fraud—An emerging threat

5.2 Fraud risk management

Fraud risk management is the structured process by which organizations anticipate, identify, assess, and respond to the risks of fraud. In the digital era, where fraudsters are highly adaptive, traditional internal controls alone are no longer sufficient. Organizations must adopt a holistic fraud risk management framework that integrates governance, technology, human awareness, and regulatory compliance. The goal is not only to detect fraud once it has occurred but also to reduce its likelihood and impact through proactive measures.

The foundation of fraud risk management lies in a clear understanding of the fraud risk universe, the full spectrum of ways in which fraud can occur, from phishing scams and unauthorized digital transactions to insider collusion and identity theft. Organizations must conduct periodic fraud risk assessments, mapping vulnerabilities across processes, technologies, and human interactions. These assessments should evaluate both internal risks (such as employee misconduct or system misuse) and external risks (such as cyberattacks, social engineering, and third-party fraud).

A robust fraud risk management framework typically includes several key pillars. The first is governance and accountability, where leadership defines clear fraud management policies and establishes oversight structures such as fraud risk committees or designated compliance officers. Without leadership commitment, anti-fraud measures often remain superficial. The second pillar is controls and prevention mechanisms, which range from segregation of duties and multi-factor authentication to transaction monitoring systems. These controls must evolve constantly, as fraudsters rapidly adapt to outdated defenses.

Another critical element is fraud detection and monitoring. Advanced analytics, artificial intelligence (AI), and machine learning (ML) are increasingly being used to analyze transaction data for anomalies, such as unusual spending patterns or login attempts from unexpected geographies. These tools allow for real-time detection, significantly reducing the window of opportunity for fraud to succeed. Complementing this is the response mechanism, clear procedures for investigation, reporting, and recovery when fraud is suspected or confirmed.

Importantly, fraud risk management extends beyond systems and policies to include human vigilance. Employees, customers, and third parties are all stakeholders in the fraud ecosystem. Training programs, awareness campaigns, and ethical culture initiatives play a central role in ensuring that individuals recognize red flags and act responsibly. Regulators such as the Reserve Bank of India (RBI) have repeatedly emphasized that customer education and grievance redressal frameworks are just as crucial as firewalls and encryption.

The effectiveness of fraud risk management depends on adopting a shared responsibility model. Banks and financial institutions must strengthen controls and monitoring, regulators must enforce standards and accountability, and customers must exercise safe practices while transacting digitally. When all three elements work together, fraud risk management transforms from a reactive activity into a proactive shield that builds trust in digital ecosystems.

As shown in Figure 5.2, fraud risk management is a layered framework that integrates governance, prevention, detection, response, and awareness.

Figure 5.2 Fraud risk management framework

5.3 Components

Fraud risk management is not a single tool or process but a composite system made up of multiple interdependent components. Each component addresses a specific dimension of fraud prevention, detection, and response. Together, they create a holistic structure that protects organizations and customers from evolving threats.

The first essential component is Governance and Oversight. Effective fraud risk management begins with a clear commitment from leadership. Boards, senior executives, and audit committees must define fraud policies, outline responsibilities, and ensure accountability. Establishing a dedicated fraud risk management unit or appointing a Chief Risk Officer helps anchor this commitment within the organizational structure. Without strong governance, even the best technological defenses risk becoming fragmented or underutilized.

The second component is Risk Assessment and Identification. Organizations must continuously analyze their exposure to fraud risks across processes, systems, and stakeholders. This involves evaluating both internal risks (such as employee collusion, insider misuse, and weak segregation of duties) and external risks (including cyberattacks, identity theft, phishing, and social engineering). Risk assessments must be dynamic, reflecting changes in business models, regulatory requirements, and the evolving tactics of fraudsters.

The third component is Internal Controls and Preventive Mechanisms. Controls act as the first line of defense, preventing fraud before it occurs. Examples include access restrictions, role-based permissions, dual authorization for high-value transactions, and strong password or biometric policies. In the case of digital banking and payments, preventive mechanisms extend to two-factor authentication, encryption, and transaction monitoring thresholds. The strength of these controls often determines how resilient an organization is to opportunistic attacks.

Fraud Detection and Monitoring form the next critical component. While prevention reduces opportunities, no system is foolproof. Organizations must deploy continuous monitoring tools to identify anomalies and suspicious activities. Advanced solutions powered by artificial intelligence (AI) and machine learning (ML) analyze vast amounts of data to flag unusual patterns, such as transactions from unfamiliar locations, repeated failed logins, or sudden spikes in fund transfers. Early detection drastically reduces financial losses and reputational damage.

Another key component is the Response and Investigation Mechanism. Detecting fraud is only the beginning; organizations must also be prepared to investigate incidents promptly and fairly. This includes setting up whistleblower channels, forensic investigation teams, and standardized reporting processes. Effective response mechanisms ensure that fraud cases are handled transparently and lessons learned are integrated back into the system.

Finally, Awareness and Training complete the framework. Employees, customers, and third-party partners all play a role in fraud ecosystems. Regular training programs for employees help them identify red flags and follow best practices, while customer awareness campaigns reduce the likelihood of social engineering scams. Regulators and industry bodies frequently emphasize this component because even the strongest technological system can be compromised by uninformed human behavior.

In essence, the components of fraud risk management—governance, risk assessment, controls, detection, response, and awareness—work together to form a cycle of protection. Each component reinforces the other, ensuring that fraud risks are not just managed reactively but continuously addressed through vigilance, accountability, and adaptation.

As illustrated in Figure 5.3, the six components of fraud risk management work as a continuous cycle integrating governance, assessment, controls, detection, response, and awareness for combating fraud.

Figure 5.3 Components of fraud risk management

5.4 Fraud detection

Fraud detection represents the critical second line of defense after preventive controls. While prevention aims to stop fraud before it occurs, detection mechanisms ensure that any fraudulent activity that bypasses controls is quickly identified, contained, and investigated. In today's fast-paced digital environment, where millions of transactions take place in real time, the speed and accuracy of fraud detection determine the difference between minor financial loss and catastrophic damage.

Traditional fraud detection methods relied heavily on manual reviews and rule-based systems. Banks and organizations used preset thresholds, such as flagging transactions above a certain value or monitoring unusual login attempts. While effective to an extent, these systems often generated high numbers of false positives and struggled to keep up with fraudsters who continually adapted their tactics. The rise of online and mobile transactions has rendered such static models insufficient.

Modern fraud detection leverages data analytics, machine learning (ML), and artificial intelligence (AI) to analyze patterns and detect anomalies. These technologies can process enormous volumes of structured and unstructured data, customer profiles, transaction histories, geolocation data, and device fingerprints to identify suspicious behavior in real time. For instance, if a customer typically makes small payments in one city and suddenly attempts a high-value transfer from another country, the system immediately raises an alert. This kind of contextual and behavioral analysis goes far beyond simple rules.

Another critical advancement in fraud detection is the use of real-time monitoring systems. Payment processors, banks, and fintech companies now deploy continuous transaction monitoring platforms that flag unusual activities within milliseconds. This minimizes the time between fraud occurrence and response, often preventing money from being withdrawn or transferred out of the system. The National Payments Corporation of India (NPCI), for example, has mandated strong monitoring systems for UPI transactions to address growing fraud concerns.

Fraud detection also involves multi-layered verification. When anomalies are detected, systems may trigger additional authentication steps such as one-time passwords (OTPs), biometric verification, or security challenge questions. These "step-up" authentication measures ensure that suspicious activities are cross-verified before completion, striking a balance between user convenience and safety.

Equally important is the role of collaborative intelligence in fraud detection. Fraudsters often target multiple institutions simultaneously, making information sharing across banks, telecom providers, and regulators crucial. Platforms that aggregate fraud reports, such as Indian Computer Emergency Response Team (CERT-In) advisories in India, help organizations detect threats that may have first emerged elsewhere.

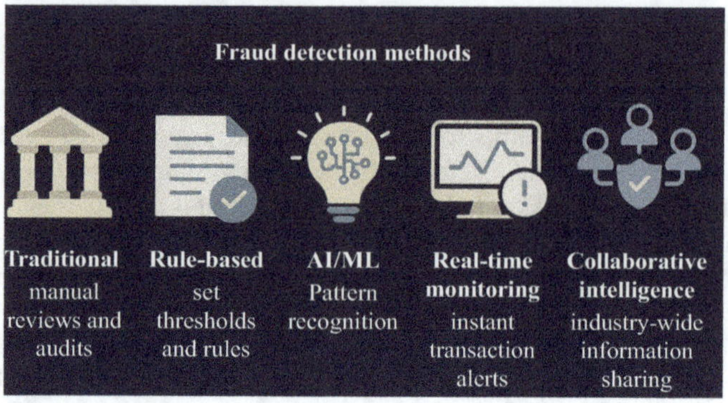

Figure 5.4 Fraud detection methods

However, detection systems face ongoing challenges. Fraudsters frequently test the boundaries of detection algorithms by making small, low-risk attempts before launching large-scale attacks. Moreover, excessive reliance on AI without human oversight can lead to "alert fatigue," where genuine fraud alerts are missed amid thousands of false positives. Thus, the most effective fraud detection strategies are hybrid models, combining automated analytics with human judgment through fraud investigation teams.

Ultimately, fraud detection is not just about catching fraud but about building resilience. By continuously monitoring systems, analyzing data intelligently, and sharing intelligence across industries, organizations can minimize the impact of fraud while reinforcing customer trust. Detection mechanisms, when integrated with prevention, response, and awareness, form the backbone of a comprehensive fraud risk management strategy.

As illustrated in Figure 5.4, fraud detection has progressed from manual reviews *and rule-based systems* to advanced AI analytics, real-time monitoring, and collaborative intelligence.

5.5 Imparting customer awareness of fraud

No matter how advanced fraud detection systems become, customers remain the first line of defense against cyber fraud. Fraudsters often exploit human psychology, curiosity, urgency, fear, or trust, rather than technical flaws. This makes customer awareness programs an essential part of fraud prevention strategies. When customers are educated about common fraud tactics and safe practices, the chances of fraud succeeding decrease dramatically.

One of the most effective awareness strategies is clear, jargon-free communication. Banks, fintech firms, and e-commerce platforms must ensure that their fraud alerts and advisories use simple language that customers of all backgrounds can understand. For example, instead of stating "Beware of phishing attempts," a message might say, "Do not click on links asking for your banking details, your bank will never ask this." Such clarity bridges the gap between technical warnings and customer comprehension.

Another key element is multichannel awareness campaigns. Fraudsters target customers through SMS, emails, calls, and fake websites; therefore, awareness must also reach customers through all possible touchpoints. SMS alerts, in-app notifications, email reminders, call center messages, and even posters in bank branches can reinforce safety habits. Successful campaigns such as the RBI's "RBI Kehta Hai" initiative in India show the value of consistent, relatable messaging in multiple languages to reach diverse audiences.

Storytelling and real-life examples are especially powerful in educating customers. Hearing about a neighbor who lost money to a SIM swap or an elderly person scammed through a gift card scheme makes fraud risks feel real, not abstract. By presenting fraud cases as stories with lessons, organizations can make awareness both engaging and memorable.

Furthermore, gamification and interactive learning are being used to increase participation. Short quizzes, fraud-awareness games, and digital simulations allow customers to test their knowledge and build practical awareness in a safe environment. This approach transforms education from passive reading into active learning.

Accessibility is also crucial. Awareness content should be available in multiple languages and formats, including text, audio, and video, to ensure that all customers, urban or rural, young or elderly, tech-savvy or not, can benefit. For instance, rural customers may be more responsive to radio ads or community workshops, while urban users may prefer app-based push notifications.

Ultimately, imparting awareness is not a one-time event but a continuous process. Fraud tactics evolve, and so must customer knowledge. Organizations that regularly update their awareness programs build a culture of vigilance, where customers instinctively pause, verify, and question before transacting. This culture significantly reduces fraud success rates and strengthens trust between customers and service providers.

In essence, empowered customers are safer customers. By providing knowledge, tools, and confidence, organizations can transform customers from passive targets into active participants in fraud prevention.

5.6 Employee awareness and training

While customers are the first line of defense, employees are the gatekeepers of organizational integrity. Cyber fraud often succeeds not only because of external attacks but also due to internal lapses, negligence, or collusion. This makes employee awareness and training a cornerstone of fraud prevention frameworks. An organization may deploy the most sophisticated fraud detection systems, but if its employees fail to recognize suspicious activity or mishandle security protocols, the entire defense collapses.

Employee awareness begins with cultivating an ethics and compliance culture. From frontline staff in banks to IT administrators in fintech firms, every employee must internalize the importance of security and understand their role in safeguarding customer trust. Training should go beyond generic modules and be role-specific. For example, customer service representatives need to identify phishing attempts when customers call with suspicious queries, while IT teams must be equipped to detect system anomalies or unauthorized access.

A major focus of training is social engineering awareness. Many fraudsters rely on manipulating employees into sharing sensitive information or bypassing protocols. Phishing emails disguised as urgent instructions from senior management, fake vendor invoices, and pretexting calls are common tactics. Employees must be trained to pause, verify, and escalate suspicious requests rather than responding impulsively. Regular mock phishing campaigns are now widely used to test employee vigilance and provide targeted feedback.

Another critical area is data protection practices. Employees must understand how to securely handle customer data, restrict access on a need-to-know basis, and avoid insecure practices such as emailing unencrypted files or using unauthorized devices. With regulations like the General Data Protection Regulation (GDPR) and India's Digital Personal Data Protection Act (DPDP Act, 2023), compliance is not just a best practice but a legal obligation. Incident response readiness is also part of effective training. Employees should know how to report suspected fraud, whom to contact, and how to preserve evidence. Delays or confusion during the first few minutes of a fraud attempt can lead to significant financial and reputational damage. Clear escalation procedures, combined with periodic drills, ensure that employees respond quickly and consistently.

Technology-driven learning platforms are increasingly used to make training more engaging. Interactive e-learning modules, scenario-based simulations, and gamified security challenges allow employees to practice fraud recognition in a safe environment. This not only enhances learning retention but also fosters a proactive security mindset.

Ultimately, employee awareness and training must be viewed as an ongoing investment rather than a one-time exercise. Fraud tactics evolve constantly, and so must employee knowledge. Organizations that prioritize continuous training build a resilient workforce capable of acting as a "human firewall" against fraud. By combining ethics, role-specific skills, and real-time readiness, employees can transform from potential weak links into powerful defenders of organizational security.

As shown in Figure 5.5, employee defense against fraud can become strong if built through ethics, role-specific training, social engineering awareness, data protection, incident readiness, and continuous learning.

Figure 5.5 Building employee defense against fraud

5.7 Fraud prevention practices

Fraud prevention is the ultimate goal of any fraud risk management framework. While detection and response are critical, the most cost-effective strategy is to prevent fraud from happening in the first place. Effective prevention is not achieved through a single control or technology but through a multi-layered defense strategy that integrates people, processes, and technology.

At the organizational level, the first step in prevention is strong governance and clear policies. Organizations must articulate zero tolerance for fraud, supported by well-defined codes of conduct, fraud policies, and escalation procedures. Employees and customers alike must be made aware that fraudulent behavior carries strict consequences. This clarity establishes a culture of deterrence, making it clear that fraud will be met with swift investigation and action.

Technological measures form the backbone of prevention. Multi-factor authentication (MFA), encryption, device fingerprinting, and AI-driven anomaly detection significantly reduce opportunities for fraudsters. For example, combining biometric verification with dynamic transaction alerts ensures that even if credentials are stolen, unauthorized activity is quickly flagged. Similarly, real-time monitoring systems allow organizations to intercept suspicious transactions before they are completed.

Access controls and segregation of duties are another fundamental practice. No single individual should be able to initiate, approve, and finalize a high-value transaction. By distributing responsibilities, the risk of insider collusion or unauthorized actions is greatly reduced. Automated access management systems that grant privileges strictly on a need-to-know basis add further protection.

From the customer's perspective, fraud prevention requires safe digital practices. Customers should never share personal identification numbers (PINs), OTPs, or passwords with anyone, regardless of the request's apparent urgency. They must also avoid transacting over public Wi-Fi networks and ensure that banking or payment apps are always downloaded from official sources. Regularly updating mobile devices and applications further strengthens security, as many fraudsters exploit outdated software.

Regulators play a crucial role by mandating industry-wide preventive standards. In India, the Reserve Bank of India (RBI) and the National Payments Corporation of India (NPCI) have issued clear guidelines on authentication, transaction limits, and liability frameworks. For example, the zero liability policy protects customers from unauthorized transactions if reported promptly, reinforcing trust in digital banking ecosystems.

Another preventive practice is fraud intelligence sharing. Since fraud schemes often target multiple organizations simultaneously, industry collaboration is essential. Shared databases of blacklisted accounts, compromised devices, or phishing domains allow institutions to block fraud attempts before they escalate. Initiatives like CERT-In advisories exemplify the importance of collective defense.

Finally, continuous monitoring and adaptation are vital. Fraudsters are dynamic, constantly modifying their tactics. Organizations must therefore treat fraud prevention as an ongoing process rather than a one-time implementation. Regular audits, red-team exercises, and technology upgrades ensure that prevention measures stay ahead of emerging threats.

In essence, fraud prevention practices combine governance, advanced technology, access controls, customer awareness, regulatory enforcement, and collaboration. By integrating these elements, organizations can shift from reactive firefighting to proactive resilience, creating digital ecosystems where fraud finds fewer opportunities to succeed.

As shown in Figure 5.6, effective fraud prevention relies on a multi-layered approach combining governance, technology, controls, customer practices, regulations, intelligence sharing, and monitoring.

Figure 5.6 Multi-layered fraud prevention practices

Key points to remember

- Cyber fraud is a technology-driven crime that exploits digital platforms, networks, and devices to deceive individuals and organizations for financial or personal gain.
- The scale of cyber fraud is global, with billions of transactions processed daily, making speed and vigilance essential to minimize risks.
- The human factor remains the weakest link—Fraudsters rely on social engineering, urgency, and fear to bypass even advanced technical controls.
- Fraud risk management provides a structured approach to anticipate, detect, and respond to fraud, turning organizations from reactive to proactive.
- Governance and oversight are foundational—Strong policies, leadership commitment, and clear accountability ensure that fraud management is prioritized.
- Risk assessment and identification must be continuous, mapping vulnerabilities in both internal processes and external threats.
- Preventive controls such as segregation of duties, multi-factor authentication, and encryption significantly reduce fraud opportunities.
- Fraud detection systems have evolved from manual reviews to AI- and ML-driven analytics that monitor anomalies in real time.
- Real-time monitoring is critical—Early detection minimizes financial losses and reputational damage by stopping fraud before escalation.

- Collaborative intelligence, such as CERT advisories and shared blacklists, strengthens fraud defense across industries.
- Customers are the first line of defense; awareness campaigns equip them to recognize phishing, fake apps, and social engineering scams.
- Clear and jargon-free communication is key; fraud warnings should be simple, relatable, and accessible across languages.
- Storytelling and gamification make customer awareness more effective by transforming abstract warnings into memorable lessons.
- Employee awareness and training are equally important, as internal lapses, negligence, or collusion often enable fraud.
- Mock phishing drills and scenario-based training build employee vigilance against social engineering and insider risks.
- Data protection practices ensure sensitive customer data is handled securely, in compliance with global and national privacy laws.
- Incident response readiness among employees reduces delays; clear escalation protocols limit fraud impact.
- Multi-layered fraud prevention integrates governance, technology, customer practices, regulations, and intelligence sharing.
- Regulatory standards such as RBI's liability frameworks and NPCI guidelines enforce accountability and build customer trust.
- Fraud prevention is a continuous process; organizations must adapt controls, update training, and revise policies as fraud tactics evolve.

Questions (Try answering them yourself)

1. Define cyber fraud and explain how it differs from traditional fraud in terms of scale, techniques, and impact.
2. Discuss the role of human behavior in enabling cyber fraud despite the presence of advanced technological defenses.
3. Explain the key pillars of a fraud risk management framework and analyze why governance is considered its foundation.
4. Evaluate the importance of fraud risk assessments in organizations. How can both internal and external risks be mapped effectively?
5. What are preventive controls in fraud risk management? Provide real-world examples from banking or fintech sectors.
6. Compare traditional rule-based fraud detection with AI/ML-driven approaches. What advantages do modern systems offer?
7. How does real-time monitoring reduce financial losses in fraud cases? Support your answer with examples.
8. Critically assess the challenges organizations face in balancing fraud detection with minimizing false positives.
9. Explain the role of collaborative intelligence in fraud detection. Why is information sharing across industries crucial?
10. Describe the RBI's "RBI Kehta Hai" initiative and discuss its effectiveness in customer fraud awareness.

11. How can storytelling and gamification improve customer awareness programs compared to conventional campaigns?
12. Discuss the barriers to customer awareness in rural and semi-urban areas. How can financial institutions overcome them?
13. Evaluate the role of employee training in preventing fraud. Why must training be role-specific?
14. What are mock phishing campaigns, and how do they contribute to strengthening employee vigilance?
15. Explain the relationship between employee negligence, insider collusion, and large-scale fraud incidents.
16. Discuss how data protection practices for employees align with global privacy regulations like GDPR or India's DPDP Act (2023).
17. Outline the key elements of incident response readiness for employees. Why are the first few minutes critical?
18. Analyze the importance of multi-layered fraud prevention. How do governance, technology, and regulations complement each other?
19. Critically evaluate RBI and NPCI's regulatory standards on digital transactions. How do they empower customers and banks alike?
20. In your opinion, what future trends in cyber fraud prevention will shape the financial sector over the next decade?

Objective questions

1. Cyber fraud primarily exploits which factor?
   (a) Physical security gaps
   (b) Human behavior and digital systems
   (c) Manual banking procedures
   (d) Government policies

2. Which organization issues advisories in India on cyber threats such as phishing?
   (a) NPCI
   (b) CERT-In
   (c) RBI
   (d) IBA

3. Fraud risk management begins with which foundational component?
   (a) Customer awareness
   (b) Governance and oversight
   (c) Access control
   (d) Encryption

4. Which of the following is NOT typically an external fraud risk?
   (a) Phishing emails
   (b) Malware attacks
   (c) Insider collusion
   (d) SIM swap scams

5. Segregation of duties in fraud prevention ensures:
   (a) Employees have maximum access
   (b) No single individual controls all steps of a transaction
   (c) Customers are directly responsible for fraud
   (d) Technology alone prevents fraud
6. AI and ML in fraud detection are primarily used for:
   (a) Eliminating governance structures
   (b) Pattern recognition and anomaly detection
   (c) Manual review replacement only
   (d) Reducing training needs
7. Which is a limitation of traditional rule-based fraud detection?
   (a) Works only in banks
   (b) Generates false positives and misses evolving tactics
   (c) Cannot detect high-value transactions
   (d) Requires too much customer awareness
8. Real-time monitoring in fraud detection helps by:
   (a) Providing end-of-month fraud reports
   (b) Stopping suspicious transactions instantly
   (c) Reducing the need for audits
   (d) Lowering employee involvement
9. Collaborative intelligence in fraud detection involves:
   (a) Competitors avoiding each other
   (b) Information sharing across industries
   (c) Restricting fraud knowledge to one organization
   (d) Customers alone reporting fraud
10. Which RBI campaign focused on fraud awareness?
   (a) Digital Bharat
   (b) RBI Kehta Hai
   (c) Secure India
   (d) Cyber Suraksha
11. Gamification in fraud awareness refers to:
   (a) Playing online games
   (b) Using interactive methods like quizzes for education
   (c) Limiting awareness to young people
   (d) Teaching through advertisements only
12. Which barrier often limits rural customer fraud awareness?
   (a) Over-dependence on AI
   (b) Lack of clear, local-language communication
   (c) Too many phishing emails
   (d) Excessive training workshops

13. Which fraud tactic specifically targets employees using manipulation?
    (a) Data encryption
    (b) Social engineering
    (c) Real-time monitoring
    (d) Transaction encryption

14. Mock phishing campaigns are designed to:
    (a) Identify fraudulent vendors
    (b) Test employee vigilance
    (c) Improve customer redressal
    (d) Train AI systems

15. Insider collusion in fraud is best described as:
    (a) Customers bypassing OTPs
    (b) Employees misusing access privileges
    (c) Vendors breaching contracts
    (d) Regulators neglecting rules

16. Which regulation focuses on personal data protection in India?
    (a) SEBI Act
    (b) DPDP Act 2023
    (c) RTI Act
    (d) IT Outsourcing Act

17. Why are the first few minutes critical in incident response?
    (a) Because fraud attempts often escalate rapidly
    (b) Because customers demand refunds immediately
    (c) Because regulators impose instant fines
    (d) Because prevention tools fail in this window

18. Multi-layered fraud prevention means:
    (a) Using only technology to stop fraud
    (b) Combining governance, technology, and awareness
    (c) Ignoring customers and focusing on employees
    (d) Reducing regulatory oversight

19. Which RBI measure protects customers from unauthorized digital transactions?
    (a) Free banking
    (b) Zero liability policy
    (c) Unlimited withdrawals
    (d) No-KYC accounts

20. Fraud prevention is best described as:
    (a) A one-time exercise
    (b) An ongoing, adaptive process
    (c) A regulator-only responsibility
    (d) A customer-only responsibility

Answer key

1 – b
2 – b
3 – b
4 – c
5 – b
6 – b
7 – b
8 – b
9 – b
10 – b
11 – b
12 – b
13 – b
14 – b
15 – b
16 – b
17 – a
18 – b
19 – b
20 – b

Further reading

[1] Reserve Bank of India. *Annual Report on Banking Frauds 2023–24*. Mumbai: RBI; 2024.
[2] National Payments Corporation of India. *UPI Safety and Security Guidelines*. Mumbai: NPCI; 2023.
[3] Indian Computer Emergency Response Team. *Cyber Security Advisories 2024*. New Delhi: Ministry of Electronics & IT; 2024.
[4] Association of Certified Fraud Examiners. *Report to the Nations: Global Study on Occupational Fraud and Abuse*. Austin: ACFE; 2022.
[5] PwC. *Global Economic Crime and Fraud Survey 2022*. London: PwC; 2022.
[6] Deloitte. *Financial Crime in a Digital World: Threats and Controls*. New Delhi: Deloitte India; 2023.
[7] KPMG. *Fraud Risk Management Framework for BFSI Sector*. Mumbai: KPMG India; 2023.
[8] Ernst & Young. *Global Fraud Survey: How to Spot and Prevent Cyber-Enabled Fraud*. London: EY; 2022.
[9] McAfee. *Cybercrime and the Economy Report 2023*. Santa Clara: McAfee; 2023.
[10] IBM Security. *X-Force Threat Intelligence Index 2023*. Armonk: IBM; 2023.

[11] Symantec. *Internet Security Threat Report*. Mountain View: Symantec; 2022.

[12] World Bank. *Financial Inclusion and Digital Fraud Risks in Emerging Economies*. Washington DC: World Bank; 2021.

[13] International Monetary Fund. *Cybersecurity Risk and Financial Stability*. Washington DC: IMF; 2020.

[14] Reserve Bank of India. *Cyber Security Framework in Banks – Circular*. Mumbai: RBI; 2016.

[15] National Payments Corporation of India. *UPI Chalega Campaign Report*. Mumbai: NPCI; 2021.

[16] SISA Information Security. *Fraud and Risk Management in Digital Payments*. Bengaluru: SISA; 2022.

[17] Indian Banks' Association. *Handbook on Cyber Security and Fraud Management in Indian Banks*. Mumbai: IBA; 2022.

[18] ESYA Centre. *Cybersecurity and Digital Payments in India: Threat Assessment*. New Delhi: ESYA; 2023.

[19] Gartner. *Fraud Detection and Prevention Solutions Market Guide*. Stamford: Gartner; 2023.

[20] CERT-In. *Cyber Crime Trends in India 2023: Annual Review*. New Delhi: Ministry of Electronics & IT; 2024.

Chapter 6
Debit and credit card frauds

Learning objectives

After going through the chapter, the reader will be able to

(a) Understand the nature and evolution of debit and credit card fraud in modern banking ecosystems.
(b) Identify and differentiate between various types of card fraud, such as skimming, cloning, phishing, and online data theft.
(c) Recognize the role of social media in enabling card-based attacks and study real-world examples of such incidents.
(d) Explain the concepts of vishing and smishing and their connection with human-centric social engineering.
(e) Evaluate preventive mechanisms and best practices for both consumers and financial institutions to ensure safe card usage.
(f) Analyze case-based scenarios of card fraud and identify warning signs, vulnerabilities, and response actions.
(g) Explore further learning resources and regulatory measures related to card security, payment authentication, and fraud monitoring systems.

6.1 Introduction

The widespread use of debit and credit cards has transformed global finance into a cash-light economy. With contactless payments, EMV (**E**uropay, **M**asterCard, and **V**isa) chips, and online shopping, consumers experience unmatched convenience but also unprecedented risk.

Fraudsters no longer need physical access to a card. A single data leak, phishing email, or manipulated QR code can lead to unauthorized withdrawals across continents.

A World Payments Report (2024) estimates that one in every 130 digital transactions globally encounters attempted fraud. The scale is daunting: losses from card fraud exceed $35 billion annually, according to the Nilson Report (2024).

Card fraud affects

- Customers: Monetary loss, emotional stress, damaged credit scores.
- Banks: Reputational damage, regulatory penalties, compensation obligations.
- Merchants: Chargebacks, compliance burden, loss of trust.

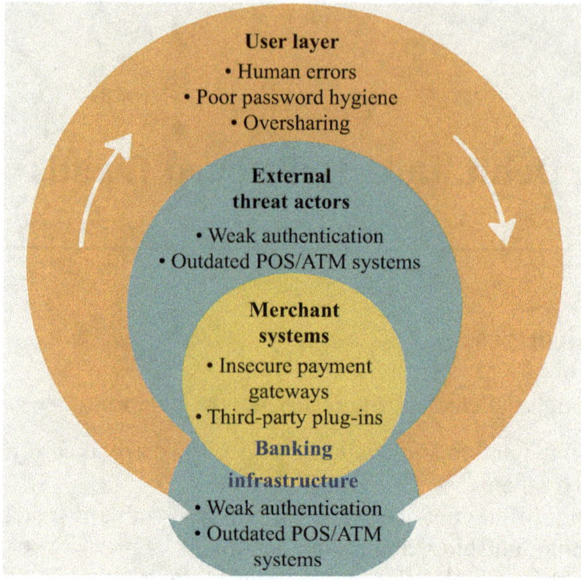

Figure 6.1 Ecosystem of card fraud—A circular model

Card fraud is thus not a single event; it is an ecosystem of vulnerabilities spanning technology, process, and human behavior. Figure 6.1 illustrates the interconnected ecosystem of card fraud, highlighting vulnerabilities across users, banking infrastructure, merchant systems, and external threat actors.

6.2 Types of possible attacks

Frauds can be classified into **Physical**, **Digital**, and **Hybrid** attacks. Below is a comprehensive categorization. One can refer to Table 6.1 to understand the common debit and credit card attack types.

Detailed explanations

1. Skimming

Process: Small devices attached to ATM slots record card data; hidden cameras or fake keypads capture PINs.

Example: In the 2023 Mumbai incident, several cloned cards were used abroad within hours.

Prevention: Tug card slots before use; prefer ATMs inside bank branches.

2. Shimming

Process: A thin "shim" sits inside the chip slot, intercepting data flow between the EMV chip and the terminal.

Risk: Creates partial replicas usable for online (card not present) purchases.

Prevention: Use contactless or mobile-based payments.

Table 6.1 Common debit and credit card attack types

Category	Attack type	Mechanism	Impact	Countermeasure
Physical	Skimming	Hidden reader copies the magnetic stripe and the camera captures PIN	Card cloning and cash withdrawal	Inspect ATMs, cover keypad, and use chip slots
	Shimming	Micro device intercepts EMV chip data	Partial duplication of chip info	Prefer contactless/ secured ATMs
Digital	Phishing	Fake emails/websites mimic banks	Credential theft	Verify URLs; do not click unsolicited links
	Malware/ Keylogger	Spyware records input during online payment	Steals CVV, PIN	Use anti-malware; avoid public Wi-Fi
	Man-in-the-Middle (MITM) Attack	Data intercepted between user and bank	Transaction manipulation	Ensure HTTPS and VPN usage
	Ecommerce Breach	Hackers steal data from merchant servers	Mass card leakage	PCI DSS compliance, tokenization
Hybrid	SIM Swap	Fraudster duplicates SIM to intercept OTPs	Bypass 2FA	Request SIM lock, report signal loss
	Social Media Scam	Fake pages and DMs posing as banks	Victim disclosure	Verify blue tick handles, no card info sharing

3. Cloning

Definition: Reproduction of card data on blank magnetic cards.

A simplified attack chain showing how skimming devices on ATMs harvest card data, enabling attackers to produce duplicates that are later used at remote terminals.

4. Phishing

Mechanism: Deceptive communication prompting users to submit card data.

Example: Fake "Visa Verification" portal with near-identical branding.

5. Malware/keyloggers

Description: Trojans monitor browser or keystrokes.

Case: "Emotet" spread via invoice attachments targeting banking credentials.

6. MITM attack

Mechanism: The attacker positions between the user and the bank, modifying packets.

Prevention: Use secured networks; banks should implement TLS (Transport Layer Security protocol) 1.3.

7. Ecommerce breaches

Example: British Airways 2018 data breach (400k cards).

Lesson: Merchants must deploy layered encryption and periodic audits.

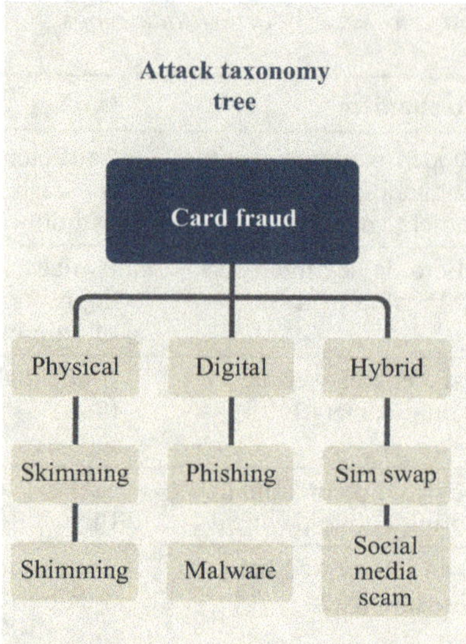

Figure 6.2 Attack taxonomy tree

8. Contactless exploits

Scenario: A criminal brushes a scanner near a crowded metro, capturing NFC signals.

Protection: RFID-blocking wallets, deactivate "tap and pay" when unused.

Figure 6.2 classifies card fraud into physical, digital, and hybrid attack families and lists representative techniques (skimming, shimming, phishing, malware, MITM, SIM swap, and social media scams).

6.3 Social media attacks with examples

Social media is an unsuspected vector for financial fraud due to trust-based interactions.

Forms of social media exploitation

1. Fake bank profiles
   - Fraudsters replicate official Facebook/Twitter pages.
   - Solicit card details in private messages under "customer support."
   - Example: Fake "@HDFCBank_Care" on Twitter collecting card info.
2. Giveaway and cashback scams
   - Victims lured by fake contests.
   - Example: "Share & Win ₹10,000 using your debit card" posts redirect to phishing forms.
3. Friend impersonation
   - Hacked accounts request money or OTPs.
   - Example: "Urgent! Need to book ticket, share your card OTP please."

Table 6.2 Indicators of a social media card fraud

Indicator	Description	Recommended action
Urgent tone/emotional manipulation	"Account blocked, verify now!"	Ignore; verify directly via the official app
Unverified handle	Missing blue tick/ mismatched name	Do not engage
External short links	Bit.ly and tinyurl in message	Hover to preview; avoid clicking
Requests for OTP or CVV	Always illegitimate	Report immediately
"Cashback" forms asking for details	Harvesting attempt	Report the post and alert others

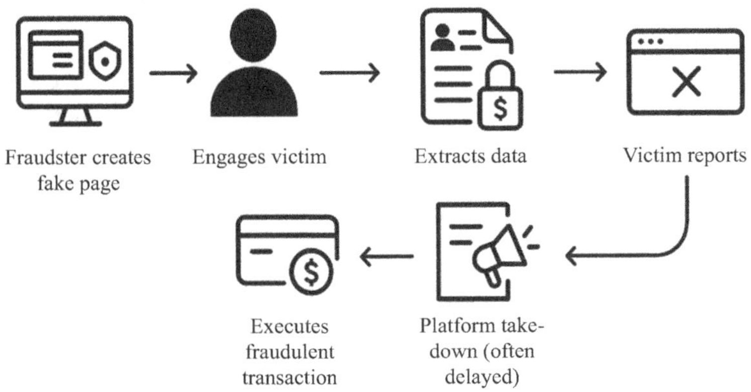

Figure 6.3 Social media fraud lifecycle

4. Malicious ads and surveys
   - Embedded trackers steal details entered into fake feedback forms.

One can refer to Table 6.2 to visualize the indicators of social media card fraud.

A stepwise flow illustrating how fraudsters create fake pages, lure victims, harvest data, conduct fraudulent transactions, and face delayed takedowns after victim reports is depicted in Figure 6.3.

6.4 Best practices to ensure safety and security

For customers

1. Activate real-time alerts for every transaction.
2. Limit daily withdrawal/spending limits to reduce exposure.
3. Use tokenized payments or virtual cards online.

4. Prefer mobile wallets with biometric authentication.
5. Regularly review statements and report anomalies within 24 hours.
6. Avoid saving card data on shopping websites.
7. Secure your SIM with a PIN to prevent OTP theft.
8. Educate family members, especially seniors and children.

For banks

1. Deploy AI/ML Fraud Analytics: Models learn user-spending patterns to flag anomalies.
2. Implement PCI DSS (Payment Card Industry Data Security Standard) v4.0 compliance: Encryption, network segmentation, and monitoring.
3. Tokenization and EMV, 3D Secure 2.0 (3DS2): Adds device-based verification.
4. Conduct Customer Awareness Drives: "Bank Never Asks" campaigns.
5. Centralized Incident Response Centers: 24/7 coordination with CERT-In.
6. Integrate Behavioral Biometrics: Detect unusual typing or transaction rhythm.

A concentric shield design representing five defense layers—user awareness, authentication, encryption and tokenization, network monitoring, and regulatory oversight—is portrayed in Figure 6.4.

Figure 6.4 Multi-layered card security model

6.5 Learn about vishing and smishing attacks

Vishing (voice phishing)

- Definition: Telephone scams where callers impersonate bank officials.
- Script example: Caller: "Sir, your debit card has been blocked. Please confirm 16 digit number for verification."
- Objective: Extract OTP or CVV under pressure of urgency.
- Psychological trigger: Fear and authority.
- Defenses:
  - Hang up immediately; call the official number printed on the card.
  - Never share OTPs.
  - Register with "Do Not Disturb" to reduce scam calls.

Smishing (SMS phishing)

- Definition: Fraudulent SMS messages containing malicious links or helpline numbers.
- Example message: "Your HDFC Card will be deactivated today. Click http://bit.ly/hdfc, verify to continue."
- Impact: Credentials harvested or malware installed.
- Defenses:
  - Do not click embedded links.
  - Check sender ID formatting (banks never use random numbers).
  - Report to Cybercrime Helpline 1930.

Table 6.3 has the comparison between vishing and smishing.

Figure 6.5 outlines the sequential stages of a phishing attack, from fake communication to bank intervention and investigation.

The timeline mapping provides the typical stages from a fake message to an eventual bank investigation, illustrating the progression of a phishing scam.

Table 6.3 Comparison: Vishing vs. smishing

Aspect	Vishing	Smishing
Medium	Voice call	SMS/Text
Primary tool	Social engineering via conversation	Link or fake number
Psychological lever	Urgency, fear of account lock	Curiosity, reward, fear
Typical data stolen	OTP, CVV, full card number	Card number, credentials
Preventive action	Verify via official helpline	Ignore/delete the message immediately

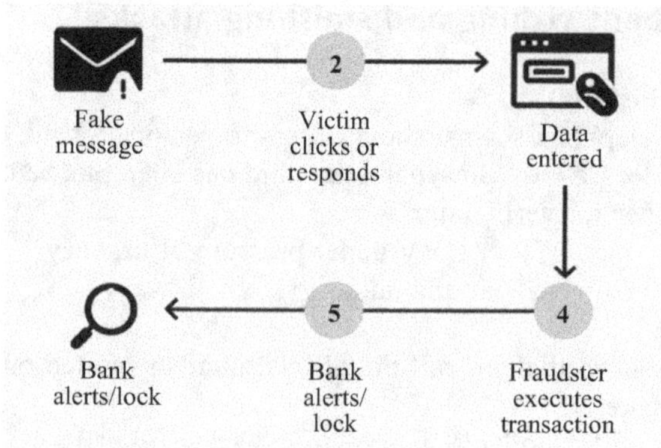

Figure 6.5 Anatomy of a phishing attempt

6.6 Possible scenarios and typical examples

Scenario 1: ATM tampering

A user withdraws ₹5,000 from an outdoor ATM. Hours later, international charges appear. Investigation reveals a skimmer and a pinhole camera installed.

Lesson: Prefer ATMs with in-person guards or inside bank premises.

Scenario 2: Phishing followed by vishing

The customer receives an "account verification" email and enters card details. Soon after, a fake "confirmation call" validates the data and drains the account.

Lesson: Sequential multi-vector attacks combine phishing and vishing.

Scenario 3: Ecommerce data leak

A popular online marketplace stored plain-text card numbers. Hackers leaked 200k records on the dark web.

Lesson: Merchant negligence is equally dangerous; demand secure payment gateways.

Scenario 4: Social media impersonation

A fake Facebook account of a bank executive "assists" a customer, stealing card info.

Lesson: Verify blue tick pages; banks never ask for private details online.

Scenario 5: SIM swap fraud

The attacker convinces the telecom provider to issue a duplicate SIM. OTPs are rerouted, enabling fraudulent transfers.

Lesson: Set SIM change alerts with your mobile operator.

Table 6.4 contains the summary of fraud scenarios and defensive actions.

Table 6.4 Summary of fraud scenarios and defensive actions

Scenario	Fraud type	User mistake	Preventive action
ATM tampering	Skimming	Uninspected ATM	Use secure ATMs, shield PIN
Phish + vish	Phishing and voice scam	Clicking a fake link	Verify emails, and never share OTP
Ecommerce leak	Merchant breach	Saving card info	Use virtual cards
Social impersonation	Social media scam	Trusting fake profiles	Verify page authenticity
SIM swap	Telecom manipulation	Not securing SIM	Enable SIM lock

6.7 Best practices to ensure safety (consolidated)

A. For individuals

- Use chip or contactless cards; disable magnetic stripes abroad.
- Enable international usage only when required.
- Use RBI's DigiSaathi for secure payment awareness.
- Store card images encrypted, not in the phone gallery.
- Shred old statements and expired cards.

B. For institutions

- Continuous monitoring using AI anomaly engines.
- Periodic ethical hacking audits.
- Mandatory two-factor authentication.
- Tie-ups with law enforcement for rapid takedowns.
- Conduct mock fraud response drills annually.

A hierarchical pyramid showing layered security, from foundational user awareness and process controls to encryption, AI-driven monitoring, and governance at the top, is illustrated in Figure 6.6. The card security pyramid emphasizes the progression from basic awareness to apex-level governance.

6.8 End of chapter summary

Debit and credit card fraud represent one of the most pervasive threats in the digital banking era. They combine technological sophistication with psychological manipulation, exploiting both system vulnerabilities and human behavior. What began as simple card cloning has evolved into a global network of coordinated cybercrime involving malware, phishing, social engineering, and large-scale data breaches.

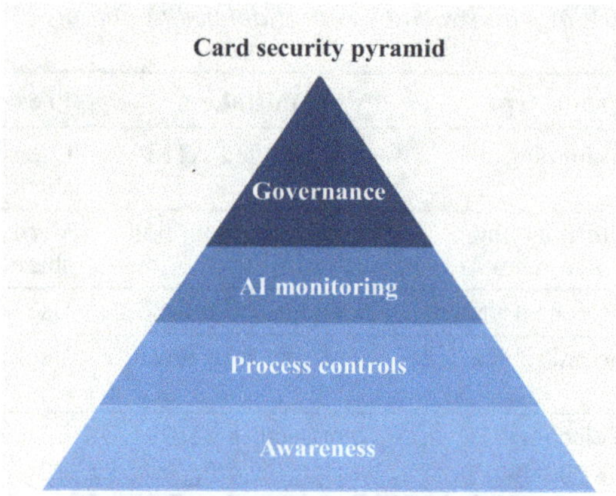

Figure 6.6 Card security pyramid

Throughout this chapter, we explored how fraudsters operate at multiple layers of the payment ecosystem, from tampering with physical ATMs to infiltrating ecommerce databases. The modern criminal toolkit includes skimmers, shimmers, malicious scripts, and even artificial intelligence that mimics legitimate user behavior. As financial systems begin to adopt new technologies such as contactless payments, digital wallets, and tokenized transactions, the threat landscape shifts correspondingly. Attackers now employ advanced analytics, deepfake voice calls, and synthetic identities to outsmart conventional detection methods.

At the same time, the human factor remains the weakest link. Phishing emails, vishing calls, and social media impersonations continue to succeed because they prey on trust and urgency. Awareness alone is no longer sufficient; users must cultivate digital skepticism, a conscious habit of questioning every message, link, or request that involves personal data. Regular education campaigns, customer communication in regional languages, and realistic simulations can transform awareness into habitual caution.

Financial institutions play an equally crucial role. Banks are investing heavily in AI-driven anomaly detection, behavioral biometrics, and predictive analytics that learn spending patterns to flag irregularities in real time. These technologies, however, are only as effective as the governance behind them. Strict adherence to frameworks such as PCI DSS 4.0, RBI's Cybersecurity Directions, and global AML/KYC norms ensures that technological defenses align with compliance and accountability.

The concept of multi-layered security has emerged as a gold standard. No single control, not even encryption, can secure the entire ecosystem. Instead, protection must be layered: secure endpoints, encrypted communication, robust authentication, continuous monitoring, and well-trained human oversight. Multifactor authentication, once viewed as an inconvenience, is now indispensable. Combined with geolocation tracking and tokenization, it forms the digital equivalent of locking, bolting, and guarding a vault simultaneously.

From the customer's perspective, vigilance translates into empowerment. Simple actions such as verifying website URLs, inspecting ATMs, covering keypads, using transaction alerts, and avoiding public Wi-Fi drastically reduce risk exposure. Equally important is prompt reporting: the sooner a suspicious transaction is flagged, the higher the chance of recovery and containment. The Government of India's (GOI) Cybercrime Helpline 1930 and cybercrime.gov.in portal have made reporting easier and more accessible.

Social media has introduced a parallel battlefield. Fraudsters leverage fake pages, cloned handles, and influencer-style giveaways to harvest card data. Awareness campaigns like "RBI Kehta Hai" and "Bank Never Asks" have proven valuable, but they must evolve with new digital habits. Collaboration between banks, regulators, telecom operators, and social media companies can ensure faster takedowns of fraudulent pages and improved content moderation against scams.

In essence, card fraud prevention is not merely a technical problem; it is a socio-technical challenge requiring cooperation among regulators, institutions, merchants, and end users. The equation of security has shifted from firewalls and passwords to trust and shared responsibility. Every participant in the financial chain, from developers designing secure payment APIs to customers authorizing a single transaction, contributes to the overall resilience of the system.

Looking ahead, emerging technologies like blockchain, quantum-safe cryptography, and explainable AI offer promising avenues for building transparent and tamper-resistant financial systems. Blockchain's immutable ledgers can prevent unauthorized transaction manipulation; quantum-resistant algorithms will safeguard encryption standards in the coming decade; and explainable AI will ensure fairness and accountability in automated fraud detection. Yet, these advances must be balanced with ethics, privacy, and inclusivity so that security innovations do not create new inequalities or biases.

Ultimately, debit and credit card fraud highlight the dynamic interplay between innovation and exploitation. As the financial world becomes smarter, so do its adversaries. The only sustainable defense is an informed, collaborative, and adaptive approach—one that combines technology, policy, and human vigilance.

By internalizing the mechanisms of fraud and the psychology behind them, banking professionals and consumers can strengthen trust in digital finance and safeguard the backbone of the global economy.

In short: proactive learning, layered security, and cooperative defense are not optional; they are the foundations of financial integrity in an interconnected world. Awareness is the new firewall, and every informed user is part of the security system.

Key points to remember

1. **Debit and credit card fraud thrive on both technical flaws and human lapses;** attackers exploit weak systems and careless behaviors simultaneously.
2. **Awareness is the first layer of defense;** informed customers can identify scams long before technology does.

3. **Social engineering remains the most common attack route,** using fear, urgency, or curiosity to extract confidential information.
4. **Skimming and shimming devices are physical threats** that silently copy card data. Inspect ATMs and POS terminals carefully.
5. **Phishing, vishing, and smishing attacks manipulate trust,** imitating banks through fake calls, emails, or SMS alerts.
6. **Social media has become a fertile ground for fraudsters,** where fake pages and giveaways harvest sensitive details.
7. **Ecommerce platforms are frequent targets;** a single database breach can expose millions of stored card numbers.
8. **Contactless and mobile payments introduce new vulnerabilities,** requiring tokenization and RFID shielding for safety.
9. **Malware and keyloggers record user activity silently,** making device hygiene and antivirus protection essential.
10. **Multifactor authentication adds a vital safety layer,** combining OTPs, biometrics, or device tokens for stronger verification.
11. **Behavioral analytics helps banks detect anomalies,** spotting spending patterns inconsistent with genuine users.
12. **AI-driven fraud detection systems reduce human error,** identifying suspicious activity faster than manual reviews.
13. **Timely reporting of suspicious transactions** increases recovery chances and limits further unauthorized activity.
14. **Transaction alerts and spending limits empower customers** to monitor activity and cap exposure automatically.
15. **Regulatory frameworks such as RBI guidelines and PCI DSS standards** ensure minimum security practices across institutions.
16. **Employee and customer education programs** bridge the gap between technical safeguards and human awareness.
17. **SIM swap and OTP interception attacks highlight telecom vulnerabilities,** emphasizing the need for SIM locks and verified changes.
18. **Card tokenization and encryption protect sensitive data in transit,** making intercepted information useless to attackers.
19. **Cybersecurity is a shared responsibility;** customers, merchants, and banks must collaborate for collective protection.
20. **Ultimately, vigilance, skepticism, and informed action** remain the strongest shields against ever-evolving card fraud threats.

Questions (Try answering them yourself)

- Explain the evolution of debit and credit card frauds and discuss how digital transformation has changed the threat landscape.
- Differentiate between card skimming and card shimming. How do these attacks operate, and what preventive steps can customers take?
- Describe how social engineering contributes to card fraud. Provide relevant examples from recent incidents.

- Discuss the role of malware and keyloggers in card data theft. How can such attacks be detected and mitigated?
- Analyze the impact of ecommerce data breaches on cardholder privacy and financial integrity.
- What are the psychological triggers used in phishing, vishing, and smishing attacks? Explain with case-based examples.
- Elaborate on the types of social media scams that target banking customers and explain how they exploit trust and urgency.
- How does multifactor authentication enhance card security? Discuss its benefits and possible limitations.
- Describe the steps involved in a Man-in-the-Middle (MITM) attack during online transactions and suggest countermeasures.
- What is card tokenization? How does it improve transaction security for online payments?
- Evaluate the role of AI and machine learning in fraud detection and prevention within card-based payment systems.
- Discuss how behavioral biometrics are being used to identify fraudulent transactions in modern banking systems.
- Explain the difference between card cloning and card counterfeiting. Provide practical examples for both.
- How can awareness campaigns like "RBI Kehta Hai" and "Bank Never Asks" help reduce debit and credit card frauds?
- Discuss the significance of PCI DSS compliance in protecting customer data and maintaining payment integrity.
- Illustrate a real-world case study of a major card fraud incident and explain what lessons can be drawn from it.
- Identify and explain five best practices for individual card users to safeguard their financial information.
- How do SIM swap and OTP interception attacks work, and why are they becoming increasingly common?
- Discuss the importance of collaboration between banks, regulators, and customers in minimizing card-related cybercrime.
- In your opinion, what emerging technologies (e.g., blockchain, quantum cryptography) could redefine card security in the next decade?

Objective questions

Q1. Which of the following best defines card skimming?
- (A) Copying data from a card's magnetic stripe using an illegal device
- (B) Blocking unauthorized IP addresses in a network
- (C) Using voice phishing to steal OTPs
- (D) Encrypting data for online payments

Q2. A shim is used by fraudsters to:
(A) Detect counterfeit cards
(B) Intercept data between an EMV chip and a card reader
(C) Clone contactless cards directly
(D) Jam wireless card readers

Q3. Which of the following is a social engineering technique targeting card users?
(A) SQL injection
(B) DDoS attack
(C) Vishing
(D) Cross-site scripting

Q4. The term phishing is most closely associated with:
(A) Voice-based scams
(B) Email- or web-based credential theft
(C) Card duplication
(D) Malware attached to ATMs

Q5. The main difference between skimming and shimming is:
(A) Skimming targets' chip cards, shimming targets' magnetic cards
(B) Skimming uses external devices; shimming uses micro inserts inside the reader
(C) Skimming is online; shimming is offline
(D) Skimming is legal data reading

Q6. The RBI's DigiSaathi initiative primarily focuses on:
(A) Cryptocurrency education
(B) Customer awareness of digital payment safety
(C) Managing blockchain networks
(D) Offering new debit card services

Q7. Which of the following attacks involves intercepting communication between a user and a bank website?
(A) Man-in-the-Middle (MITM)
(B) Keylogger
(C) Denial of service
(D) SIM swap

Q8. Smishing attacks are delivered via:
(A) Social media messages
(B) Voice calls
(C) SMS messages
(D) Email attachments

Q9. What is the primary goal of card tokenization?
(A) Store card data in plain text
(B) Replace card data with a unique encrypted code
(C) Track spending habits
(D) Eliminate the need for OTPs

Q10. A contactless payment exploit often involves:
(A) Skimming with cameras
(B) Remote scanning of RFID/NFC signals
(C) Manually entering card data online
(D) Phone number spoofing

Q11. Which of the following organizations sets the global payment data security standards?
(A) NASSCOM
(B) PCI Security Standards Council
(C) IMF
(D) RBI

Q12. Which fraud type occurs when criminals duplicate a SIM card to receive OTPs?
(A) Phishing
(B) SIM swap
(C) Spoofing
(D) Data breach

Q13. Behavioral analytics in banking is used to:
(A) Block websites automatically
(B) Identify spending anomalies based on user patterns
(C) Encrypt magnetic stripe data
(D) Generate virtual cards

Q14. A keylogger attack steals card information by:
(A) Recording user keystrokes
(B) Redirecting payments to fake sites
(C) Tampering with ATMs
(D) Modifying DNS entries

Q15. Which of the following best describes vishing?
(A) Voice-based phishing attempt
(B) Video-based card skimming
(C) Visual authentication for cards
(D) Verification via fingerprint

Q16. Which of these practices should be followed by every cardholder for safety?
(A) Sharing card details only with family
(B) Clicking on promotional links from banks
(C) Regularly checking transaction alerts and statements
(D) Saving card images in the mobile gallery

Q17. The most effective way to avoid ATM skimming is to:
- (A) Withdraw during off-peak hours
- (B) Inspect the card slot and cover the keypad during PIN entry
- (C) Avoid using chip cards
- (D) Disable OTP for transactions

Q18. The PCI DSS framework is mainly applicable to:
- (A) Telecom operators
- (B) Payment processors and merchants
- (C) Government departments
- (D) Insurance companies

Q19. What is the primary motivation behind social media card scams?
- (A) Increase page followers
- (B) Build user engagement
- (C) Trick users into revealing financial details
- (D) Promote legitimate bank offers

Q20. The best way to report digital payment fraud in India is to contact:
- (A) Cybercrime Helpline 1930 or cybercrime.gov.in
- (B) Nearest police station only
- (C) Ministry of Commerce
- (D) Internet service provider

Answer key

Q. No.	*Answer*
1	A
2	B
3	C
4	B
5	B
6	B
7	A
8	C
9	B
10	B
11	B
12	B
13	B
14	A
15	A
16	C
17	B
18	B
19	C
20	A

Further reading

[1] PCI Security Standards Council. *Payment Card Data Security Standards (PCI DSS)*. 2024.

[2] Barney N. *What Is PCI DSS? Definition, Requirements, Benefits*. TechTarget; 2024.

[3] Secureframe. *What's New in PCI DSS 4.0? Key Updates Explained*. 2024.

[4] Wickramanayake B, Geeganage DK, Ouyang C, and Xu Y. A survey of online card payment fraud detection using data mining, based methods. *arXiv [Preprint]*. 2020 Nov 27.

[5] Fariha N, Moin Khan N, *et al.* Advanced fraud detection using machine learning models: Enhancing financial transaction security. *arXiv [Preprint]*. 2025 June 12.

[6] Tiwari P, Mehta S, Sakhuja N, Kumar J, and Singh AK. Credit card fraud detection using machine learning: a study. *arXiv [Preprint]*. 2021 Aug 23.

[7] EY. *The Digital Payments Ecosystem of India*. EY Global; 2025.

[8] PwC India. *Combating Payments Fraud in India's Digital Payments Landscape*. 2025.

[9] RBI. *FAQs on Master Directions on Fraud Risk Management. Reserve Bank of India*. 2025.

[10] Economic Times. *Experts Welcome RBI's Digital Payment Authentication Overhaul*. 2025.

[11] Economic Times. *RBI's Digital Payments Intelligence Platform to Flag Risky Transactions*. 2025.

[12] Times of India. *Internet, Card Frauds Halve in FY25: RBI Data*. 2025.

[13] Reuters. *India Central Bank Allows Risk, Based Checks in New Digital Payment Guidelines*. 2025.

[14] Secureframe (blog). *PCI DSS 4.0 Compliance Checklist*. 2024.

[15] CrowdStrike. *PCI DSS Compliance: 12 Requirements*. 2023.

[16] AuditBoard. *The 12 PCI DSS Compliance Requirements: What You Need to Know*. 2023.

[17] IT Governance. *PCI DSS: What It Is and How to Comply*. 2024.

[18] VikingCloud. *PCI DSS: What It Is and How to Comply*. 2024.

[19] Controller, UCSF. *Understanding Payment Card Industry Data Security Standard (PCI DSS)*. 2024.

[20] IT Governance. *PCI DSS 4.0.1 – Latest Update*. 2024.

[21] Wikipedia contributors. *Payment Card Industry Data Security Standard*. Wikimedia Foundation; 2024.

[22] Wikipedia contributors. *PADSS (Payment Application Data Security Standard)*. Wikimedia Foundation; 2025.

[23] Wikipedia contributors. *Point, to, Point Encryption*. Wikimedia Foundation; 2025.

[24] *Loksabha Questions – Government of India*. Digital payment/card fraud statistics. 2025.

[25] Times of India/The Cyber Express. *RBI Tightens Noose on Digital Payment Frauds*. 2024.

Chapter 7
Money laundering

Learning objectives

After completing this chapter, readers will be able to

(a) Define money laundering and explain why it poses serious risks to financial stability and cybersecurity.
(b) Understand the three stages of money laundering: Placement, layering, and integration, with modern digital examples.
(c) Interpret the essence of the FinCEN 2016 Guide and its relevance to financial institutions worldwide.
(d) Examine how Anti-Money-Laundering (AML) frameworks intersect with cybersecurity controls.
(e) Recognize the importance of prompt cyber-event reporting and cross-border cooperation.
(f) Analyze famous money-laundering incidents to identify governance lapses and lessons learned.
(g) Explore further learning resources and current global initiatives combating illicit financial flows.

7.1 Money laundering! Do we have to worry?

Money laundering is the process of concealing the origins of illegally obtained money by passing it through legitimate channels to make it appear clean. While the phrase evokes images of criminal gangs and offshore accounts, today's laundering activities are far more sophisticated; they exploit digital banking, cryptocurrencies, prepaid cards, and even online gaming platforms.

According to the *United Nations Office on Drugs and Crime (UNODC)*, global money-laundering transactions account for 2–5% of global GDP (approx. US $2 trillion annually).

Banks, fintech companies, and payment aggregators face immense pressure to detect suspicious patterns without obstructing genuine transactions.

Why worry? Because laundering funds fuels terrorism, corruption, cybercrime, and human trafficking, it destabilizes entire economies. It also erodes trust in the financial system, leading to reputational damage and heavy regulatory penalties for institutions that fail to detect it.

Figure 7.1 outlines the classic three-stage process of money laundering: placement, layering, and integration.

Table 7.1, presented below, reveals the common methods of money laundering.

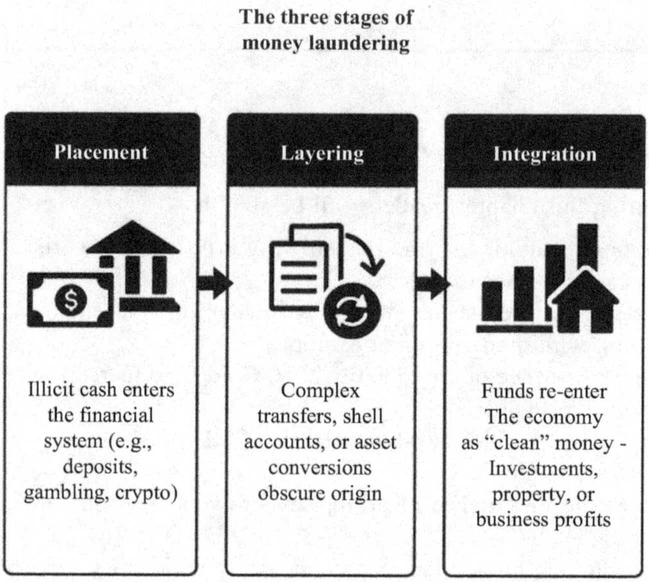

Figure 7.1 The three stages of money laundering

Table 7.1 Common methods of money laundering

Stage	Method	Description	Example/digital angle
Placement	Structuring (Smurfing)	Breaking large cash deposits into smaller ones	Multiple ₹49,000 deposits to avoid reporting limit
	Cash-intensive businesses	Co-mixing illicit and legal cash	Restaurants, gas stations
Layering	Shell companies and offshore accounts	Creating distance between criminal and funds	Complex ownership across three jurisdictions
	Cryptocurrency tumblers	Mixing crypto to hide the source	Bitcoin mixers or privacy coins
Integration	Investment in assets	Buying property, art, gold	Digital gold or NFT (Non-Fungible Token) purchases
	Loan-back schemes	A criminal lends his own clean money to himself	Fake lending platforms

7.2 The FinCEN 2016 Guide

The *Financial Crimes Enforcement Network (FinCEN)*, a bureau of the US Department of the Treasury, issued in 2016 a landmark guide titled "Advisory to Financial Institutions on Cyber-Events and Cyber-Enabled Crime." This guide redefined how banks view and report suspicious activity linked with cyber incidents.

Core highlights

1. Integration of cyber and AML reporting: FinCEN emphasized that cyber-events—malware, data theft, credential compromise—can be directly tied to money-laundering attempts.
2. Suspicious Activity Report (SAR) Enrichment: Financial institutions must include technical indicators (IP addresses, domain names, and malware hashes) in SARs.
3. Cross-agency collaboration: Encouraged coördination between IT security, compliance, and law enforcement teams to ensure holistic detection.
4. Focus on cyber-enabled crime: Highlighted emerging channels such as digital wallets, virtual currencies, and peer-to-peer transfers.
5. Proactive Information Sharing (314(b) Program): Allowed institutions to share cyber-related suspicious data legally within the financial community.

Figure 7.2 depicts the FinCEN reporting flow, from event detection to regulatory feedback provided back to banks.

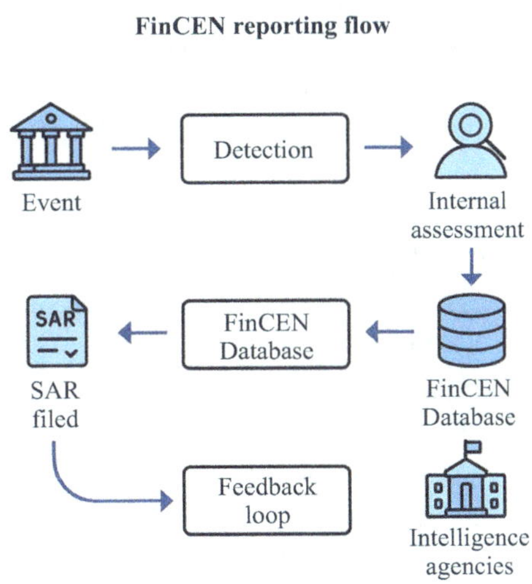

Figure 7.2 FinCEN reporting flow

7.2.1 Key takeaway

The 2016 Guide transformed AML compliance from a purely financial monitoring exercise to a **cyber-intelligence discipline**, merging two once-separate worlds.

7.3 Anti-Money-Laundering (AML) and cybersecurity

AML and cybersecurity are two sides of the same coin. A cyber-breach that leaks credentials can immediately be exploited to launder stolen funds. Likewise, effective AML controls require a secure digital infrastructure to ensure reliable data.

7.3.1 Convergence of functions

Traditionally, AML teams focused on transaction monitoring, while cybersecurity teams handled system protection.

Modern risk frameworks integrate both, sharing real-time alerts and common analytics dashboards.

7.3.2 Use of AI and machine learning

AI models detect unusual transaction clusters, while cybersecurity tools identify compromised accounts, jointly reducing false positives.

7.3.3 Blockchain and RegTech

Blockchain enables transparent transaction trails, and RegTech (Regulatory Technology) automates compliance checks through smart rules.

7.3.4 Cyber Threat Intelligence (CTI)

Banks now collect indicators of compromise (IoCs) from dark-web forums to prevent laundering of stolen or ransomware proceeds.

Table 7.2 presents the clear details of the intersection of AML and cybersecurity.

Table 7.2 Intersection of AML and cybersecurity

AML activity	Cybersecurity parallel	Combined outcome
Know Your Customer (KYC)	Digital identity verification, biometrics	Prevent fake accounts
Transaction monitoring	Network anomaly detection	Early warning for fraud
Suspicious activity reporting	Incident Response Reporting	Unified regulatory view
Data retention and audit trail	Secure log management	Forensic readiness
Compliance training	Phishing and social-engineering awareness	Human defense enhanced

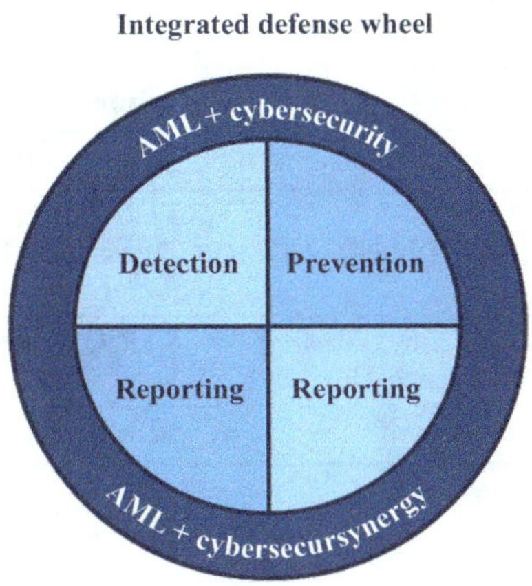

Figure 7.3 Integrated defense wheel

Figure 7.3 illustrates the Integrated Defense Wheel, highlighting detection, prevention, response, and reporting within an AML–cybersecurity synergy framework.

7.4 Reporting cyber-events

Timely and transparent reporting is the cornerstone of an effective AML cyber framework.

7.4.1 Why reporting matters!

- Helps trace cross-border money trails.
- Enables regulators to link cyberattacks with illicit fund flows.
- Reduces systemic risk through early warnings.

7.4.2 Global reporting mechanisms

Table 7.3 below summarizes the global reporting mechanisms.

7.4.3 Challenges

- Delays in data correlation between cyber and compliance teams.
- Fear of reputational loss discourages disclosure.
- Fragmented reporting standards across countries.

7.4.4 Best practices

- Maintain joint Incident Response and Compliance playbooks.
- Automate SAR/STR triggering via SIEM (Security Information and Event Management) tools.
- Conduct post-incident AML reviews to close control gaps.

Table 7.3 Global reporting mechanisms

Jurisdiction	Reporting entity	Primary channel	Timeline
USA	FinCEN	SAR Portal	Within 30 days
India	FIU-IND (Financial Intelligence Unit - India)	STR (Suspicious Transaction Report) Portal	7 working days
UK	NCA (National Crime Agency) - Financial Intelligence Unit	SAR Online	Prompt
EU	Europol FIU Network	GoAML System	Variable

Figure 7.4 Cyber-event reporting cycle

Figure 7.4 illustrates the cyber-event reporting lifecycle, tracing the flow from detection through assessment, classification, regulatory reporting, law enforcement action, and feedback.

7.5 Famous money-laundering incidents

Studying historical cases illuminates how loopholes are exploited and how policies evolved.

7.5.1 HSBC Case (2012)

- **Nature:** Failure to prevent laundering by Mexican drug cartels.
- **Outcome:** US $1.9 billion fine.
- **Lesson:** Global banks need unified AML monitoring; fragmented compliance breeds risk.

7.5.2 Danske Bank Estonia Case (2018)

- **Nature:** €200 billion suspicious flows through the Baltic branch.
- **Cause:** Weak KYC controls for nonresident accounts.
- **Lesson:** Local compliance cannot ignore cross-border exposure.

7.5.3 Wirecard Scandal (Germany, 2020)

- **Nature:** Falsified revenues and shell accounts to mask fund movement.
- **Lesson:** Fintech oversight must match that of traditional banks.

7.5.4 Punjab National Bank Fraud (India, 2018)

- **Nature:** Fake Letters of Undertaking (LoUs) and layered offshore transfers.
- **Lesson:** Combine AML and cybersecurity controls for trade-finance operations.

7.5.5 OneCoin Cryptocurrency Scheme (2014–2019)

- **Nature:** $4 billion Ponzi marketed as a crypto investment.
- **Lesson:** Virtual-asset providers require AML licensing and blockchain analytics.

One can have a quick look at Table 7.4 to understand the summary of famous cases and their respective insights.

Table 7.4 Summary of case insights

Case	Country	Primary failure point	Penalty/impact
HSBC	USA/ Mexico	Inadequate transaction monitoring	$1.9 billion fine
Danske Bank	Estonia/ EU	Weak nonresident KYC	Bank exit from Estonia
Wirecard	Germany	Fake accounts and audit failures	Collapse of firm
PNB	India	Trade finance fraud and SWIFT misuse	$2 billion loss
OneCoin	Bulgaria/ Global	Crypto laundering	Founder arrested/ongoing trial

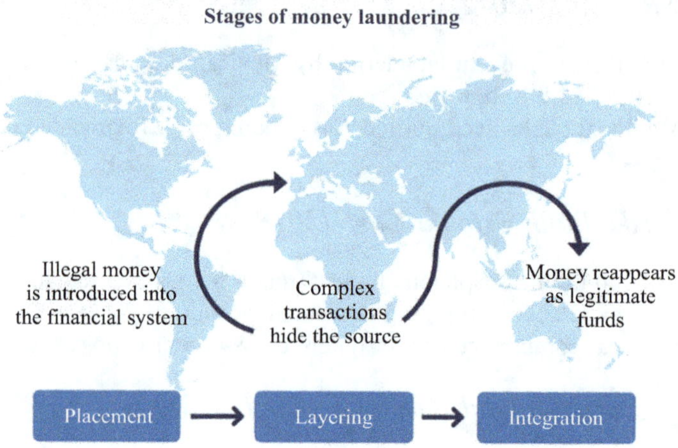

Figure 7.5. Global money-laundering map

Figure 7.5 shows global money-laundering patterns, mapping cross-border fund movement routes across key jurisdictions.

7.6 End of chapter summary

Money laundering is not only a financial offense but also a digital-age enabler of global crime. As payment ecosystems expand, criminals adapt by using crypto wallets, online shells, and stolen identities. The FinCEN 2016 Guide marked the turning point by merging cyber intelligence with financial compliance. Today, effective defense demands integrated AML cyber strategies, automated analytics, and transparent governance.

From HSBC's lapses to India's trade-finance frauds, every incident underscores the same truth: financial integrity is a collective responsibility. Only through cooperation among banks, regulators, and vigilant customers can economies remain resilient against the invisible flows that erode trust and national security.

7.6.1 Key points to remember

1. Money laundering disguises illicit funds through placement, layering, and integration.
   It typically follows a three-stage process. In the placement stage, illicit cash is introduced into the financial system through methods like deposits, gambling, or converting to digital assets. The layering stage involves complex transfers, shell companies, or asset conversions designed to obscure the fund's origin. Finally, in the integration stage, these funds reappear as seemingly legitimate investments, business profits, or property purchases. Understanding these

stages is fundamental for banks and regulators to build targeted controls against money laundering.

2. Digital transformation has created new laundering channels like crypto and e-wallets.
   With the growth of financial technology, criminals exploit cryptocurrencies, online wallets, and peer-to-peer apps for laundering. These platforms provide anonymity, speed, and cross-border flexibility, making traditional monitoring mechanisms less effective. For instance, a launderer can move illicit proceeds through decentralized exchanges, convert them into privacy coins, and withdraw them globally. This evolution requires regulators and financial institutions to upgrade detection systems for emerging channels. Digital risk management has become an urgent priority.
3. The FinCEN 2016 Guide bridged the gap between cyber incidents and AML reporting.
   The 2016 FinCEN Guidance recognized that cyber incidents often have money-laundering links, urging banks to integrate AML reporting with cybersecurity events. This meant that Suspicious Activity Reports (SARs) must also consider data breaches, account takeovers, or ransomware payments. It bridged the historical gap between financial compliance and IT security teams. The guidance was a landmark step in aligning financial integrity with cyber resilience. Many global regulators followed similar frameworks thereafter.
4. AML and cybersecurity convergence enhance resilience against financial crime.
   Traditionally, AML teams and cybersecurity teams worked in silos. Now, their convergence creates stronger defense mechanisms by correlating financial transaction patterns with network anomalies. For example, combining AML suspicious transaction alerts with SIEM logs can reveal sophisticated cross-channel fraud. Institutions that integrate these domains respond faster and reduce detection blind spots. This synergy is seen as the future of financial crime compliance.
5. Timely SAR/STR filing is crucial for legal compliance and intelligence gathering.
   Suspicious Activity Reports (SARs) or Suspicious Transaction Reports (STRs) are a legal obligation for banks and regulated entities. Delays or inaccuracies can lead to penalties and missed opportunities for law enforcement to stop ongoing laundering. Timely filing enables intelligence agencies to connect dots across multiple institutions. For instance, one bank's SAR could reveal a small piece of a larger global laundering scheme. Regulators increasingly measure compliance effectiveness by timeliness and quality of reporting.
6. AI, ML, and blockchain analytics are redefining detection capabilities.
   Artificial intelligence and machine learning enable pattern recognition, anomaly detection, and predictive analysis in vast transaction datasets. Blockchain analytics provide traceability on crypto transactions, mapping wallets, and identifying illicit clusters. These technologies reduce false positives, which traditionally overwhelmed compliance teams. They also empower

proactive fraud detection by flagging suspicious activity before funds move further. The adoption of these technologies is transforming AML compliance from manual to intelligent.

7. Real-time collaboration between banks, regulators, and law enforcement is essential.
   Financial crime is rarely isolated to one institution. Real-time collaboration, supported by data-sharing platforms and joint intelligence groups, is essential to disrupting laundering networks. Public-private partnerships such as the UK's Joint Money Laundering Intelligence Taskforce (JMLIT) are examples of successful collaboration. This model ensures quicker responses to cross-border laundering schemes. The stronger the cooperation, the harder it becomes for criminals to exploit jurisdictional loopholes.
8. Weak KYC controls remain the root cause in most laundering cases.
   Despite advanced tools, Know Your Customer (KYC) weaknesses remain the most exploited gap in the financial system. Fake identities, incomplete documentation, or inadequate verification allow criminals to set up accounts that later facilitate laundering. Regulators stress continuous KYC updates and enhanced due diligence for high-risk clients. Strengthening KYC is not only a regulatory mandate but also a business necessity to protect institutional reputation. Many large laundering scandals trace back to poor onboarding processes.
9. Reputational and financial penalties for noncompliance are enormous.
   Failure to comply with AML regulations has led to multi-billion-dollar fines for global banks. Beyond monetary losses, reputational damage erodes customer trust and investor confidence. Institutions named in laundering scandals often face long-term operational restrictions. Proactive investment in AML systems is therefore seen as cheaper than regulatory fallout. A single compliance failure can undo years of brand equity.
10. Public-private partnerships strengthen systemic defense.
    Public-private partnerships (PPPs) align the interests of regulators, law enforcement, and financial institutions. They help share typologies, red flags, and intelligence that a single institution may not detect on its own. These partnerships also foster innovation in AML technology and compliance standards. Countries with strong PPP ecosystems report higher laundering disruption rates. Collaboration is now considered a central pillar in combating financial crime.
11. Training staff to recognize cyber-enabled red flags is vital.
    Technology can only go so far if employees are not vigilant. Training front-line staff to spot red flags like rapid transfers, unusual crypto activity, or suspicious communication patterns is critical. Cyber-enabled laundering often begins with account compromise, which human operators may notice before algorithms do. Regular awareness campaigns build a culture of compliance. Human vigilance complements technological defenses.
12. Cross-border data sharing improves visibility into layered transactions.
    Layering in laundering thrives when jurisdictions fail to share data. Cross-border cooperation enables regulators and banks to see the full transaction

chain. Initiatives like the Egmont Group of Financial Intelligence Units promote such international information exchange. Enhanced data visibility breaks down laundering schemes that rely on fragmented oversight. Harmonized data-sharing frameworks are essential in today's interconnected economy.

13. Crypto exchanges must adopt AML licensing and blockchain tracing tools.
    Cryptocurrency exchanges serve as gateways between fiat and digital assets, making them prime laundering targets. Regulators now require exchanges to hold AML licenses, conduct KYC, and implement transaction monitoring. Blockchain tracing tools like Chainalysis or Elliptic allow compliance teams to detect illicit wallets. Without these measures, crypto adoption risks are being overshadowed by laundering concerns. Responsible exchanges must embrace transparency to earn legitimacy.
14. Integration of SIEM and AML systems reduces detection latency.
    Security Information and Event Management (SIEM) platforms track IT events, while AML systems track financial ones. Their integration reduces latency in detecting fraud by correlating cyber incidents with suspicious financial transactions. For example, a compromised account login identified by SIEM can instantly trigger AML checks on subsequent transfers. This convergence strengthens both cybersecurity and financial compliance. Many institutions are investing in unified monitoring systems.
15. Ethical corporate culture underpins successful compliance programs.
    Rules and technologies cannot replace an ethical organizational culture. Institutions with leadership committed to compliance build more resilient frameworks. Conversely, companies with profit-driven negligence often end up in scandals. Ethics-driven cultures encourage employees to speak up, adhere to controls, and act in the institution's long-term interest. Compliance begins at the top.
16. Transparency and whistleblower mechanisms deter internal complicity.
    Employees are sometimes complicit in laundering schemes. Whistleblower channels provide safe mechanisms to report such misconduct. Transparency in governance discourages collusion between insiders and launderers. Strong reporting frameworks, backed by legal protections, foster accountability. These measures ensure that compliance is not undermined internally.
17. Proactive governance transforms compliance from reactive to preventive.
    Governance should not only respond to regulatory breaches but also anticipate risks. Proactive governance integrates AML into business strategy, risk management, and digital transformation. Boards that prioritize compliance see fewer surprises and greater resilience. Preventive frameworks also reduce costs compared to reactive investigations. Governance maturity is a competitive differentiator in finance.
18. Money laundering threatens economic stability and national security.
    Laundering funds often finances organized crime, terrorism, and corruption, posing threats to societies at large. Large-scale laundering destabilizes financial systems by distorting markets and weakening trust. It can also

undermine foreign investment if a country is perceived as a money laundering haven. Therefore, AML is not only about compliance but also about national and global security. Strong AML systems protect economies as much as they protect institutions.

19. Awareness and accountability at all levels build trust in digital finance.
    From frontline staff to senior executives, shared accountability ensures effective AML frameworks. Customer awareness also plays a role, as educated clients can avoid scams and report suspicious activity. Trust in digital finance grows only when all stakeholders demonstrate accountability. This holistic awareness strengthens the resilience of financial ecosystems. Shared responsibility is the bedrock of sustainable compliance.
20. Combating laundering requires a unified approach combining law, technology, and ethics.
    No single tool or regulation can eliminate laundering. The most effective defense blends legal enforcement, advanced technology, and ethical conduct. Laws set the boundaries, technology enhances detection, and ethics ensure integrity. Institutions embracing this triad move from basic compliance to systemic resilience. Ultimately, unity across these dimensions is the only path to long-term success in the fight against money laundering.

7.6.2 Objective questions

Q1. Which of the following best defines money laundering?
- (A) The process of investing in foreign currencies
- (B) The process of concealing the origins of illegally obtained money
- (C) The transfer of money between banks for trade purposes
- (D) The act of converting cryptocurrency into fiat currency

Q2. What are the three primary stages of money laundering?
- (A) Hiding, Stealing, Spending
- (B) Deposit, Transfer, Withdrawal
- (C) Placement, Layering, Integration
- (D) Identification, Reporting, Verification

Q3. The FinCEN 2016 Guide focuses primarily on:
- (A) Managing foreign exchange reserves
- (B) Linking cyber-events with suspicious financial activity
- (C) Promoting mobile banking
- (D) Encouraging cryptocurrency adoption

Q4. Which organization issued the FinCEN 2016 Advisory on Cyber-Enabled Crime?
- (A) IMF (International Monetary Fund)
- (B) FATF (Financial Action Task Force)
- (C) US Department of the Treasury
- (D) European Central Bank

Q5. What does AML stand for in financial security terminology?
- (A) Advanced Malware Layer
- (B) Anti-Money Laundering
- (C) Asset Management Ledger
- (D) Automated Market Listing

Q6. The placement stage in money laundering involves:
- (A) Using illicit money for legitimate purchases
- (B) Introducing illegal funds into the financial system
- (C) Transferring money to multiple offshore accounts
- (D) Returning funds to the criminal in a legitimate form

Q7. Which of the following methods belong to the Layering stage?
- (A) Smurfing
- (B) Casino deposits
- (C) Offshore shell companies
- (D) Property purchase

Q8. Integration in money laundering means:
- (A) Depositing cash below reporting limits
- (B) Mixing illegal funds with legitimate income
- (C) Reintroducing laundered money as legal assets
- (D) Hiding funds using cryptocurrency

Q9. The main purpose of Suspicious Activity Reports (SARs) is to:
- (A) Record customer satisfaction
- (B) Inform regulators about potential illicit transactions
- (C) Track bank profits
- (D) Issue tax refunds

Q10. The Financial Intelligence Unit – India (FIU-IND) receives:
- (A) Trade data
- (B) Stock exchange reports
- (C) Suspicious Transaction Reports (STRs)
- (D) ATM transaction logs

Q11. Which of the following technologies can aid AML monitoring?
- (A) Machine Learning
- (B) 3D Printing
- (C) Virtual Reality
- (D) Optical Networking

Q12. Which international body sets global AML standards?
- (A) FATF
- (B) UNESCO (United Nations Educational, Scientific and Cultural Organization)
- (C) UNDP (United Nations Development Programme)
- (D) WHO (World Health Organization)

Q13. Which of the following is an example of cyber-enabled money laundering?
- (A) Cash deposits in local banks
- (B) Transferring cryptocurrency through mixers
- (C) Purchasing gold in person
- (D) Physical smuggling of cash

Q14. Structuring (or smurfing) means:
- (A) Large-value single deposits
- (B) Breaking large amounts into smaller deposits to avoid detection
- (C) Withdrawing funds from multiple ATMs
- (D) Donating money to charity for concealment

Q15. What was the main cause of the Danske Bank Estonia scandal?
- (A) Data breach in customer accounts
- (B) Weak KYC controls for nonresident clients
- (C) Server misconfiguration
- (D) Ransomware attack

Q16. Which of the following is a key objective of AML–Cybersecurity integration?
- (A) Faster customer onboarding
- (B) Reducing false positives and improving detection
- (C) Enhancing marketing insights
- (D) Supporting cryptocurrency trading

Q17. The HSBC 2012 case primarily involved:
- (A) Trade mispricing
- (B) Laundering drug cartel money through bank accounts
- (C) Crypto-exchange manipulation
- (D) Insider trading

Q18. What is the global platform for cross-border AML cooperation under the UN?
- (A) Interpol Data Hub
- (B) Egmont Group
- (C) SWIFTNet (Society for Worldwide Interbank Financial Telecommunication)
- (D) Euroclear

Q19. Which Indian institution enforces KYC and AML rules for banks?
- (A) NITI (National Institution for Transforming India) Aayog
- (B) SEBI (Securities and Exchange Board of India)
- (C) Reserve Bank of India (RBI)
- (D) Ministry of Home Affairs

Q20. Why is money laundering a cybersecurity concern?
- (A) It weakens encryption standards
- (B) It exploits online systems to transfer illicit funds anonymously
- (C) It helps improve customer privacy
- (D) It reduces the number of online crimes

Answer key

Q. No.	*Answer*
1	*B*
2	*C*
3	*B*
4	*C*
5	*B*
6	*B*
7	*C*
8	*C*
9	*B*
10	*C*
11	*A*
12	*A*
13	*B*
14	*B*
15	*B*
16	*B*
17	*B*
18	*B*
19	*C*
20	*B*

Further reading

[1] Financial Crimes Enforcement Network. *Advisory to Financial Institutions on Cyber-Events and Cyber-Enabled Crime*. Washington, DC: FinCEN; 2016.

[2] Financial Crimes Enforcement Network. *Advisory on Ransomware and the Use of the Financial System to Facilitate Ransom Payments*. Washington, DC: FinCEN; 2021.

[3] Naheem MA. AML compliance: A banking nightmare? The HSBC case study. *Int J Disclosure Governance*. 2015;12(4):300–310.

[4] Naheem MA. Risk of money laundering in the US: HSBC case study. *J Money Laundering Control*. 2016;19(3):234–258.

[5] Deprez B, Vanderschueren T, Baesens B, Verdonck T, and Verbeke W. Network analytics for anti-money-laundering – a systematic literature review and experimental evaluation. *INFORMS Journal on Data Science*. 2025, Ahead of print, https://doi.org/10.1287/ijds.2024.0042.

[6] Diop MB. Combating money laundering in the age of digital payments: Legislative experiences of Türkiye and Nigeria. *Glob Finance J*. 2025; 67:101061.

[7] Anonymous. Analysis of the main techniques and tools to combat money laundering. *J Money Laundering Control*. 2025;28(2):188–203.

[8] Anonymous. Enhancing AML compliance: A machine-learning approach to detect suspicious activity. *J Money Laundering Control*. 2025;28(3):215–228.
[9] Anonymous. Strengthening anti-money-laundering and counter-terrorist financing through integrated cybersecurity and compliance measures. *J Fin Crime*. 2024;31(4):901–918.
[10] University of Strathclyde. *Using Automation and AI to Combat Money Laundering*. Glasgow: University of Strathclyde White Paper; 2024.
[11] Cornell Law School. HSBC Bank PLC – The preferred financial institution for drug cartels and money launderers. *Cornell Int Law J*. 2017;50(2):445–470.
[12] Anonymous. Effectiveness of US anti-money-laundering regulations and the HSBC case study. *Res J Finance Accounting*. 2024;15(1):52–60.
[13] Seven Pillars Institute. *The Case of HSBC, Its Money Laundering, and Its Non-Prosecution*. Kansas City, MO: Seven Pillars Institute; 2013.
[14] LearnSignal Ltd. *HSBC's Money Laundering Scandal: A Comprehensive Overview*. Dublin: LearnSignal; 2024.
[15] Guardian News and Media Ltd. *HSBC's Swiss Private Banking Arm Breached Money-Laundering Rules, Regulator Finds*. London: The Guardian; 2024.
[16] Investopedia Inc. *HSBC's Money Laundering Scandal*. New York: Investopedia; 2023.
[17] Financial Action Task Force. *International Standards on Combating Money Laundering and the Financing of Terrorism and Proliferation*. Paris: FATF; 2024.
[18] Reserve Bank of India. *Master Direction on Know Your Customer (KYC) and Anti-Money-Laundering (AML) Compliance*. Mumbai: RBI; 2024.
[19] United Nations Office on Drugs and Crime. *Global Report on Illicit Financial Flows 2023*. Vienna: UNODC; 2023.
[20] Deloitte Touche Tohmatsu Ltd. *Anti-Money-Laundering and Financial Crime Trends 2025*. London: Deloitte; 2025.
[21] PwC India. *AML in Digital Payments – Outlook 2025*. New Delhi: PricewaterhouseCoopers Private Ltd; 2025.
[22] Organisation for Economic Co-operation and Development. *Beneficial Ownership Transparency Report 2024*. Paris: OECD; 2024.
[23] Basel Committee on Banking Supervision. *Sound Management of Risks Related to Money Laundering and Financing of Terrorism*. Basel: BIS; 2023.
[24] Europol. *Internet Organised Crime Threat Assessment (IOCTA) 2024*. The Hague: Europol; 2024.
[25] Transparency International. *Global Corruption Barometer 2024*. Berlin: Transparency International; 2024.

Chapter 8

Harnessing the power of AI and ML for cybersecurity in banking

Learning objectives

After completing this chapter, the reader will be able to

1. Understand how Artificial Intelligence (AI) and Machine Learning (ML) transform cybersecurity in the banking sector.
2. Differentiate between machine learning and Deep Learning, with emphasis on their role in cybersecurity.
3. Explore real-world case studies of AI/ML applications in fraud detection, intrusion prevention, and regulatory compliance.
4. Analyze success stories from global banking institutions deploying AI-driven security.
5. Evaluate the challenges, ethical concerns, and future outlook for AI/ML in banking security.

8.1 AI for cybersecurity—a new perspective

The banking sector has always been a high-value target for cybercriminals due to the sheer volume of financial transactions it handles daily. Historically, banks have relied on firewalls, intrusion detection systems, and rule-based monitoring tools to safeguard against fraud and breaches. However, the evolution of cybercrime has outpaced these traditional methods. Attackers today use advanced persistent threats, polymorphic malware, phishing campaigns, and insider collusion, which static systems fail to detect quickly.

Artificial intelligence introduces a new paradigm in cybersecurity. Unlike rule-based systems that rely on preprogrammed instructions, AI models can learn from historical data, adapt to new attack strategies, and make predictions about possible threats. For example, AI systems can detect unusual login attempts across geographies in real time, flagging them as potential account takeovers even before money is transferred.

In the banking industry, AI is not just a technical addition; it is a business enabler. By reducing fraud, ensuring compliance, and improving customer trust, AI helps institutions achieve financial resilience. Its value also extends to regulatory compliance, where AI-driven solutions automatically generate Suspicious Activity Reports (SARs), reducing human error.

Table 8.1 presents a summary of the comparison between traditional and AI-driven cybersecurity.

This concentric circle infographic (Figure 8.1) illustrates how artificial intelligence strengthens banking cybersecurity through multiple functions, anomaly detection, fraud prevention, phishing defense, insider threat monitoring, security automation, and compliance automation, forming an integrated defense ecosystem around AI at the core.

Table 8.1 Traditional vs. AI-driven cybersecurity

Parameter	Traditional security	AI-driven security in banking
Approach	Reactive, rule-based	Proactive, adaptive, predictive
Speed of detection	Manual log analysis	Real-time automated detection
Scalability	Limited	Highly scalable (big data)
Accuracy	High false positives	Reduced false positives
Adaptability	Needs manual updates	Learns from new attack patterns

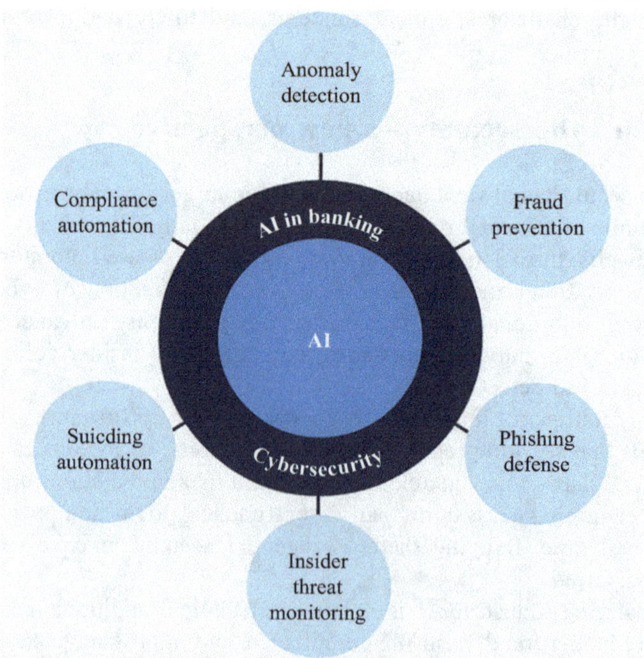

Figure. 8.1 AI in banking cybersecurity

8.2 Machine learning

Machine Learning is a subset of AI that focuses on enabling systems to learn patterns from data and improve performance without being explicitly programmed. In the banking context, ML is particularly powerful because of the vast amounts of structured data (transaction histories, account balances, payment flows) and semi-structured data (user logs, communication metadata).
Types of ML in banking cybersecurity

1. Supervised learning: Models are trained on labeled data. For example, transactions are labeled as "fraudulent" or "genuine." The system learns these distinctions and applies them to new, unseen data.
2. Unsupervised learning: Applied when data is not labeled. These models cluster or group transactions to identify anomalies. For instance, unsupervised ML can flag accounts with activity patterns that deviate from normal customer behavior.
3. Reinforcement learning: A feedback-driven learning method. In cybersecurity, it can adaptively learn authentication patterns or fine-tune firewalls based on ongoing feedback.

Applications of ML in banking security

- Credit card fraud detection: Identifies irregular patterns, such as sudden spending spikes in unfamiliar geographies.
- Anomaly detection: Flags suspicious withdrawals or multiple failed login attempts.
- Customer identity verification: Cross-checks biometric or Know Your Customer (KYC) data with behavioral patterns.
- Predictive risk scoring: Provides banks with a risk profile for new accounts based on historical fraud cases.

Table 8.2 summarizes the ML techniques in cybersecurity applications.

This flow diagram (Figure 8.2) illustrates how machine learning operates within a banking cybersecurity framework, beginning with data collection and preprocessing, progressing through supervised or unsupervised model training, and culminating in real-time fraud detection that triggers automated alerts to bank staff for rapid response.

Table 8.2 ML techniques in cybersecurity applications

ML technique	Banking cybersecurity application
Supervised learning	Fraud detection in card transactions
Unsupervised learning	Clustering unusual account behavior
Reinforcement learning	Adaptive multi-factor authentication
Ensemble methods	Improving the accuracy of fraud alerts

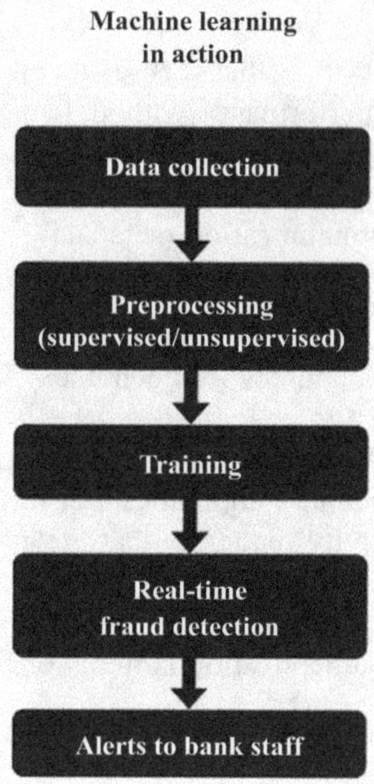

Figure 8.2 Machine learning in action for banking fraud detection

8.3 Deep learning—how is it different from machine learning?

Deep Learning (DL) is a specialized branch of ML that uses artificial neural networks to mimic human decision-making. Unlike ML, which often requires manual feature engineering (human intervention to decide what data attributes matter), DL automatically extracts patterns from raw data.

Differences between ML and DL in banking

- Data requirements: ML can work with smaller datasets, while DL thrives on massive amounts of data.
- Complexity: ML works best with structured data (transaction histories), whereas DL can process unstructured data like voice calls, emails, or scanned KYC documents.
- Use cases: DL is particularly effective in behavioral biometrics, detecting fraud from typing speed, touchscreen pressure, or facial recognition during mobile banking.

Case example: A major European bank implemented DL models to analyze millions of login attempts across devices. By correlating typing patterns, device orientation, and geolocation, the system reduced account takeover attempts by 30% within six months.

Table 8.3 ML vs. DL for banking cybersecurity

Aspect	Machine learning	Deep learning
Data requirement	Small/medium datasets	Large datasets (millions of records)
Feature engineering	Requires manual input	Learns features automatically
Processing speed	Faster on small tasks	Slower but highly accurate for complex tasks
Use cases	Detects anomalies in transactions	Voice authentication, image-based KYC

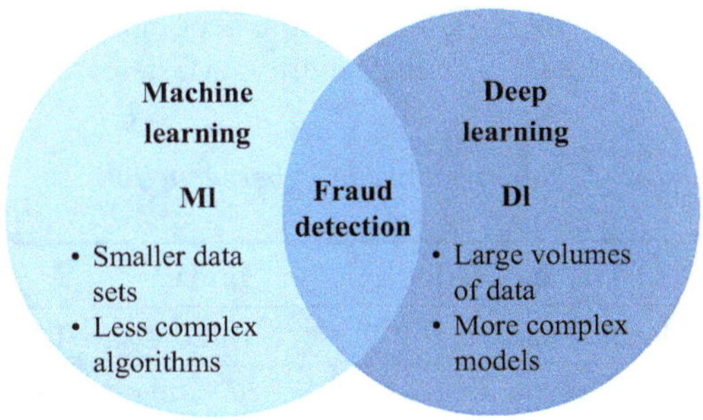

Figure 8.3 Machine Learning vs. Deep Learning in Fraud Detection

Table 8.3 summarizes the differences between ML and DL for banking cybersecurity.

This Venn diagram (Figure 8.3) compares Machine Learning (ML) and Deep Learning (DL), highlighting their overlap in fraud detection applications while distinguishing them by data volume requirements, algorithmic complexity, and model interpretability.

8.4 Machine learning and deep learning for cybersecurity—case studies

8.4.1 Case study 1: Mastercard—fraud detection

Mastercard leverages ML combined with deep neural networks to analyze billions of transactions daily. The system detects fraud in real time, reducing losses by billions annually.

8.4.2 Case study 2: HSBC—AI for Anti-Money Laundering (AML)

HSBC (Hongkong and Shanghai Banking Corporation) integrated ML into its AML compliance systems, leading to a **20% reduction in false positives** for suspicious transaction reports. This saved compliance staff thousands of hours annually.

8.4.3 Case study 3: JP Morgan Chase—insider threat detection

JP Morgan uses DL to analyze internal employee communications for signs of collusion or malicious intent. It prevents phishing attempts and reduces insider-driven fraud.

8.4.4 Case study 4: PayPal—real-time fraud analytics

PayPal's DL system processes transactions in **milliseconds**, filtering out fraudulent ones while ensuring legitimate transactions go through smoothly.

Table 8.4 presents the details of global bank AI deployments in cybersecurity.

This world map of Figure 8.4 illustrates the geographic distribution of leading banks employing AI and ML in cybersecurity, Mastercard for fraud detection,

Table 8.4 Global bank AI deployments in cybersecurity

Bank/institution	AI/ML application	Impact
Mastercard	Fraud detection	Billions saved annually
HSBC	AML monitoring	20% fewer false positives
JP Morgan Chase	Insider threat detection	Phishing attempts mitigated
PayPal	Real-time fraud detection	Faster, smoother customer experience

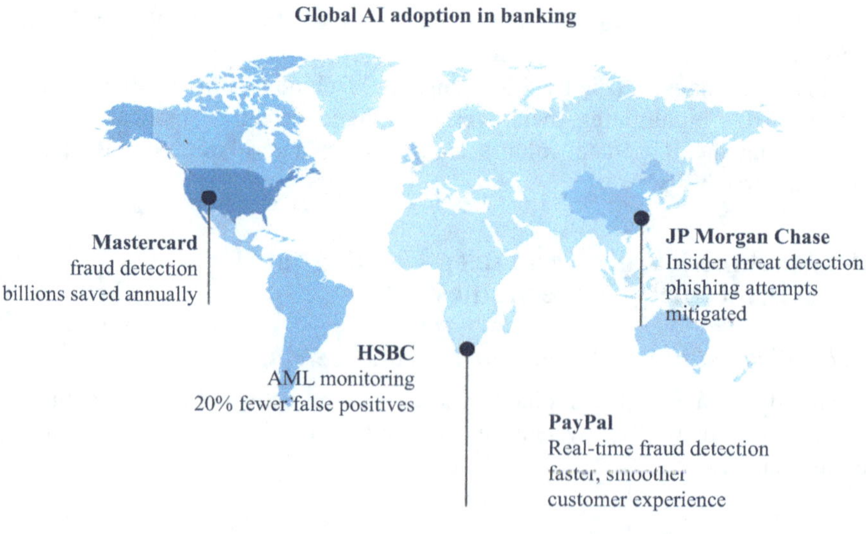

Figure 8.4 Global AI adoption in banking

HSBC for AML monitoring, JP Morgan Chase for insider threat detection, and PayPal for real-time fraud detection, highlighting measurable impacts such as cost savings, improved accuracy, and enhanced customer experience.

8.5 Success stories—a quick recap

8.5.1 Wells Fargo—AI chatbots and fraud alerts integration

8.5.1.1 Overview

Wells Fargo, one of the largest US-based financial institutions, has been a pioneer in implementing AI-powered conversational interfaces that extend far beyond customer service. By integrating AI-driven fraud alert systems into its chatbots and online platforms, Wells Fargo has significantly improved its cyber defense while simultaneously enhancing user experience.

8.5.1.2 Technology and functionality

The AI chatbot system, deployed on Wells Fargo's mobile and web banking channels, leverages Natural Language Processing (NLP) and machine learning models to interact intelligently with customers. When a transaction is flagged as suspicious by the bank's fraud detection algorithms, the chatbot engages the user instantly, seeking confirmation or clarification before allowing the transaction to proceed.

The system draws data from multiple sources

- Transaction metadata (time, location, amount, merchant ID).
- Behavioral analytics (spending frequency, device patterns).
- Historical fraud models trained on millions of transaction outcomes.

Through real-time anomaly detection, the chatbot distinguishes legitimate deviations (e.g., travel-related spending) from actual fraud. This reduces false positives and minimizes customer frustration from unnecessary transaction holds.

8.5.1.3 Security architecture

The backend architecture integrates

- AI Decision Engine: Built on supervised learning models, trained using labeled fraud and non-fraud transaction datasets.
- Multi-Channel Orchestration Layer: Connects chatbots, email alerts, and SMS channels.
- Dynamic Authentication Protocols: Adds adaptive verification methods (OTP, voice recognition, or facial ID) based on transaction risk.

This AI–human hybrid system enables Wells Fargo to act within seconds, crucial in preventing unauthorized withdrawals or card misuse.

8.5.1.4 Business and customer impact

According to internal metrics published in fintech reviews (2024), Wells Fargo achieved:

- 35% faster fraud detection-to-alert time compared to traditional call-center workflows.
- Reduction of 22% in false alarms, improving customer trust.
- 24/7 intelligent fraud response, removing dependency on human-only teams.

The chatbot acts not merely as an assistant but as a cyber-sentinel, capable of learning from ongoing fraud trends and continuously refining alert models.

8.5.1.5 Lessons learned

The Wells Fargo case demonstrates that AI and customer interaction can coexist with cybersecurity, a paradigm shift where automation does not replace empathy but reinforces protection. The success lies in contextual personalization, quick escalation, and AI transparency.

8.5.2 ING Bank—AI-driven biometric authentication

8.5.2.1 Overview

ING (International Netherlands Group) Bank, headquartered in the Netherlands, has established itself as a leader in AI-driven authentication and behavioral biometrics. Recognizing the vulnerabilities of passwords and PINs, ING has implemented multi-modal biometric verification, combining facial, voice, and behavioral analysis, to safeguard mobile banking access.

8.5.2.2 Technology framework

The system uses deep learning convolutional neural networks (CNNs) for facial recognition and recurrent neural networks (RNNs) for speech pattern analysis. Behavioral biometric parameters include typing cadence, device motion, and screen interaction patterns. These unique identifiers collectively form a continuous authentication system, verifying user legitimacy throughout the session rather than only at login.

8.5.2.3 Integration with AI systems

- Anomaly detection: AI models analyze real-time deviations from baseline user profiles.
- Secure encryption: Biometric data is encrypted using homomorphic encryption, allowing verification without exposing raw biometric data.
- Adaptive risk scoring: The AI dynamically adjusts security checks depending on contextual data (e.g., device type, location variance).

8.5.2.4 Benefits and impact

The impact of ING's system is profound:

- Login accuracy rate above 99.3% across mobile platforms.
- Drastic reduction in credential theft incidents, since no static passwords exist.
- Seamless user experience, maintaining an average login time under three seconds.

- Full compliance with the EU's PSD2 (Payment Services Directive 2) and GDPR (General Data Protection Regulation) data protection standards.

8.5.2.5 Challenges and strategic insights

Although early user skepticism around privacy existed, ING mitigated this through transparency campaigns, explaining encryption methods and privacy controls. The implementation underscores a vital principle: security should be invisible but reliable, blending into customer journeys rather than disrupting them.

8.5.3 Citibank—partnering with RegTech firms for AI-enabled compliance

8.5.3.1 Overview

Citibank, one of the most globally networked banks, faces monumental compliance obligations across multiple jurisdictions. To manage this complexity, Citibank has partnered with leading RegTech (regulatory technology) firms to embed AI-driven regulatory monitoring and reporting systems across its global operations.

8.5.3.2 The role of RegTech and AI

Citibank's collaboration with RegTech vendors such as Ayasdi and Feedzai has led to the creation of AI engines capable of:

- Parsing thousands of pages of changing financial regulations across 90+ markets.
- Mapping regulatory updates to internal operational processes.
- Automating the generation of compliance reports for regulators.

These systems rely on Natural Language Understanding (NLU) and knowledge graphs to interpret legal texts semantically. The AI converts regulatory language into actionable workflows, a previously manual, error-prone task.

8.5.3.3 Benefits of AI in compliance

- Efficiency: Reporting timelines reduced by 60%–70%.
- Accuracy: AI identifies conflicting compliance clauses or redundant procedures.
- Risk mitigation: Predictive analytics forecast compliance lapses before they occur.

Through these partnerships, Citibank transformed compliance from a cost center into a strategic advantage, where the same data used for compliance informs business risk and customer profiling.

8.5.3.4 The cybersecurity link

Citibank's RegTech AI framework doubles as a cyber-risk management engine. It monitors transaction data for patterns suggestive of AML breaches or insider trading, automatically linking anomalies to regulatory alerts. This synergy aligns regulatory compliance with real-time security, a unification many institutions struggle to achieve.

8.5.3.5 Broader implications

Citibank's initiative exemplifies how AI can interpret, reason, and act upon human laws, setting the stage for automated regulatory ecosystems. It showcases the shift from reactive compliance to predictive governance, an emerging benchmark in financial integrity.

8.5.4 ICICI Bank (India)—AI-powered facial recognition for KYC

8.5.4.1 Overview

ICICI (Industrial Credit and Investment Corporation of India) Bank, one of India's largest private-sector banks, has been at the forefront of digital identity transformation. In alignment with India's "Digital India" and "Faceless Banking" initiatives, ICICI introduced AI-based facial recognition systems for Know Your Customer (KYC) verification.

8.5.4.2 System design and function

The KYC process traditionally required manual verification of identity documents. ICICI replaced this with a facial biometrics solution integrated into its mobile app and branch onboarding systems. The solution uses deep convolutional neural networks (CNNs) trained on large face datasets to match real-time selfie captures with government-issued ID photos (Aadhaar, PAN, passport, etc.).

Key technical elements include

- Liveness detection: Ensures real faces, not printed or screen images.
- 3D facial mapping: Handles pose variations and lighting differences.
- Edge computing: Processes biometric data locally on secure devices to minimize data transmission risks.

8.5.4.3 Benefits and impact

- Onboarding time reduced by 50%.
- Enhanced security: Eliminated document forgery and impersonation attempts.
- Compliance automation: Seamless integration with RBI's eKYC and AML guidelines.
- Scalability: Deployed across 5,000+ branches and millions of mobile users.

The system has been lauded by the Indian Banking Association for aligning with data minimization principles and supporting inclusive financial access, particularly in rural banking contexts.

8.5.4.4 Ethical and security considerations

ICICI's approach balances innovation with privacy. Data retention is limited to regulatory requirements, and facial data is tokenized. AI bias mitigation mechanisms are also embedded to ensure equitable accuracy across age, gender, and ethnicity groups.

8.5.4.5 Strategic takeaways

This initiative highlights India's transition from manual KYC to AI-enhanced digital trust frameworks, enabling faster, safer, and more inclusive banking. ICICI's project illustrates how AI in compliance is as much about social responsibility as it is about efficiency.

8.5.5 Comparative insights across case studies

A comparative analysis is provided in Table 8.5.

8.5.6 Key learnings

8.5.6.1 AI–human collaboration creates the strongest defense

The most effective cybersecurity systems are **hybrid in nature**, combining the analytical speed of AI with the contextual judgment of human experts. While artificial intelligence can process millions of transactions in milliseconds and detect statistical anomalies invisible to humans, it lacks the cognitive nuance to interpret *intent*, *motive*, or *ethical context*. Human analysts, conversely, bring intuition and domain expertise, understanding behavioral subtleties, geopolitical implications, and socio-economic factors influencing fraud trends.

For instance, Wells Fargo's AI-powered chatbots rapidly flag irregular transactions, but the ultimate confirmation of fraud often depends on human analysts interpreting behavioral cues and customer history. Similarly, Citibank's RegTech models might predict compliance anomalies, but human compliance officers assess the broader legal implications.

Lesson: AI should not replace human analysts but rather **amplify their efficiency**. This collaboration forms a "human-in-the-loop" architecture, where AI

Table 8.5 Comparative insights across case studies

Bank/ institution	AI/ML application	Primary impact	Strategic lesson
Wells Fargo	AI Chatbots for Fraud Alerts	Faster detection, reduced false positives	Human-centric automation enhances trust
ING Bank	Biometric Authentication	Seamless security, compliance with PSD2	Security must blend with user experience
Citibank	RegTech Partnerships for AI Compliance	Automated, predictive reporting	AI can operationalize complex regulations
ICICI Bank	Facial Recognition KYC	Secure, scalable onboarding	Digital identity verification builds inclusion

performs detection, and humans make informed final decisions. The result is faster, fairer, and more accurate fraud mitigation.

8.5.6.2 Contextual intelligence is vital for fraud alert precision

A common limitation of early-generation fraud detection systems is their tendency to trigger **excessive false positives**. Customers faced unnecessary transaction holds simply because the system lacked contextual understanding. Modern AI systems incorporate **contextual intelligence**, the ability to interpret transactions within the broader behavioral, geographic, and temporal context of a user.

For example, if a customer regularly makes purchases in multiple countries due to frequent travel, a traditional rules-based system might flag such transactions as suspicious. In contrast, an AI model trained with contextual parameters, travel frequency, device fingerprints, and location geotags can intelligently distinguish between legitimate deviations and true anomalies.

Wells Fargo and PayPal have implemented contextual learning loops where each resolved case (whether confirmed or false alarm) retrains the model, refining future accuracy.

Lesson: Contextual awareness converts static rule engines into **adaptive learning systems** that evolve with the customer. It also reduces customer friction and improves satisfaction while maintaining rigorous fraud defense.

8.5.6.3 Ethical AI frameworks: transparency, fairness, and accountability

As AI becomes central to decision-making in financial systems, **ethical governance** is no longer optional; it is imperative. Biases in datasets, opaque algorithmic reasoning, and a lack of explainability can lead to discriminatory outcomes or regulatory violations. Banks that deploy AI in risk management, fraud detection, or compliance must ensure that models are both **technically robust and ethically sound**.

Key pillars of ethical AI in banking include

- **Transparency:** Every AI decision must be traceable. For example, if a credit application is rejected or a transaction is flagged, there should be clear documentation of *why*.
- **Fairness:** AI models must be audited for bias, ensuring equitable accuracy across genders, regions, income levels, and ethnic groups.
- **Accountability:** Financial institutions must have governance frameworks where AI decisions can be overridden or reviewed by authorized humans.

ING Bank's biometric authentication program is a model example. Before deploying facial recognition at scale, ING conducted bias analysis on its dataset to prevent accuracy discrepancies among diverse demographics. Similarly, ICICI Bank implemented tokenization to prevent facial data misuse, addressing both privacy and equity concerns.

Lesson: An ethical AI system is not just a compliance requirement; it is a **trust multiplier**. Transparency, fairness, and accountability ensure that technology enhances inclusion, not exclusion, and that it protects rather than exploits user data.

8.5.6.4 Interconnected compliance and cybersecurity

Historically, **compliance** (focused on regulations and audits) and **cybersecurity** (focused on technical protection) functioned in silos. However, recent financial incidents, such as the *HSBC* and *Danske Bank* money laundering cases, revealed that separating these domains allows threats to slip through the cracks. Modern institutions are now merging the two into a **unified risk governance framework**.

Citibank exemplifies this integration through its partnership with RegTech firms, embedding AI-driven regulatory monitoring into its cybersecurity infrastructure. When an AI engine detects abnormal data flows, it simultaneously triggers compliance alerts aligned with AML and KYC regulations. This dual approach ensures that **cyber events are not only mitigated but also reported within regulatory timelines**.

Such interconnected frameworks enable

- Real-time compliance checks on digital transactions.
- Automated cross-referencing of suspicious activity with AML watch lists.
- Coordinated investigations between cybersecurity and compliance teams.

Lesson: Interlinking compliance and cybersecurity reduces duplication, strengthens governance, and enables a **proactive defense posture**. It transforms compliance from a reactive obligation into a predictive shield that prevents both regulatory penalties and cyber breaches.

8.5.6.5 Localization of AI adoption ensures legal adherence and public trust

While AI technologies are inherently global, **their deployment must be localized** to align with national regulations, data residency laws, and cultural expectations. Financial institutions operating across jurisdictions cannot adopt a one-size-fits-all approach. The *context of regulation* and *societal trust* differs dramatically between markets such as the US, Europe, and India.

ICICI Bank's facial recognition KYC system is a prime example of localization done right. The system is designed around India's **RBI eKYC** norms and Aadhaar-based authentication framework, ensuring full legal compliance while promoting customer inclusivity. Localization also extends beyond legal parameters to cultural dimensions, building user trust through regional language interfaces, privacy assurances, and data protection aligned with local expectations.

In contrast, ING Bank's biometric authentication in Europe prioritizes **GDPR-compliant data minimization** and privacy-by-design principles. These tailored implementations allow each institution to maintain regulatory harmony and societal acceptance.

Lesson: Localized AI not only complies with local laws but also enhances legitimacy. When users see that AI systems respect their regional values, data sovereignty, and linguistic needs, they engage with greater confidence, transforming **trust into long-term customer loyalty**.

Synthesis: The future of AI in banking cybersecurity.

The collective lessons from these global case studies reinforce a central theme: **AI is not an isolated technology but a systemic enabler of trust, compliance, and resilience**. To succeed, banks must move from siloed automation toward **intelligent orchestration**, where AI, human judgment, regulation, and culture intersect seamlessly.

AI-driven security is not simply about preventing fraud: it is about **sustaining confidence in digital finance**, protecting the reputation of institutions, and ensuring equitable access to secure services worldwide. By combining ethical principles, contextual intelligence, and human collaboration within localized frameworks, the banking sector can harness AI as both a *technological tool* and a *moral compass* for the future of cybersecurity.

The journey of Wells Fargo, ING, Citibank, and ICICI Bank showcases the evolving maturity of AI in the global financial sector. From conversational fraud detection to predictive regulatory analytics and AI-based identity management, each represents a critical node in the transformation of cyber-secure digital banking.

These banks demonstrate that AI's greatest success in finance is not automation alone but intelligent augmentation, empowering institutions to stay resilient, adaptive, and customer-centric in an age of relentless cyber risk.

Key points to remember

1. AI transforms banking security from reactive to predictive. Traditional systems often respond after a breach occurs, whereas AI enables proactive defense by identifying threats in real time. This predictive capability drastically reduces fraud losses and improves customer confidence.
2. Machine learning thrives on transactional data to detect anomalies. Banks process millions of daily transactions, making manual oversight impossible. ML models flag deviations, such as sudden overseas transfers or abnormal withdrawal patterns, helping to prevent fraud.
3. Deep learning adds power by analyzing unstructured and complex data. Unlike ML, DL can interpret emails, voice calls, and biometric patterns. This allows banks to extend cybersecurity into areas like voice authentication and document scanning.
4. The combination of AI and AML compliance strengthens resilience. AI tools automate suspicious activity detection and regulatory reporting. This ensures banks meet global compliance standards while minimizing operational burdens.
5. AI reduces false positives in fraud detection systems. False alerts overwhelm compliance teams and waste resources. AI models refine detection accuracy, focusing only on genuine high-risk cases, which improves both efficiency and morale.
6. AI-driven cybersecurity fosters real-time decision-making. From detecting compromised accounts to freezing suspicious transactions, AI allows decisions to be made within seconds. This speed prevents cascading financial damage.

7. Machine learning supports adaptive authentication systems. Reinforcement learning adapts login security based on evolving threats. For example, it may request extra biometric checks when unusual behavior is detected.
8. Behavioral biometrics provide an invisible layer of security. AI can analyze keystrokes, touchscreen pressure, and device handling. This makes fraud harder, as behavior is difficult for criminals to replicate.
9. AI integration reduces compliance costs in large banks. Banks like HSBC report millions saved annually by cutting down false alerts. The efficiency gained allows compliance teams to focus on high-priority investigations.
10. Insider threat detection is significantly enhanced with AI. AI systems analyze employee communication patterns and access logs. Suspicious activity, such as unusual database queries, can be identified before it escalates.
11. Global case studies highlight tangible benefits of AI. Institutions like Mastercard, PayPal, and JP Morgan Chase demonstrate AI's effectiveness in fraud prevention and compliance. These examples provide templates for wider adoption.
12. AI enhances customer trust in digital banking channels. Consumers feel more secure when fraud alerts are precise and timely. This builds loyalty and reduces the fear of adopting online or mobile banking services.
13. AI and ML require strong, clean data pipelines to succeed. Poor-quality or biased data can undermine detection accuracy. Banks must invest in data governance and preprocessing to ensure reliable AI outcomes.
14. Cross-border money-laundering risks are mitigated by AI analytics. AI can trace layered transactions across jurisdictions. Recognizing hidden patterns aids regulators in tackling complex international fraud schemes.
15. AI enables real-time monitoring of crypto transactions. With the rise of digital assets, blockchain analytics powered by AI identify illicit wallets and trace flows. This ensures crypto adoption aligns with AML standards.
16. Integration of SIEM and AML tools provides unified monitoring. When cybersecurity and compliance systems share intelligence, threats are detected faster. This reduces latency in fraud response and enhances situational awareness.
17. Ethical AI practices are essential to responsible cybersecurity. AI must avoid discriminatory practices, such as unfairly flagging certain customer groups. Transparency in AI decision-making is critical for trust and compliance.
18. Staff training complements AI to create a human-AI defense ecosystem. Employees must learn to interpret AI alerts and escalate critical cases. Human judgment remains vital, especially in gray areas where AI predictions are uncertain.
19. AI adoption requires regulatory alignment across jurisdictions. Banks operating globally must ensure that their AI frameworks comply with multiple regulators. Unified standards will streamline adoption and improve interoperability.
20. The future of banking cybersecurity is hybrid: AI + human oversight. While AI automates detection and analysis, human experts handle strategic

decisions and ethics. This synergy ensures resilience, accountability, and adaptability in a constantly evolving threat landscape.

Questions (Try answering them yourself)

1. Explain how artificial intelligence has transformed cybersecurity in the banking sector. What advantages does it offer compared to traditional systems?
2. Discuss the three primary types of machine learning (supervised, unsupervised, and reinforcement) with examples of their application in banking cybersecurity.
3. Compare and contrast machine learning and deep learning in terms of their data requirements, feature engineering, and use cases in fraud detection.
4. How do AI-driven systems reduce false positives in fraud detection? Why is this reduction significant for compliance teams?
5. Analyze the role of behavioral biometrics in enhancing banking security. Provide examples of how banks deploy such systems.
6. Describe the importance of AI in supporting Anti-Money Laundering (AML) compliance. How does AI improve SAR/STR filing?
7. Critically evaluate the challenges banks face in implementing AI-powered cybersecurity solutions, particularly regarding data governance and ethical concerns.
8. Explain the impact of integrating SIEM systems with AML tools. How does this integration improve fraud detection and response time?
9. How do AI-powered insider threat detection systems function? Discuss their advantages and potential risks of misuse.
10. Assess the contribution of deep learning in analyzing unstructured data for banking security (e.g., emails, voice logs, images). Why is this important?
11. Discuss global case studies (e.g., HSBC, Mastercard, PayPal) that highlight the successful deployment of AI in banking security. What lessons can other banks learn?
12. How can AI analytics mitigate risks of cross-border money laundering? Provide examples of techniques or frameworks that could be used.
13. Explain the role of AI in monitoring cryptocurrency transactions. What tools and techniques are banks using to ensure compliance?
14. Analyze how AI fosters customer trust in digital banking platforms. What are the long-term implications for banks adopting such systems?
15. Discuss the ethical challenges of using AI for cybersecurity in banking. How can transparency and fairness be ensured in AI-driven systems?
16. Evaluate how reinforcement learning can be used in adaptive authentication. Provide an example of how this improves security.
17. How does AI transform regulatory compliance in banking? Discuss with reference to efficiency, timeliness, and accuracy of reporting.
18. Describe the future of banking cybersecurity as a hybrid model of AI and human oversight. Why is this balance important?

19. Discuss how staff training complements AI in building effective cybersecurity defenses. Why can't AI replace human decision-making entirely?
20. "AI in cybersecurity is not just a technical necessity but a strategic imperative for banks." Critically analyze this statement with examples.

Objective questions

1. Which of the following best describes artificial intelligence in banking cybersecurity?
   (a) A rule-based static monitoring system
   (b) A self-learning system that adapts to threats
   (c) A manual log analysis tool
   (d) A simple firewall configuration
2. Which machine learning method is commonly used for anomaly detection in transactions?
   (a) Supervised learning
   (b) Reinforcement learning
   (c) Unsupervised learning
   (d) Deep learning
3. In deep learning, feature extraction is:
   (a) Always manual
   (b) Automated by neural networks
   (c) Not required at all
   (d) Only applicable to structured data
4. Which of the following is NOT a common banking use case of machine learning?
   (a) Predictive risk scoring
   (b) Transaction anomaly detection
   (c) ATM cash dispensing
   (d) Fraudulent transaction flagging
5. What does AML stand for in banking compliance?
   (a) Advanced machine learning
   (b) Anti-money laundering
   (c) Automated monitoring layer
   (d) Artificial model learning
6. Which global bank reported a 20% reduction in false positives after adopting AI for AML?
   (a) HSBC
   (b) Wells Fargo
   (c) Citibank
   (d) ICICI Bank

7. Which type of learning is feedback-driven and adapts security based on actions and outcomes?
   (a) Supervised learning
   (b) Unsupervised learning
   (c) Reinforcement learning
   (d) Deep learning

8. Behavioral biometrics in banking can include:
   (a) Transaction amount
   (b) Typing speed and swipe pressure
   (c) Loan repayment history
   (d) Customer age

9. The integration of SIEM with AML tools mainly improves:
   (a) Compliance costs
   (b) Fraud detection latency
   (c) Loan approvals
   (d) Cash withdrawal rates

10. Which of these technologies is most suitable for analyzing unstructured financial data like emails?
    (a) Rule-based systems
    (b) Supervised ML
    (c) Deep Learning
    (d) Regression models

11. Which company uses deep neural networks to process billions of transactions daily for fraud detection?
    (a) PayPal
    (b) Mastercard
    (c) ING Bank
    (d) Citibank

12. In cybersecurity, false positives refer to:
    (a) Correct detection of fraud
    (b) Legitimate transactions wrongly flagged as fraud
    (c) Missed fraudulent transactions
    (d) Transactions approved without verification

13. Which is a key advantage of deep learning over machine learning?
    (a) Lower data requirements
    (b) Real-time report filing
    (c) Automatic feature extraction
    (d) Simple computation

14. Which of the following best defines adaptive authentication?
    (a) A static password-based login
    (b) Authentication that adjusts based on user behavior

   (c) Two-factor authentication only
   (d) Manual verification by a bank officer

15. What is the primary function of blockchain analytics in banking security?
   (a) Approving cryptocurrency trades
   (b) Detecting illicit wallets and tracing funds
   (c) Issuing tokens for customer onboarding
   (d) Predicting loan defaults

16. Which of the following is a limitation in adopting AI for banking security?
   (a) Improved fraud detection
   (b) Dependence on high-quality data
   (c) Reduction in false positives
   (d) Enhanced compliance speed

17. Which of these is considered an insider threat detection use case for AI?
   (a) Monitoring phishing attempts
   (b) Analyzing employee communication logs
   (c) Approving KYC automatically
   (d) Reducing transaction fees

18. Which of the following banks is known for AI-driven biometric authentication in mobile banking?
   (a) ING Bank
   (b) JP Morgan Chase
   (c) HSBC
   (d) Wells Fargo

19. Which ethical challenge is most associated with AI in banking?
   (a) Faster fraud detection
   (b) Algorithmic bias and transparency issues
   (c) Improved customer satisfaction
   (d) Higher efficiency of compliance

20. The future of banking cybersecurity is best described as:
   (a) Entirely human-driven
   (b) Entirely AI-driven
   (c) A hybrid of AI automation and human oversight
   (d) Dependent only on regulations

Answer key

1. b) A self-learning system that adapts to threats
2. c) Unsupervised learning
3. b) Automated by neural networks
4. c) ATM cash dispensing
5. b) Anti-Money Laundering
6. a) HSBC

7. c) Reinforcement learning
8. b) Typing speed and swipe pressure
9. b) Fraud detection latency
10. c) Deep Learning
11. b) Mastercard
12. b) Legitimate transactions wrongly flagged as fraud
13. c) Automatic feature extraction
14. b) Authentication that adjusts based on user behavior
15. b) Detecting illicit wallets and tracing funds
16. b) Dependence on high-quality data
17. b) Analyzing employee communication logs
18. a) ING Bank
19. b) Algorithmic bias and transparency issues
20. c) A hybrid of AI automation and human oversight

Further reading

[1] Jada I, *et al.* The impact of artificial intelligence on organisational cybersecurity: A systematic literature review. *Comput. Secur.* 2024;138: 103679.

[2] Asmar M, *et al.* Integrating machine learning for sustaining cybersecurity in digital banking. *Heliyon*. 2024;10(8): e30256.

[3] Kovačević A, Radenković SD, and Nikolić D. Artificial intelligence and cybersecurity in the banking sector: Opportunities and risks. *Strategic Management*. 2024;29(3): 15–27.

[4] Aldasoro I, Doerr S, Gambacorta L, Notra S, and Whyte D. Generative artificial intelligence and central banks' cybersecurity. *BIS Papers*. 2024; 145: 1–40.

[5] Ndukwe ER, *et al.* A graphical and qualitative review of literature on AI and cyber threat intelligence. *Eur. J. Eng. Res. Sci*. 2023;8(6): 37–43.

[6] Gyau EB, *et al.* Transforming banking: Examining the role of AI technology innovation. *J. Bank. Financ*. 2024;163: 107052.

[7] Hamid I, *et al.* AI, machine learning and deep learning in cyber risk management: A systematic review. *Environ. Syst. Decis*. 2025;45(1): 87–103.

[8] Khan AR, *et al.* FinSafeNet: securing digital transactions using optimized deep learning. *Sci. Rep*. 2024;14(1): 76214.

[9] Eskandarany A, *et al.* Adoption of artificial intelligence and machine learning in the banking sector: Defending against financial fraud. *J. Financ. Crime*. 2024;31(3): 678–693.

[10] Al-Dosari K, *et al.* Artificial intelligence and cyber defense system for banking. *J. Inf. Computer Secur*. 2022;30(5): 813–827.

[11] Fursov I, Morozov M, Kaploukhaya N, et al. Adversarial attacks on deep models for financial transaction records. *Proceedings of the 27th ACM SIGKDD Conference on Knowledge Discovery & Data Mining*. 2021;3121–3129.

[12] Zhang Y, and Zhu H. Additively homomorphic encryption-based deep neural network for asymmetrically collaborative machine learning. *Inf. Sci.* 2021; 580: 570–586.

[13] Ling L, Gao Z, Silas MA, Lee I, and Le Doeuff E. An AI-based, multi-stage detection system of banking botnets. *J. Inf. Secur. Appl.* 2020;55: 102599.

[14] Kiwia D, Dehghantanha A, Choo KK-R, and Slaughter J. A cyber kill chain-based taxonomy of banking Trojans for evolutionary computational intelligence. *Future Gener Comput Syst.* 2019;100: 531–543.

[15] Hassani H, Silva E, Unger S, and Gupta R. Deep learning and its implementations in banking. *Ann Oper. Res.* 2020;297(1): 403–427.

[16] Tran TN, *et al.* Cybersecurity in banking: A systematic literature review. *Inf. Syst Front.* 2025;27(2): 455–478.

[17] Kokina J, Davenport TH. The potential for artificial intelligence in fraud detection in accounting and banking. *J Emerg Technol Account.* 2017;14(2): 91–108.

[18] Kshetri N. Artificial intelligence in banking: applications and challenges. *IT Professional.* 2021;23(2): 62–66.

[19] Singh A, and Razaque A. Deep learning approaches for fraud detection in mobile banking transactions. *Int J Inf Manag Data Insights.* 2022;2(2): 100082.

[20] Alom MZ, Taha TM, Yakopcic C, *et al.* The history, evolution, and future of deep learning in cybersecurity. *IEEE Access.* 2019; 7: 99524–99545.

[21] Alsaadi E, *et al.* Artificial intelligence applications in enhancing banking cybersecurity resilience. *J Cyber Digital Trust.* 2023; 5(1): 55–69.

[22] Barakat M, *et al.* Explainable AI for fraud detection in digital financial transactions. *Expert Syst Appl.* 2024; 244: 122958.

[23] Kiran BR, Thomas D, and Parthasarathy S. An overview of deep reinforcement learning in banking security systems. *ACM Comput Surv.* 2021; 54(5): 1–36.

[24] Aldasoro I, Frost J, Gambacorta L, and Whyte D. Cyber risk in the financial sector: An overview. *BIS Quarterly Review.* 2020; 1–16.

[25] Bhattacharya J, *et al.* Artificial intelligence, big data and cybersecurity in banking: A convergence approach. *J. Bank. Regul.* 2023; 24(3): 211–230.

Chapter 9

Blockchain technology in banking

Learning objectives

After going through the chapter, readers will gain a clear understanding of

(a) The fundamental principles of blockchain technology and its relevance to the banking and financial services industry.
(b) The role of decentralization, transparency, and immutability in enhancing trust and security in banking transactions.
(c) Different types of blockchains (public, private, and consortium) and their suitability for various banking use cases.
(d) Smart contracts and their application in automating banking operations, such as loan approvals and trade finance.
(e) Identifying the potential of blockchain in improving payment systems, cross-border remittances, and settlement processes.
(f) Assessing the risks, regulatory challenges, and compliance requirements associated with adopting blockchain in the banking sector.
(g) Exploring the integration of blockchain with existing banking infrastructure and strategies for overcoming adoption barriers.
(h) Investigation of real-world case studies of blockchain implementations in banking, such as Know Your Customer (KYC) sharing platforms and syndicated lending.

9.1 Introduction to blockchain

Blockchain technology was first conceptualized in 2008 through a groundbreaking white paper authored by an individual or group under the pseudonym Satoshi Nakamoto. This whitepaper introduced a revolutionary concept for conducting digital transactions securely, transparently, and without reliance on centralized authorities such as banks or governments. Unlike conventional systems, where a trusted intermediary validates and authorizes transactions, blockchain enables a distributed approach in which participants collectively maintain and verify records, thereby reducing dependency on a single entity.

At its core, blockchain functions as a decentralized digital ledger where data is recorded in units called *blocks*, as shown in Figure 9.1. These blocks are

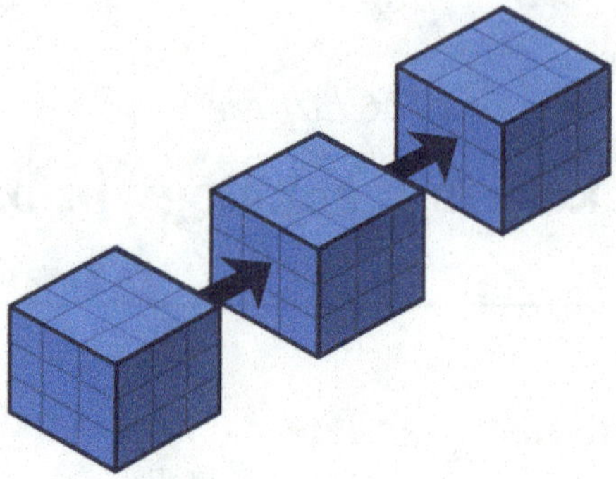

Figure 9.1 Blockchain

chronologically linked, creating a continuous and immutable chain of records. Each block contains a set of transactions, and once a block is added to the chain, it cannot be altered without modifying all subsequent blocks. This design makes blockchain highly resistant to tampering or manipulation, as altering even a single entry would require enormous computational resources and consensus approval from the majority of participants in the network.

A critical feature of blockchain is its consensus-driven verification system. Transactions are not validated by a central authority but instead by a network of distributed participants who use consensus mechanisms such as Proof of Work (PoW) or Proof of Stake (PoS) to agree on the validity of transactions. This collaborative approach eliminates the risk of unilateral control, ensuring integrity and trust across the system. By distributing authority across many nodes, blockchain achieves both resilience and robustness, even in the presence of potentially untrusted actors.

Although blockchain was originally designed as the technological foundation for Bitcoin, its scope has grown significantly over time. Beyond cryptocurrency, blockchain has demonstrated remarkable versatility and applicability across numerous industries. In the financial sector, it is being explored for payment systems, settlement processes, and fraud prevention. In supply chain management, it improves traceability and transparency, while in healthcare, it secures sensitive patient records. Governments, too, are exploring blockchain for digital identity management and transparent governance models.

Ultimately, blockchain represents the beginning of a new era of trustless, transparent, and decentralized systems. By shifting reliance away from central authorities and enabling verifiable, tamper-proof records, blockchain paves the way for more secure, efficient, and accountable digital ecosystems. Its principles of decentralization, transparency, and immutability are driving innovation across industries, and its evolution continues to redefine how organizations, governments, and individuals approach trust and collaboration in the digital age.

Decentralized trust
Traditional financial systems rely on central authorities to validate and authorize transactions, often leading to inefficiencies and vulnerabilities. Blockchain decentralizes this trust by enabling a network of distributed participants to collectively maintain a synchronized, transparent, and tamper-proof ledger.

Immutable ledger
Blockchain's core advantage lies in its immutable design. Cryptographic hashing and consensus algorithms ensure that once data is recorded in a block, altering it retroactively would require control over the majority of the network—an almost impossible task. This immutability fosters transparency and significantly enhances auditability.

Consensus and security
Different blockchain platforms implement consensus mechanisms like Proof of Work (PoW), Proof of Stake (PoS), and Practical Byzantine Fault Tolerance (PBFT) to validate transactions without centralized control. These protocols enable agreement among distributed nodes and uphold the integrity of the ledger even in the presence of untrusted participants.

Expanding beyond cryptocurrency
While originally tailored for Bitcoin, blockchain's scope has rapidly expanded. Financial institutions have identified their potential to streamline operations in areas like payments, asset management, loan processing, clearing, and identity management. The ability to build trust without intermediaries has driven interest in decentralized finance (DeFi) and smart contracts.

Implications for the banking sector
Banks worldwide are exploring blockchain to enhance efficiency, security, and customer experience. From cross-border payments and fraud detection to real-time settlement and digital identities, blockchain is reshaping financial infrastructure. By offering real-time, shared access to verified information, it challenges the traditional, siloed approach of banking systems.

> "Blockchain is not merely a technological upgrade; it represents a shift in how trust, value, and data are managed in modern banking."

As we delve deeper into this book, we will explore how blockchain is redefining core banking processes and examine real-world case studies that highlight its transformative impact.

9.1.1 Evolution and development

Blockchain technology has undergone a rapid transformation from a simple transaction ledger to a foundational pillar of modern digital ecosystems. Initially focused on recording financial exchanges, blockchain soon revealed its potential to support programmable contracts, decentralized applications, and secure data management across various industries. As the technology matured, new platforms emerged that addressed the limitations of early systems, including challenges related to scalability, interoperability, and energy consumption. The development of smart contracts, tokenization models, and enterprise-grade blockchains has expanded their reach far beyond finance, enabling innovative solutions in supply chain logistics, healthcare, identity management, and governance. With ongoing research into faster consensus algorithms, enhanced privacy mechanisms, and regulatory integration, blockchain continues to evolve, promising a more decentralized, secure, and efficient digital future. In the section below, we will see the evolution of blockchain.

- **2008**: Satoshi Nakamoto publishes the whitepaper "Bitcoin: A Peer-to-Peer Electronic Cash System," introducing blockchain as the underlying technology for Bitcoin.
- **2009**: The Bitcoin network is launched, and the first block, known as the Genesis Block, is mined.
- **2013**: Vitalik Buterin proposes Ethereum, a blockchain platform enabling decentralized applications (DApps) through smart contracts.
- **2015**: Ethereum network goes live, significantly expanding the potential use cases for blockchain technology beyond cryptocurrency.
- **2017**: Initial Coin Offering (ICO) boom leverages blockchain for fundraising, although it also attracts regulatory scrutiny due to fraud and speculation.
- **2020**: Decentralized Finance (DeFi) applications gain popularity, allowing users to engage in financial services like lending and borrowing without traditional intermediaries.
- **2021**–Present: Blockchain technology sees increasing adoption across various industries, including supply chain management, healthcare, and finance, with significant investment in research and development.

9.1.2 Key features of blockchain and use cases

In Section 9.1, we have discussed the features of blockchain. Table 9.1 explains the features with a real-life use case.

9.1.3 Types of blockchains

Blockchain systems are categorized into different types depending on how access, participation, and control are managed. Each type serves distinct needs, from open public interaction to confidential enterprise use.

9.1.3.1 Public blockchain

Public blockchains are completely open networks where anyone can read, write, or participate in the validation process. They are fully decentralized, relying on consensus mechanisms like Proof of Work (PoW) or Proof of Stake (PoS) to maintain integrity. These blockchains prioritize transparency and trustlessness but can face scalability challenges.

Table 9.1 Features of blockchain and its use case

Characteristics	Description	Real-life banking use case
Decentralization	Eliminates central authority, improving reliability and system resilience	JPMorgan's Onyx Network enables peer-to-peer bank transfers without central clearing houses
Transparency	Shared ledger view ensures visibility and accountability	Santander's One Pay FX (foreign exchange) shows real-time international payment details via Ripple's network
Immutability	Once recorded, data cannot be changed without full network consensus	HSBC uses we.trade for secure, tamper-proof trade finance documentation
Security	Cryptographic protection ensures data is safe from unauthorized access	Standard Chartered's KYC blockchain improves document safety and user privacy
Smart Contracts	Automates transaction processing, reduces manual intervention	AXA's Fizzy triggers automatic flight delay insurance payouts through blockchain
Traceability	Tracks the complete transaction history from source to endpoint	ING Bank tracks digital trade documents and asset movements for enhanced auditability

Example

- **Bitcoin**: A decentralized digital currency operating on a public blockchain, allowing anyone to transact without intermediaries.
- **Ethereum**: A blockchain enabling smart contracts and decentralized applications (DApps), widely used for DeFi, • Non-Fungible Tokens (NFTs), and more.

9.1.3.2 Private blockchains

Private blockchains restrict participation to specific users who are granted permission. A single organization or a designated authority typically manages these networks, providing greater control over data privacy, access, and transaction processing speed. Although faster and more scalable, they are less decentralized.

Example

- **Hyperledger Fabric:** A permissioned blockchain framework designed for businesses needing secure, high-speed, private transactions.
- **Corda:** A platform aimed at regulated industries like finance, where selective data sharing and privacy are critical.

9.1.3.3 Consortium blockchains

Consortium blockchains are governed by a group of organizations rather than a single entity. They provide a partially decentralized environment where selected participants share responsibility for maintaining the network. This type is suitable for industries where collaboration among competitors is necessary.

Example

- **Marco Polo Network:** A blockchain consortium streamlining trade finance processes across multiple banks.
- **Energy Web Chain:** Designed for the energy sector to support decentralized energy systems through a trusted network.

9.1.3.4 Hybrid blockchain

Hybrid blockchains combine elements of both public and private models. Organizations can keep sensitive data restricted while allowing selective interaction with a public blockchain for verification purposes. This setup offers flexibility, security, and scalability in a balanced way.

Example

- **IBM Food Trust**: A solution enhancing food supply chain transparency, blending public traceability with private data protection.
- **Dragonchain**: A hybrid platform enabling businesses to selectively interact with public blockchains while maintaining private operations.

9.2 Importance of blockchain

Blockchain technology addresses several critical issues in traditional systems, including:

Trust: Blockchain fosters trust among participants by maintaining a transparent, tamper-proof ledger where all transactions are permanently recorded. This reduces dependence on centralized authorities or intermediaries.
Efficiency: By automating processes through smart contracts and eliminating manual verification steps, blockchain significantly cuts down transaction times and operational costs, leading to faster and more seamless operations.
Security: The decentralized nature of blockchain, combined with strong cryptographic mechanisms, makes it highly resistant to hacking, data breaches, and fraudulent activities, offering enhanced protection for sensitive information.
Transparency: Every transaction on a blockchain is visible to authorized participants and cannot be altered once recorded, ensuring full traceability and accountability and reducing the risk of misconduct or corruption.

9.2.1 Famous blockchain platforms

Bitcoin: Launched in 2009, Bitcoin is the first and most widely known blockchain network, designed to enable peer-to-peer digital currency transactions without the need for a central authority. It uses the Proof of Work (PoW) consensus mechanism to secure the network and validate transactions, with Bitcoin (BTC) as its native cryptocurrency.

Ethereum: Proposed by Vitalik Buterin in 2013 and launched in 2015, Ethereum extends blockchain capabilities beyond simple transactions by introducing smart contracts and decentralized applications (DApps). It transitioned from Proof of Work to Proof of Stake (PoS) with Ethereum 2.0, and its native cryptocurrency, Ether (ETH), fuels transactions and computational services on the network.

Hyperledger: Initiated by the Linux Foundation, Hyperledger is an umbrella project of open-source blockchains and related tools tailored for enterprises. It supports private and permissioned blockchain systems like Hyperledger Fabric and Hyperledger Sawtooth, aiming to streamline operations across industries such as supply chain, healthcare, and finance.

Corda: Developed by R3, Corda is a blockchain-inspired platform specifically built for businesses, particularly in the banking and financial sectors. Unlike traditional blockchains, Corda allows for permissioned access and is designed to facilitate direct, secure transactions between trusted parties without broadcasting data to the entire network.

Stellar: Created by Jed McCaleb in 2014, Stellar focuses on simplifying global money transfers. Its consensus protocol allows for fast, low-cost transactions, making it ideal for connecting financial institutions, payment systems, and individuals across borders, with an emphasis on financial inclusion.

EOS: Launched by Block.one, EOS is a blockchain platform engineered to support scalable decentralized applications. It features a Delegated Proof of Stake (DPoS) consensus model, which improves transaction throughput and efficiency, and offers a developer-friendly environment with flexible governance and minimal transaction fees.

9.2.2 State of the art

Blockchain technology continues to evolve, with ongoing research and development focused on improving scalability, interoperability, and sustainability. Innovations include:

- **Layer 2 Solutions**: Technologies like the Lightning Network (for Bitcoin) and Plasma (for Ethereum) aim to increase transaction throughput and reduce fees by processing transactions off-chain.
- **Interoperability Protocols**: Projects like Polkadot and Cosmos facilitate communication and interoperability between different blockchain networks.
- **Consensus Mechanisms**: New consensus algorithms, such as Proof of Stake (PoS), aim to improve energy efficiency and security. Ethereum's transition to Ethereum 2.0 is a notable example.
- **Decentralized Finance (DeFi)**: A rapidly growing sector leveraging blockchain for financial services like lending, borrowing, and trading without intermediaries.
- **Non-Fungible Tokens (NFTs)**: Unique digital assets represented on the blockchain, gaining popularity in art, gaming, and entertainment.

9.3 Banking and blockchain technology—the combination

9.3.1 Advantages for the banking sector

The banking sector, traditionally built on centralized trust models, faces ongoing challenges related to security, transparency, operational efficiency, and cost optimization. Blockchain technology offers a transformative approach by addressing many of these issues through its decentralized, secure, and transparent architecture. Its integration into banking operations promises not just incremental improvements but fundamental shifts in how financial services are delivered and managed.

One of the most significant advantages of blockchain in banking is **enhanced security**. Through cryptographic techniques and decentralized validation, blockchain minimizes the risk of fraud, cyberattacks, and unauthorized data manipulation. Every transaction is encrypted and linked to the previous transaction, forming an immutable chain that is virtually tamper-proof. This drastically reduces vulnerabilities associated with centralized databases, which have historically been attractive targets for malicious actors.

Operational efficiency is another major benefit. Blockchain eliminates the need for multiple intermediaries and redundant verification processes, which are common in traditional banking systems. With smart contracts, banks can automate tasks like loan approvals, cross-border payments, and clearing settlements. These automated workflows speed up transaction times from days to minutes, significantly lowering administrative costs and improving customer satisfaction.

Transparency and auditability are natural outcomes of blockchain's design. Since every participant in the network has access to a real-time, synchronized ledger, auditing processes become faster, simpler, and more reliable. Regulators and compliance officers can verify transactions in near real-time without relying solely on reports provided by banks, enhancing trust and regulatory compliance.

Blockchain also introduces **cost savings** by streamlining backend processes. In areas such as cross-border payments, blockchain reduces dependence on multiple correspondent banks and cuts down transaction fees. Platforms like Ripple have already demonstrated that blockchain can lower the cost and complexity of international money transfers.

Another critical advantage is **financial inclusion**. Blockchain-powered banking services can reach underbanked and unbanked populations by providing secure, low-cost alternatives to traditional banking. Decentralized finance (DeFi) models, built on blockchain, allow individuals without access to formal banking systems to save, borrow, and invest securely via mobile devices.

Moreover, **improved customer identity management** is possible through blockchain. Solutions based on decentralized identity frameworks enable banks to maintain up-to-date, verified customer records without the need for repeated Know Your Customer (KYC) processes across different financial institutions. Customers gain greater control over their data, while banks benefit from reduced onboarding costs and enhanced customer experiences.

Finally, blockchain enables **new business models**. Tokenization of assets, programmable money, and decentralized exchanges present opportunities for banks to create innovative financial products and services, thus remaining competitive in a rapidly evolving market landscape.

9.3.2 Applications in banking

Refer to Figure 9.2 for the applications of blockchain in the banking sector.

9.3.2.1 Cross-border payments

Cross-border payments are financial transactions where the payer and the recipient reside in different countries. Traditionally, these payments rely on a complex network of correspondent banks, central clearing systems, and multiple intermediaries, often resulting in high transaction costs, lengthy settlement times, a lack of transparency, and limited traceability.

Challenges in traditional cross-border systems

- **Settlement delays**: Transactions can take 3–5 business days due to multiple bank handovers and time zone differences.
- **High costs**: Each intermediary adds a fee, including currency conversion charges.
- **Lack of transparency**: Senders and recipients often cannot track payment status or view the full breakdown of charges.
- **Error rates**: Manual handling and inconsistent data formats across systems can lead to mismatches and rejections.

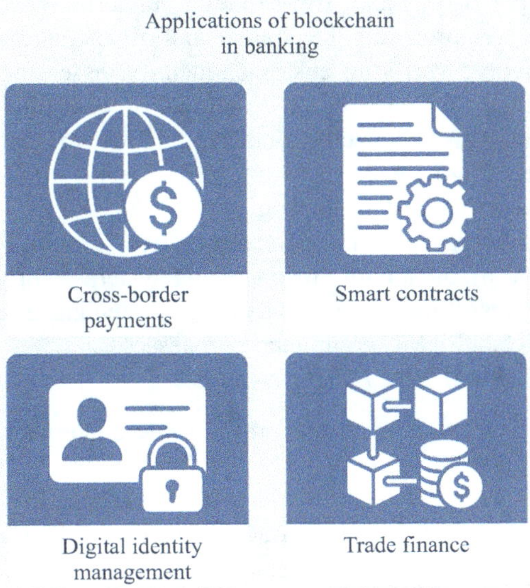

Figure 9.2 Applications of blockchain in banking

Blockchain technology offers a transformative alternative by enabling real-time, peer-to-peer international transfers that are faster, more cost-effective, and highly secure. Through the use of distributed ledger technology (DLT), blockchain removes the need for intermediaries and central clearing, providing a single, immutable source of truth across the network.

How it works—Simplified workflow

1. **Sender initiates payment**: The sender's bank creates a blockchain-based transaction.
2. **Transaction verified**: Network nodes verify and record the transaction in real time.
3. **Smart contract executes**: If applicable, a smart contract validates terms like exchange rate and KYC compliance.
4. **Receiver's bank updates ledger**: The funds are reflected in the receiver's account in the local currency.
5. **Instant confirmation**: Both parties can view the transaction status and completion time instantly.

Stakeholder benefits

- **Banks:** Reduced operational costs, improved liquidity management, and enhanced auditability.
- **Customers:** Faster transfers, lower fees, full visibility of payment flow, 24/7 availability.

9.3.2.2 Know Your Customer (KYC) and Anti-Money Laundering (AML)

Know Your Customer (KYC) and Anti-Money Laundering (AML) regulations are critical compliance requirements for banks and financial institutions globally. These processes involve verifying customer identity, assessing risk profiles, and continuously monitoring transactions to detect and prevent illicit activities such as money laundering, terrorism financing, and fraud. However, traditional KYC/AML workflows are often fragmented, slow, and costly, with duplicate efforts across institutions and challenges in data sharing.

Blockchain technology presents a transformative solution by enabling secure, decentralized, and verifiable identity management systems. Through shared ledgers and permissioned access, blockchain can significantly enhance the accuracy, speed, and security of KYC and AML compliance processes.

Challenges in traditional KYC/AML systems

- **Redundancy**: Customers must submit the same documents repeatedly to different institutions.
- **Manual Processing**: Verification and risk scoring are slow and error-prone.
- **Limited Data Sharing**: Privacy concerns and incompatible systems hinder collaboration between banks and regulators.
- **Cost**: KYC compliance costs banks billions annually in onboarding and monitoring.

Blockchain introduces a shared digital identity layer, allowing authorized institutions to access verified KYC data on a permissioned ledger. Once a customer's identity is verified and recorded, it can be reused across institutions, reducing duplication. Smart contracts can automate compliance checks and flag suspicious patterns based on preset AML rules, ensuring timely reporting and intervention.

How it works—Simplified workflow

1. **Customer onboarding**: One-time KYC verification is conducted by a trusted institution.
2. **Blockchain record creation**: Verified identity and documents are hashed and stored on the blockchain.
3. **Permissioned sharing**: Other authorized banks or institutions can request and view the verified data.
4. **Smart contract monitoring**: AML rules coded into smart contracts monitor transactions and flag anomalies.
5. **Regulatory reporting**: Suspicious activity reports are auto-generated and shared with regulatory bodies in real time.

Stakeholder benefits

- Banks: Reduced compliance costs, faster onboarding, fewer redundancies
- Customers: Greater control of personal data, faster account setup
- Regulators: Real-time insights, improved monitoring, and easier enforcement

Regulatory alignment and compliance

Blockchain-based KYC/AML systems can align with existing compliance standards, such as:

FATF (Financial Action Task Force) recommendations

- GDPR (General Data Protection Regulation) and local data protection regulations
- Regional KYC utilities (e.g., India's CKYC—Central Know Your Customer, European Union's electronic Identification, Authentication and Trust Services—EU's eIDAS)

By offering tamper-resistant audit trails and secure sharing mechanisms, blockchain not only meets but also enhances regulatory expectations around financial transparency and accountability.

9.3.2.3 Trade finance

Trade finance refers to the set of financial instruments and products used by companies to facilitate international trade and commerce. It includes processes like issuing letters of credit (LC), bills of lading, invoice financing, and payment guarantees. However, traditional trade finance is heavily paper-based, involves multiple intermediaries, and suffers from inefficiencies, a lack of transparency, and fraud vulnerabilities.

Blockchain technology offers a secure, transparent, and digitized solution that transforms how trade finance operates. By enabling a shared ledger for all parties—including exporters, importers, banks, insurers, and customs authorities—blockchain ensures real-time visibility, reduces paperwork, and eliminates delays in document verification and fund transfers.

Challenges in traditional trade finance

- **Manual paperwork**: Documents like LCs and invoices are exchanged physically, causing delays.
- **Fraud risks**: Duplicate invoices, false shipments, and forged documents are hard to detect.
- **Limited transparency**: Trade participants operate in silos, with limited visibility into the status of goods and documents.
- **Slow settlement**: Verifications across multiple parties extend the payment cycle significantly.

Blockchain introduces a single, immutable record of all trade-related transactions and documents accessible to all authorized participants in the supply chain. Smart contracts automate the release of payments based on real-time updates (e.g., proof of shipment). Document authenticity and provenance can be verified instantly through digitally signed, timestamped entries on the blockchain.

How it works—Simplified workflow

1. **Trade agreement recorded**: Purchase orders and contracts are digitized and logged on the blockchain.
2. **Documents shared in real time**: Invoices, bills of lading, and certificates are uploaded and instantly accessible.
3. **Smart contracts execute payments**: Once goods are shipped and conditions met, payments are automatically triggered.
4. **Bank finances or guarantees**: Banks issue digital LCs or invoice financing based on verified documents.
5. **Audit and compliance logs maintained**: All interactions are timestamped and verifiable for future audits.

Stakeholder benefits

- Banks: Faster LC issuance, reduced fraud, improved customer experience.
- Exporters/Importers: Lower paperwork burden, faster payment cycles, and better transparency.
- Regulators: Easier compliance and auditing through tamper-proof digital records.

Integration with other technologies

If we integrate blockchain with technologies like IoT, we can achieve enhanced results as given below.

- **IoT sensors**: Can provide real-time updates on temperature, location, and condition of goods.
- **AI (**Artificial Intelligence**)/ML (**Machine Learning): Enhance risk scoring and fraud detection.

- **ERP (Enterprise Resource Planning) Systems**: Blockchain platforms can plug into ERP systems for seamless enterprise workflows.

9.3.2.4 Syndicated loans

Syndicated loans are large loans jointly issued by a group of lenders—usually banks or financial institutions to a single borrower, typically a corporation or a government body. These loans are common in large infrastructure projects, mergers, or corporate expansions, where the borrowing amount and risk need to be distributed among multiple parties. Despite their widespread use, syndicated loans remain highly manual, opaque, and slow-moving, often taking weeks to months for processing and settlement.

Blockchain technology introduces a modern alternative that can transform the syndicated loan process. By providing a shared, immutable, and transparent digital ledger, blockchain streamlines the complex coordination among parties, accelerates settlement, and ensures trust and auditability across all stakeholders.

Challenges in traditional syndicated loans

- **Manual paperwork**: High dependency on physical documentation and manual approval chains.
- **Lengthy settlement times**: Loan origination, allocation, and settlement often take several weeks.
- **Coordination complexity**: Involves multiple lenders, agents, legal teams, and back-office systems working asynchronously.
- **Lack of transparency**: Limited visibility across stakeholders into real-time status, documents, and changes.
- **Operational risks**: Prone to errors, reconciliation delays, and communication breakdowns.

Blockchain enables a unified, digital loan record accessible to all participating parties—borrowers, lenders, agents, legal teams, and regulators. Through smart contracts, loan terms, repayment schedules, interest calculations, and covenants can be codified and enforced automatically. Document flows, approvals, and cash disbursements become traceable, auditable, and faster.

How it works—Simplified workflow

1. **Loan agreement setup**: Borrower and lead bank define loan terms and digitally encode them in smart contracts.
2. **Syndicate formation**: Other lenders join the loan via blockchain-based registration.
3. **Loan issuance**: Funds are disbursed through tokenized representation or traditional rails tracked on-chain.
4. **Loan servicing**: Interest, fees, and repayments are auto-calculated and distributed as per the smart contract logic.
5. **Ongoing reporting**: All stakeholders have a synchronized view of balances, schedules, and compliance events.

Stakeholder benefits

- Banks/Lenders: Lower processing costs, reduced settlement time, improved communication
- Borrowers: Faster loan access, transparent terms, better reporting
- Agents: Easier coordination, simplified loan management, lower reconciliation effort
- Auditors/Regulators: Real-time audit trails and automated compliance checks

9.3.2.5 Syndicated loans

Asset tokenization is the process of representing real-world or financial assets as digital tokens on a blockchain. These tokens serve as verifiable, transferable representations of ownership or rights in assets such as real estate, equities, commodities, art, or intellectual property. Tokenization enhances liquidity, transparency, and fractional ownership by converting traditionally illiquid assets into easily tradable digital instruments.

Blockchain technology underpins this transformation by offering secure, immutable ledgers and programmable smart contracts that facilitate transparent asset issuance, transfer, and settlement—without the need for intermediaries.

Challenges in traditional asset management

- **Limited liquidity**: High-value assets like property, artwork, or private equity are hard to trade or subdivide.
- **High entry barriers**: Many investment opportunities are reserved for institutional investors due to minimum capital requirements.
- **Inefficiencies and delays**: Manual processing, third-party verification, and clearing can delay settlements.
- **Lack of transparency**: Ownership records, valuations, and transaction histories are often siloed and difficult to verify.

Blockchain enables the creation of **digital tokens** that represent partial or full ownership of an asset. These tokens are stored and traded on-chain, with each transaction automatically verified and recorded in a decentralized ledger. Smart contracts facilitate compliance, dividend distribution, and rights management, reducing reliance on legal and administrative intermediaries.

How it works—Simplified workflow

1. **Asset selection**: A real-world asset is identified and valued.
2. **Legal structuring**: A framework is established to link token ownership to legal rights in the asset.
3. **Token issuance**: Digital tokens representing the asset are created on a blockchain.
4. **Investor onboarding**: KYC/AML checks are done before distributing tokens to investors.
5. **Secondary trading**: Investors can trade tokens on a compatible digital asset exchange.
6. **Lifecycle management**: Smart contracts handle dividends, interest, or usage rights.

Table 9.2 Challenges and considerations of blockchain in banking

Challenge/consideration	Description
Scalability	Blockchain networks often face transaction speed and volume limitations, which can hinder their ability to support high-frequency banking operations.
Regulatory uncertainty	Ambiguous and evolving laws around blockchain, cryptocurrencies, and data privacy pose legal and compliance risks for banks.
Interoperability	Integrating blockchain with existing banking systems and other blockchains remains complex due to a lack of standardization.
Security risks	Vulnerabilities such as smart contract bugs, wallet breaches, and potential network attacks require specialized cybersecurity strategies.
Cost of implementation	High initial investments in infrastructure setup, employee training, and compliance adaptations can deter adoption, especially for smaller banks.
Privacy concerns	Public blockchain transparency may conflict with the need for confidentiality in banking, demanding careful design choices around data privacy.

Stakeholder benefits

- Asset owners: Access to global investors, faster liquidity, and lower issuance costs
- Investors: Broader access to asset classes, fractional ownership, and transparency
- Regulators: Improved auditability and built-in compliance enforcement

9.3.3 Challenges and considerations

While blockchain technology offers immense potential for transforming banking operations, it also presents a set of complex challenges and considerations that financial institutions must address carefully before widespread adoption. Table 9.2 portrays the challenges and considerations of blockchain in the banking sector.

In summary, while blockchain has the potential to revolutionize banking by enhancing transparency, efficiency, and security, successful adoption demands careful planning, regulatory alignment, technological innovation, and a thoughtful approach for integrating new solutions into complex financial systems.

9.4 Case study—how blockchain can improve security in the banking domain?

Case study: Santander's blockchain initiative

Background: Traditional cross-border payments have long been associated with delays, high transaction fees, and a lack of transparency. Santander, one of the largest banks in Europe, recognized these challenges and sought a solution to enhance their international payment services.

Problem statement:

Customers experienced transaction settlement times of up to 3–5 days for international transfers. The process involved multiple intermediary banks, leading to additional costs, delayed funds availability, and a lack of real-time visibility into the payment status.

Blockchain-based solution:

Santander adopted a blockchain solution to power its international payments through a platform called Santander One Pay FX. Built in collaboration with Ripple's blockchain network, the system allows customers to execute same-day or next-day international transactions with full transparency on costs and timing.

How was blockchain used?

- Transactions are recorded on Ripple's distributed ledger, allowing banks to directly connect with one another without multiple intermediaries.
- Smart contracts automate settlement processes, reducing the need for manual intervention and verification steps.
- Payment tracking is integrated, providing customers with end-to-end visibility into the status of their funds.

Benefits achieved:

Speed: Transaction times were reduced from several days to within 24 hours, with some transfers happening almost instantly.
Cost efficiency: By minimizing the number of intermediaries, transaction fees were significantly lowered.
Transparency: Customers could track the status and exchange rates of their payments in real time, improving trust and satisfaction.
Security: Blockchain's cryptographic validation ensured secure, tamper-proof transaction records.
Impact: Santander successfully demonstrated that blockchain technology could be used not just for backend settlement but as a customer-facing innovation. The bank strengthened its competitive position in the global payments market and set a benchmark for other financial institutions considering blockchain adoption.

Key points to remember

1. Blockchain was introduced in 2008 by Satoshi Nakamoto as the foundation for Bitcoin.
2. It enables secure, transparent, decentralized transactions without a central authority.

3. Core features include decentralization, transparency, immutability, and security.
4. Consensus mechanisms (PoW, PoS, PBFT) ensure trust and integrity in transactions.
5. Blockchain extends beyond cryptocurrency into banking, supply chain, and healthcare.
6. In banking, it improves efficiency, security, real-time settlement, and customer trust.
7. Smart contracts automate operations like loan approvals, trade finance, and insurance payouts.
8. Types of blockchains include public (Bitcoin, Ethereum), private (Hyperledger, Corda), consortium (Marco Polo), and hybrid (IBM Food Trust).
9. Major platforms: Bitcoin, Ethereum, Hyperledger, Corda, Stellar, and EOS serve diverse financial use cases.
10. Key applications in banking:Cross-border payments, KYC/AML compliance, trade finance, syndicated loans, and asset tokenization.
11. Benefits include cost savings, faster transactions, reduced fraud, improved transparency, and financial inclusion.
12. Challenges involve scalability, regulatory uncertainty, interoperability, security risks, and high implementation costs.
13. Blockchain integration requires balancing privacy with transparency in financial data.
14. Santander's case study shows blockchain reducing settlement time, cutting costs, enhancing transparency, and improving security in cross-border payments.
15. Overall, blockchain promises a fundamental shift in banking operations, but success depends on careful adoption, regulatory alignment, and technological innovation.

Questions (try answering yourself)

1. Explain how the fundamental principles of decentralization, transparency, and immutability make blockchain relevant to the banking and financial services industry.
2. Describe the structure of a blockchain block and how cryptographic hashing contributes to the immutability of the ledger.
3. Compare Proof of Work (PoW), Proof of Stake (PoS), and Practical Byzantine Fault Tolerance (PBFT) as consensus mechanisms in the context of banking applications.
4. Trace the evolution of blockchain from the Bitcoin whitepaper in 2008 to its current role as a foundation for decentralized finance (DeFi) and enterprise solutions.
5. Differentiate between public, private, consortium, and hybrid blockchains, and discuss suitable banking use cases for each type.

6. Using Table 9.1, discuss how decentralization, transparency, immutability, security, smart contracts, and traceability individually benefit banking operations.
7. Explain the role of smart contracts in automating banking processes such as loan approvals, trade finance, or insurance payouts, with suitable examples.
8. Evaluate how blockchain can improve efficiency, security, and customer experience in cross-border payment systems.
9. Discuss the challenges of traditional cross-border payments and how a blockchain-based workflow addresses settlement delays, costs, and transparency issues.
10. Describe how blockchain-based KYC and AML systems can reduce redundancy, speed up onboarding, and support regulatory compliance.
11. Analyze the potential integration of blockchain with existing KYC/AML frameworks such as FATF recommendations, GDPR, CKYC, and eIDAS.
12. Explain how blockchain transforms trade finance processes, highlighting the role of shared ledgers and smart contracts in reducing fraud and paperwork.
13. Discuss how combining blockchain with IoT, AI/ML, and ERP systems can further enhance trade finance and supply chain visibility.
14. Describe the end-to-end lifecycle of a syndicated loan on a blockchain platform and explain how smart contracts improve servicing and reporting.
15. Define asset tokenization and analyze its impact on liquidity, fractional ownership, and investor access in the banking and investment domains.
16. Critically examine the main challenges and considerations for banks adopting blockchain, including scalability, interoperability, security risks, and implementation costs.
17. Discuss how famous platforms such as Bitcoin, Ethereum, Hyperledger, Corda, Stellar, and EOS differ in design and suitability for banking use cases.
18. Evaluate how blockchain can promote financial inclusion and what limitations or risks may still hinder inclusion for underbanked populations.
19. Using Santander's One Pay FX initiative as a case study, discuss how blockchain improved speed, cost efficiency, transparency, and security in cross-border payments.
20. Do you think blockchain will fundamentally replace existing core banking systems or primarily act as a complementary technology? Justify your answer with arguments from the chapter.

Objective questions

1. **Blockchain was originally introduced as the underlying technology for which system?**
   (A) Ethereum
   (B) Ripple
   (C) Bitcoin
   (D) Hyperledger Fabric

2. **Which of the following is NOT a key feature of blockchain?**
   (A) Immutability
   (B) Decentralization
   (C) Transparency
   (D) Centralized validation

3. **What ensures that once data is recorded on blockchain, it cannot be altered without network consensus?**
   (A) Smart contracts
   (B) Cryptographic hashing
   (C) Cloud backup
   (D) Multi-factor authentication

4. **Which consensus mechanism was used in Bitcoin's original implementation?**
   (A) Proof of Authority (PoA)
   (B) Proof of Work (PoW)
   (C) Proof of Stake (PoS)
   (D) Delegated Proof of Stake (DPoS)

5. **Which of the following is a permissioned blockchain platform widely used in banking?**
   (A) Bitcoin
   (B) Ethereum
   (C) Hyperledger Fabric
   (D) Dogecoin

6. **Which type of blockchain is governed by a group of organizations rather than a single entity?**
   (A) Public blockchain
   (B) Private blockchain
   (C) Consortium blockchain
   (D) Hybrid blockchain

7. **Smart contracts are primarily used to:**
   (A) Encrypt transactions
   (B) Automate predefined business rules
   (C) Detect malware
   (D) Issue cryptocurrency rewards

8. **Which platform is commonly used for cross-border payments using blockchain?**
   (A) Ripple
   (B) EOS
   (C) Solana
   (D) Polygon

9. **What is a major limitation of traditional cross-border payment systems?**
   (A) Instant finality
   (B) High speed
   (C) Multiple intermediaries
   (D) Fixed exchange rates
10. **In blockchain-based KYC systems, what enables secure sharing of verified identity data?**
   (A) Public broadcasting
   (B) Permissioned ledgers
   (C) SMS verification
   (D) Cloud databases
11. **Which regulation focuses on identity, authentication, and trust services in the European Union?**
   (A) FATF
   (B) eIDAS
   (C) GDPR
   (D) CKYC
12. **In trade finance, blockchain's biggest advantage is:**
   (A) Increased paperwork
   (B) Real-time shared visibility
   (C) Higher currency conversion fees
   (D) Manual document verification
13. **Which technology combination enhances blockchain-based trade finance with real-time shipment updates?**
   (A) Blockchain + IoT Sensors
   (B) Blockchain + Keyboard Input
   (C) Blockchain + Printing Machines
   (D) Blockchain + VPN
14. **In syndicated loans, smart contracts help automate:**
   (A) Social media approvals
   (B) Loan terms, repayment schedules, and covenants
   (C) ATM cash withdrawals
   (D) Customer surveys
15. **Asset tokenization refers to:**
   (A) Creating physical tokens for ATM use
   (B) Representing real-world assets as digital tokens
   (C) Converting crypto back to fiat money
   (D) Printing digital receipts
16. **Which challenge relates to blockchain facing transaction volume and speed issues?**
   (A) Interoperability
   (B) Scalability

(C) Regulatory uncertainty
(D) Privacy concerns

17. **Which blockchain platform is specifically designed for financial institutions and selective data sharing?**
    (A) Corda
    (B) Ethereum
    (C) Stellar
    (D) Tezos

18. **Santander's One Pay FX primarily improved cross-border payments by:**
    (A) Increasing settlement time
    (B) Reducing transparency
    (C) Reducing costs and enabling faster transfers
    (D) Removing mobile access

19. **Which blockchain platform is known for fast, low-cost global payments and financial inclusion?**
    (A) EOS
    (B) Stellar
    (C) Filecoin
    (D) Avalanche

20. **What is one of the biggest barriers to blockchain adoption in banking?**
    (A) Too many skilled blockchain developers
    (B) Low infrastructure costs
    (C) Regulatory uncertainty and compliance issues
    (D) Overly simple integration with legacy systems

Answers

1. C
2. D
3. B
4. B
5. C
6. C
7. B
8. A
9. C
10. B
11. B
12. B
13. A
14. B
15. B
16. B

17. A
18. C
19. B
20. C

Further learning

[1] Drescher D. *Blockchain Basics: A Non-Technical Introduction in 25 Steps*. New York: Apress; 2017.

[2] Tapscott D, and Tapscott A. *Blockchain Revolution: How the Technology Behind Bitcoin Is Changing Money, Business, and the World*. New York: Penguin; 2016.

[3] King B. *Bank 4.0: Banking Everywhere, Never at a Bank*. Hoboken, NJ: Wiley; 2018.

[4] World Economic Forum, Deloitte Insights. *Blockchain in Financial Markets and Beyond*. Geneva: WEF; 2016.

[5] Bashir I. *Mastering Blockchain: Unlocking the Power of Cryptocurrencies, Smart Contracts, and Decentralized Applications*. 3rd ed. Birmingham: Packt Publishing; 2020.

[6] Mougayar W. *The Business Blockchain: Promise, Practice, and the Application of the Next Internet Technology*. Hoboken, NJ: Wiley; 2016.

[7] Sharma T. *Blockchain Applications in Finance*. Mumbai: Blockchain Council Press; 2019.

[8] Rubini A. *Fintech Founders: Inspiring Tales from the Entrepreneurs that Are Changing Finance*. Berlin: Walter de Gruyter; 2020.

[9] De Filippi P, and Wright A. *Blockchain and the Law: The Rule of Code*. Cambridge, MA: Harvard University Press; 2018.

[10] Skinner C. *Digital Bank: Strategies to Launch or Become a Digital Bank*. Singapore: Marshall Cavendish International; 2014.

[11] Lipovyanov P. *Blockchain for Business: Discover How Blockchain Will Transform Financial Services*. London: Packt Publishing; 2019.

[12] Rahman SMM, Yii KJ, Masli EK, and Voon ML. The blockchain in the banking industry: A systematic review and bibliometric analysis. *Cogent Business & Management*. 2024;11(1):2407681.

[13] Javaid M, Haleem A, Pratap Singh R, Suman R, and Khan S. A review of blockchain technology applications for financial services. *BenchCouncil Transactions on Benchmarks, Standards and Evaluations*. 2022;2(3):100073.

[14] Patel R, Migliavacca M, and Oriani ME. Blockchain in banking and finance: A bibliometric review. *Research in International Business and Finance*. 2022; 62:101718.

[15] Wu H, Yao Q, Liu Z, *et al.* Blockchain for finance: A survey. *IET Blockchain*. 2024;4(2):101–123.

[16] Rahman SMM, Saif ANM, Kabir S, *et al*. Blockchain in the banking industry: Unravelling thematic drivers and adoption barriers. *IET Blockchain*. 2025;5:e12093.

[17] Varma JR. Blockchain in Finance. *Vikalpa: The Journal for Decision Makers*. 2019;44(4):1–13.

[18] Ahmed IE. Analyzing the impact of blockchain technology on banking transaction costs using the random forest method. *Front. Blockchain*. 2025; 8:1551970.

[19] Journal of International Technology and Information Management. Blockchain adoption model for the global banking industry. *J Int Technol Inf Manage*. 2020;28(4):5.

[20] Singh S, Jaiswal R, Gupta S, and Kumar C. What we know and what should we know about the future of blockchain in finance. *F1000Res*. 2024;13:1051.

[21] Goghie AS. Tokenization and the banking system: Redefining authority in the digital era. *Compet Change*. 2024;28(5):663–682.

[22] University at Buffalo, State University of New York. *Blockchain Specialization*. Coursera; 2021. Available from: https://www.coursera.org

[23] Berkeley X. *Blockchain Technology*. edX; 2021. Available from: https://www.edx.org

[24] Udacity. *Blockchain Developer Nanodegree*. Udacity; 2021. Available from: https://www.udacity.com

Chapter 10
Social engineering attacks

10.1 Introduction to social engineering

In today's interconnected world, cybersecurity threats extend beyond technical vulnerabilities to human weaknesses. Social engineering attacks exploit human psychology to manipulate individuals into divulging confidential information, granting access, or performing actions that compromise security. Unlike traditional cyberattacks that target software or hardware, social engineering focuses on exploiting trust, fear, urgency, or curiosity to achieve malicious objectives.

These attacks can take many forms, including phishing emails, impersonation, pretexting, baiting, and tailgating. The common thread across all methods is the strategic manipulation of human behavior rather than system flaws. Attackers often conduct thorough research to craft convincing narratives that deceive their targets, making social engineering both difficult to detect and challenging to defend against using conventional security measures alone.

As technology evolves, so do the techniques used by social engineers, making it crucial for individuals and organizations to remain vigilant. Understanding the various tactics, recognizing warning signs, and promoting a culture of skepticism are essential steps in strengthening defenses. This chapter delves into the different types of social engineering attacks, real-world examples, and strategies to build resilience against one of the most potent threats in the cybersecurity landscape.

10.1.1 Understanding the concept and its relevance

Social engineering is defined as the use of deception and influence to manipulate people into taking actions that may compromise information or systems. It bypasses traditional technical barriers by appealing to natural human tendencies like trust and helpfulness.

10.1.1.1 Why is it critical in cybersecurity?

- A majority of breaches stem from human error, not technical flaws.
- These attacks often go unnoticed, as victims may not realize they have been manipulated.
- It can serve as an entry point to more damaging exploits like ransomware or credential theft.

10.1.2 The human element in security weaknesses

Human behavior often represents the most vulnerable part of a security system. Unlike hardware or software, which can be patched, people can be misled—especially under stress or pressure.

10.1.2.1 Key vulnerabilities include

- **Lack of training**: Employees may not recognize suspicious behavior or phishing attempts.
- **Routine behavior**: Predictable actions like clicking email links or downloading attachments are exploitable.
- **Overconfidence**: People assume they are too cautious to be fooled.
- **Oversharing online**: Public posts about job roles, routines, or systems create an easy roadmap for attackers.

A well-designed attack can manipulate even a security-aware individual, especially when combined with information harvested from social media or internal documents.

10.2 How does it differ from traditional cyberattacks?

Traditional cyberattacks primarily focus on finding and exploiting flaws in technology, such as weaknesses in software, networks, or hardware systems. Attackers use technical methods like viruses, malware, hacking tools, or network attacks to breach systems and steal or disrupt data.

On the other hand, social engineering attacks target human behavior instead of technological gaps. These attacks manipulate individuals into giving up confidential information or performing risky actions, often by playing on emotions like trust, fear, or urgency. The success of a social engineering attack depends more on psychological tactics than on technical skills.

Defending against traditional cyberattacks usually involves strong firewalls, antivirus software, and system updates. However, protecting against social engineering requires continuous user education, strict identity verification, and creating a culture of skepticism and alertness among users.

10.3 Types of social engineering attacks

Social engineering attacks can take many forms, depending on the channel used, the target, and the psychological strategy behind them. Attackers often blend technology with manipulation techniques to trick individuals into compromising secure systems. Refer to Figure 10.1 for the social engineering attack flow. The major categories of social engineering attacks, each with real-world relevance and examples, are given below.

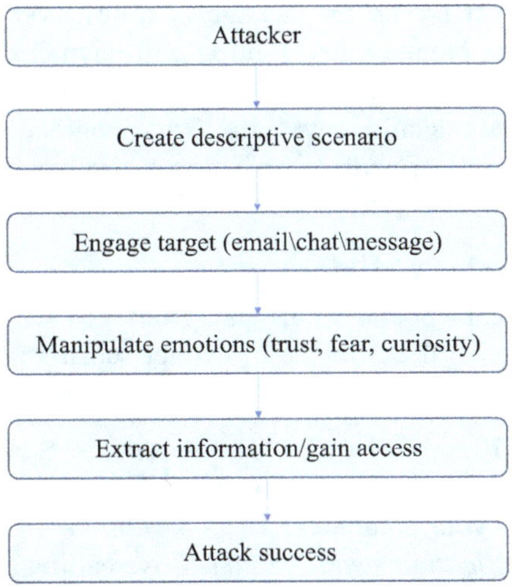

Figure 10.1 Social engineering attack flow

10.3.1 Phishing

Phishing is one of the most common and effective social engineering methods. It typically involves fraudulent communication—usually via email—that appears to come from a trusted source. The message often contains malicious links or attachments designed to steal credentials or infect devices.

10.3.1.1 Variants include

- **Email phishing**: Mass messages that lure users into clicking harmful links or revealing login details.
- **Spear phishing**: Highly personalized emails targeting specific individuals using researched information (e.g., role, organization).
- **Whaling**: Targets high-level executives or decision-makers with tailored messages involving urgent financial actions.
- **Clone phishing**: Sends a replica of a previously legitimate email but replaces original links or attachments with malicious ones.

10.3.2 Smishing and vishing

These forms of phishing use phones rather than emails to deceive victims.

10.3.2.1 Smishing (SMS phishing)

Text messages claiming to be from banks, delivery services, or government bodies prompt users to click on malicious links or disclose personal data.

> ***Example 1: Fake bank alert:*** Unusual login attempt detected on your account. If this wasn't you, verify immediately: [http://hdabc-alerts.com/verify]

Example 2: Delivery scam: Your package is waiting. Pay ₹35 customs fee to avoid return. Complete payment here: [http://dml-payment.in]
Example 3: KYC update fraud: Your bank KYC is outdated. Account will be frozen in 24 hrs. Update details now: [http://kyc-revalidation.com]
Example 4: Government subsidy trap: You are eligible for ₹6000 PM subsidy. Confirm Aadhaar & PAN at [http://gov-benefits.in]

10.3.2.2 Vishing (voice phishing)

Attackers make phone calls posing as officials from tech support, law enforcement, or HR (Human Resources) departments to extract sensitive details or gain system access.

Example 1: Fake IT support call: "Hello, this is Sandeep from Microsoft Security. We've detected a malware infection on your system. To remove it, I'll need remote access to your computer."
Example 2: Bank verification scam: "This is Priya calling from ICICI Bank fraud division. We noticed a ₹35,000 withdrawal attempt. To cancel it, please verify your OTP and card number immediately."
Example 3: Telecom provider impersonation: "Good evening, sir. I'm calling from Jio. Your SIM will be deactivated in 2 hours due to KYC failure. Please tell me your Aadhaar number to update the records."
Example 4: Fake government officer: "This is Officer Singh from the Income Tax Department. Your PAN is flagged in a financial investigation. To avoid a warrant, I need your bank details to verify identity."

10.3.3 Baiting

Baiting tricks the target into acting by offering something enticing—often a free gift or benefit. It can occur both physically and digitally.

10.3.3.1 Examples

- **Physical baiting**: Leaving infected USB drives in public spaces, hoping someone plugs them into a corporate device.
- **Online baiting**: Offering free downloads (music, movies, games) that secretly install malware.

10.3.4 Pretexting

Pretexting involves the attacker fabricating a believable scenario or identity to gain the victim's trust and extract sensitive information.

10.3.4.1 Common scenarios

- Pretending to be an IT technician requesting access to systems.
- Impersonating an auditor or HR official needing personal or financial data.
- Calling as a service provider requesting verification information.

Unlike phishing, which relies on urgency, pretexting depends on building credibility and appearing legitimate over time.

10.3.5 Quid pro quo

This tactic involves offering a benefit or favor in return for information or access. The promise could be as simple as tech help, a reward, or even participation in a survey.

10.3.5.1 Examples

- A fake IT agent offers to resolve a system issue in exchange for login credentials.
- Fraudsters offer free movie tickets for completing a "banking habits" survey.

10.3.6 Tailgating/piggybacking

Tailgating involves unauthorized physical access to a secure area by following an authorized person—often without their knowledge.

10.3.6.1 How it happens

These attacks often target data centers, offices, or restricted zones, bypassing security protocols using human courtesy.

- An attacker waits near a door and enters behind someone with valid access, often by appearing polite or carrying heavy items.
- In piggybacking, the authorized individual knowingly allows the attacker in, usually unaware of the risk.

10.4 Social engineering attack lifecycle

Social engineering attacks are rarely random—they follow a deliberate, step-by-step process that allows attackers to gather information, gain trust, and execute the attack with minimal detection. Understanding this lifecycle is essential for identifying where preventive measures can be most effective.

The lifecycle typically consists of five key stages:

10.4.1 Reconnaissance (information gathering)

In this initial phase, the attacker collects detailed information about the target. This could involve individuals, organizations, or departments.

Tactics used

- **Passive methods:** Browsing social media, LinkedIn profiles, corporate websites, press releases, and job boards.
- **Active methods:** Calling help desks or conducting surveys under false pretenses.

Example: An attacker learns from an employee's LinkedIn profile that they work in finance and use SAP software—information later used in a spear-phishing email.

10.4.2 Engagement (initial contact)

Once enough information is gathered, the attacker initiates contact with the target using a convincing pretext. This could be through email, phone, text message, or even in person.

Channels used

- Phishing emails (posing as HR or IT)
- Fake customer support calls (vishing)
- SMS alerts (smishing)
- Physical interactions (tailgating or impersonation)

Example: The attacker sends a crafted email to the target, pretending to be the company's IT team, requesting a password reset due to suspicious activity.

10.4.3 Exploitation (manipulation and breach)

In this phase, the attacker manipulates the victim into performing an action that compromises security.

Common outcomes

- Revealing login credentials
- Downloading malware
- Granting remote access
- Approving unauthorized financial transactions

Example: Believing the email is genuine, the target clicks on the link and enters their corporate credentials into a fake login page.

10.4.4 Execution (action taken)

The attacker now takes advantage of the access or information gained. This could involve data theft, account takeovers, malware deployment, or lateral movement within a network.

Activities include

- Exfiltrating sensitive data
- Escalating privileges
- Installing spyware or ransomware
- Defrauding internal systems (e.g., invoice fraud)

Example: The attacker uses the stolen credentials to log into internal financial systems and initiate fraudulent wire transfers.

10.4.5 Exit and cover-up

After the attack is complete, the attacker attempts to remove traces of their actions to avoid detection.

Tactics

- Deleting logs or emails
- Erasing malware or backdoors
- Using anonymized accounts or Virtual Private Networks (VPNs)
- Leaving false trails (misdirection)

Example: The attacker deletes emails from the victim's inbox and log files on the compromised server to prevent forensic investigation.

Understanding this lifecycle allows cybersecurity professionals to identify, interrupt, and respond to attacks more effectively. Prevention measures can be applied at each stage, from limiting data exposure during reconnaissance to using monitoring tools that detect unusual access patterns during execution.

Let us see a case study and map the lifecycle with it.

Case study: The 2020 Twitter Bitcoin scam

Target: High-profile Twitter accounts (Elon Musk, Barack Obama, Apple, Uber, etc.) **Impact**: Over $100,000 in stolen Bitcoin within a few hours. **Attack type**: Social engineering and insider manipulation

Stage 1: Reconnaissance

The attackers conducted research to identify Twitter employees with administrative privileges. They likely used public sources such as LinkedIn and other job-related platforms to determine who had access to Twitter's internal systems.

- Method: Social media profiling, organizational research
- Objective: Identify targets with elevated access rights

Stage 2: Engagement

Using spoofed phone numbers, the attackers contacted selected employees, impersonating Twitter's IT support. They claimed to be addressing urgent technical issues and used persuasive language to gain trust.

- Method: Vishing (voice phishing)
- Tactic: Impersonation of internal technical staff

Stage 3: Exploitation

Believing the attackers to be legitimate support personnel, at least one employee shared credentials or logged into a phishing site controlled by the attackers. This granted unauthorized access to Twitter's account management tools.

- Weakness exploited: Trust in internal communication
- Outcome: Credential compromise and backend system access

Stage 4: Execution

Once inside the system, the attackers used the tools to take control of multiple verified accounts. They posted fraudulent messages promising to double any Bitcoin sent to a specific wallet address.

- Action taken: Unauthorized posts made from compromised accounts.
- Result: Thousands of users responded, transferring over $100,000 in Bitcoin.

Stage 5: Exit and cover-up

The attackers attempted to conceal their tracks by using VPNs and spreading the stolen funds across multiple cryptocurrency wallets, making it harder for law enforcement to trace the origin or destination of the funds.

- Method: Use of anonymizing tools and transaction complication
- Response: Twitter disabled affected accounts and initiated an internal investigation

Key takeaways

- Social engineering can bypass even the most sophisticated security systems.
- Insider threats and employee manipulation are critical risks.
- Proper security awareness training and robust identity verification protocols are essential.
- Limiting privileged access and enforcing multi-factor authentication can mitigate such risks.

10.5 Psychological triggers used in social engineering attacks

Social engineering exploits predictable psychological patterns to manipulate individuals into compromising information, systems, or resources. Understanding these cognitive triggers is crucial to recognize, prevent, and defend against such attacks. These triggers are often subtle but effective, especially when coupled with urgency, authority, or fear.

10.5.1 Authority

People are more likely to comply with requests from individuals who appear to be in positions of power or knowledge. Attackers often impersonate IT staff, managers, law enforcement, or executives to exploit this trigger.

Case example

In the 2015 Ubiquiti Networks attack, fraudsters impersonated company executives via email and tricked employees into wiring over $46 million to offshore accounts. Refer to Table 10.1.

Table 10.1 Authority techniques

Technique	Tactic used
Impersonation	Fake CEO (Chief Executive Officer)/Manager Email
Use of jargon	Technical language in messages

10.5.2 Urgency

Creating a false sense of time pressure is a common tactic. By convincing the target that immediate action is required, the attacker limits their ability to think critically or verify information.

Case example

In the 2020 Twitter breach, attackers impersonated internal IT staff and claimed accounts needed immediate "security verification," prompting staff to hand over credentials under pressure.

Common scenarios

- "Your account will be locked in 15 minutes unless you reset your password."
- "We've detected unauthorized activity; click here to stop it now."

10.5.3 Fear and anxiety

Fear-based triggers cause targets to act impulsively, especially when threats involve penalties, job loss, or law enforcement. It is effective because fear often overrides logic and verification.

Example phrases

- "Your tax filing has irregularities. Legal action will follow unless verified now."
- "Your access has been flagged for suspicious activity. Confirm your credentials immediately."

Case example

In a widespread phishing campaign in 2019, cybercriminals posed as tax authorities and frightened victims into providing financial information under threat of arrest.

10.5.4 Reciprocity

People are wired to return favors. An attacker might offer assistance, a gift, or an exclusive opportunity in exchange for login details or sensitive information. Refer to Table 10.2.

Examples

- Offering free software or tools in return for registration details
- Pretending to help with a tech issue and asking for remote access

Table 10.2 Reciprocity exploits

Reciprocity exploits	Action taken by the victim
Free document templates	Shares email or credentials
Tech help offer	Grants remote desktop access

10.5.5 Curiosity

Curiosity can be a powerful motivator—used effectively in phishing emails, USB baiting, or unexpected attachments.

Examples

- "Payroll changes for June - see attached."
- "Confidential update: CEO resignation letter enclosed."

Case example

In a 2016 attack simulation, employees at a financial firm found USB drives in the parking lot labeled "Layoff List." A majority plugged them into their systems, activating hidden malware.

10.5.6 Social proof

Humans tend to follow the actions or recommendations of others, especially when uncertain. Messages like "most people have already verified their account" subtly pressure individuals into compliance.

Example phrases

- "90% of your coworkers have completed this security update. Don't be left out."
- "As per company policy, all staff must acknowledge this compliance form."

10.5.7 Scarcity

Limited availability or exclusive access creates a perception of increased value and urgency. Refer to Table 10.3.

Examples

- "Only 3 licenses left for the full version – claim yours now!"
- "Your promotional reward expires in 30 minutes."

Social engineering attacks succeed not because of weak technology, but because of how humans naturally think, feel, and act. Attackers carefully exploit psychological tendencies and emotional triggers to manipulate their targets into revealing sensitive information or taking insecure actions. Understanding the psychological foundations behind these attacks is crucial for building stronger defenses.

Table 10.3 Scarcity techniques

Scarcity tactic	**Intended outcome**
Limited-time reward	Prompt click without thinking
"Last chance" message	Bypass of normal caution

10.6 Real-world case studies of social engineering

Examining real-life incidents of social engineering helps contextualize the risks, tactics, and outcomes of these attacks. These stories also highlight vulnerabilities in systems and behaviors that can be addressed through strategic interventions.

10.6.1 Case study 1: Google and Facebook invoice scam

Between 2013 and 2015, a Lithuanian hacker impersonated Quanta Computer, a legitimate hardware supplier to Google and Facebook. The attacker sent forged invoices and corporate communications via spoofed email accounts. As a result, both companies were tricked into wiring over $100 million to fraudulent overseas accounts.

- **Vulnerability exploited**: Lack of vendor verification and email spoofing detection
- **Outcome**: Legal proceedings led to arrest; partial funds recovered
- **Lesson**: Reinforce verification protocols for financial transactions

10.6.2 Case study 2: RSA Security breach (2011)

RSA (Rivest – Shamir – Adleman algorithm), a major provider of two-factor authentication tokens, fell victim to a social engineering attack when an employee opened a phishing email titled "2011 Recruitment Plan." The email contained a malicious Excel file that installed a backdoor, enabling attackers to steal data related to RSA's SecureID products.

- **Vulnerability exploited**: Employee trust and lack of email attachment filtering
- **Outcome**: Potential compromise of defense contractor systems
- **Lesson**: Implement strict email screening and security training

10.6.3 Case study 3: Colonial Pipeline attack (2021)

Although primarily a ransomware attack, the Colonial Pipeline breach was made possible by compromised credentials, likely harvested via social engineering or password reuse. The attackers gained access to a legacy VPN system, leading to the shutdown of fuel operations across the US East Coast.

- **Vulnerability exploited**: Weak password hygiene and lack of Multi-Factor Authentication (MFA)
- **Outcome**: Fuel shortages, emergency declarations, ransom payment
- **Lesson**: Enforce multi-factor authentication and access auditing

10.7 Social engineering in the digital age

As the digital landscape expands, so do the sophistication and reach of social engineering attacks. Traditional scams have evolved into multi-vector digital threats, capitalizing on the rapid adoption of cloud computing, artificial intelligence, remote work, and social media. Modern attackers exploit not only the weaknesses in systems but also the abundance of information individuals and organizations share online—often unknowingly.

Unlike earlier eras, where attackers might rely on basic phishing emails or phone scams, today's threat actors use a blend of automated scripts, Artificial Intelligence (AI)-generated media, and behavioral profiling to craft highly targeted attacks. These campaigns are often coordinated across several platforms, including email, mobile messaging, social networks, and collaboration tools. The digital environment provides them with tools for mass customization, rapid deployment, and high scalability, all while remaining anonymous and also difficult to trace.

Compounding the risk is the growing reliance on digital identities, remote collaboration platforms, and third-party integrations. Employees working from home may lack access to the same security infrastructure available in office settings, making them easier targets. At the same time, deepfake technologies and AI-enhanced impersonation are closing the gap between fiction and reality, blurring the lines of trust in digital communication. The section below covers the various dimensions of social engineering technologies and their impact on cybersecurity.

10.7.1 AI and deepfake technologies

Artificial Intelligence (AI) has revolutionized the field of cyber deception. Among the most alarming innovations are deepfakes, hyperrealistic but fabricated audio, video, or images generated using AI algorithms such as Generative Adversarial Networks (GANs). These tools enable attackers to convincingly mimic the voices, facial movements, and gestures of real people, making fraudulent communications appear authentic.

One prominent application is voice cloning, where attackers replicate the tone and speech patterns of a CEO or executive to issue fake orders for wire transfers or confidential data disclosure. These synthetic voices are so realistic that even trained employees may not suspect fraud. For instance, a 2020 incident involved a UK-based energy firm that lost over €220,000 after an employee received a voice call from what sounded exactly like their CEO, instructing them to transfer funds to a vendor.

Deepfake videos can also be deployed to impersonate public figures, executives, or authorities during video calls or recorded messages. In virtual meeting environments where face verification is limited and urgency is high, these videos can be used to spread disinformation or execute real-time deception.

AI also enables automation in spear phishing. Language models can now generate highly personalized emails at scale, mimicking a company's communication style and referencing past interactions. This significantly reduces the effort needed to target multiple individuals with convincing messages, increasing the success rate of attacks.

As these technologies become more accessible, even low-skilled attackers can use pretrained models and online tools to launch sophisticated campaigns. This democratization of AI-based attack tools poses a major challenge for security professionals and emphasizes the need for robust identity verification methods and digital media authentication tools.

10.7.2 Social media mining

Social media platforms have become valuable exploration tools for social engineers. Attackers actively mine public profiles on platforms like LinkedIn, Facebook, Instagram, and Twitter to gather detailed information about individuals, teams, and organizational structures. This publicly available data enables attackers to craft tailored, believable phishing emails and pretexts.

LinkedIn, for example, often contains up-to-date job titles, reporting structures, technology stacks, and contact details. A cybercriminal targeting a tech company might learn from LinkedIn that an employee just got promoted to DevOps Manager and uses AWS (Amazon Web Services) and Jenkins. With that information, the attacker can craft an email posing as an internal colleague, referencing recent changes or tools, and include a malicious "team update" attachment or link.

Facebook and Instagram offer insights into personal lives—birthdays, vacations, hobbies, and even recent purchases. This information allows attackers to build rapport, impersonate friends or family, or create emotionally resonant scenarios that increase the likelihood of a successful breach.

Moreover, social media is also used to identify employee routines and vulnerabilities. A post like "Starting my first day at XYZ Corp!" or "Traveling for a client meeting this week" informs attackers when a person may be distracted, unavailable, or outside a secure environment, making them easier to target.

Beyond individuals, company pages also reveal upcoming events, policy updates, or new product launches that can be used to time attacks for maximum believability. For instance, an attacker could exploit the announcement of a new ERP system by sending fake "onboarding instructions" with credential-stealing links.

To combat this, organizations should implement social media awareness training and enforce privacy best practices. Employees should be encouraged to limit the visibility of sensitive personal and professional details and avoid sharing security-related information like badge photos, internal apps, or infrastructure tools.

Example: A targeted email to an HR manager references a real job opening posted online, making it look like an applicant reply, but with a malicious attachment.

10.7.3 Multi-channel campaigns

Modern social engineering attacks increasingly rely on multi-channel approaches to maximize effectiveness and minimize detection. Rather than relying solely on a single email or phone call, attackers now orchestrate a combination of email, SMS, phone calls, and social media messages to build a more convincing narrative. These coordinated interactions reinforce each other, creating a sense of legitimacy and urgency that lowers the victim's defenses.

For example, an attacker might begin with a spear-phishing email claiming to be from the company's IT support team, alerting the user to a security issue requiring immediate action. Within minutes, the target receives a follow-up SMS reminding them of the email and urging them to act promptly. Shortly afterward, the attacker may call the victim, posing as an IT representative and referencing the previous communications, further solidifying the credibility of the scam.

This layered technique makes it harder for the target to pause and verify the request, especially under the illusion of consistent and urgent communication across trusted channels. The perceived legitimacy of one channel boosts the trustworthiness of the others.

Example

In one well-documented case, attackers targeted an HR executive using a fake email from the company's CEO requesting urgent payroll updates. Shortly after the email, the victim received a text message "confirming" the urgency of the situation. A follow-up call from someone impersonating the CEO's assistant pressured the HR executive to change direct deposit details for several employees, redirecting funds to attacker-controlled accounts.

This approach exploits the assumption that no attacker would have the capability to communicate so seamlessly across multiple platforms. It also leverages psychological triggers such as urgency, authority, and consistency.

10.7.4 Business Email Compromise (BEC)

Business Email Compromise (BEC) is a sophisticated form of social engineering attack where cybercriminals infiltrate or spoof a company's email system to manipulate employees into transferring funds, revealing sensitive data, or altering financial records. Unlike spam-based phishing attacks, BEC is highly targeted, leveraging prior investigation to craft convincing messages that appear to originate from executives, suppliers, or internal departments.

Key characteristics

- Targets key personnel in finance, HR, or executive roles
- Messages often involve urgent financial or administrative requests
- Exploits trust in internal communication channels

Techniques used

- **Email spoofing**: Forging sender addresses to appear legitimate
- **Credential theft**: Using phishing emails to gain access to executive mailboxes
- **Conversation hijacking**: Monitoring real email threads and inserting fraudulent replies
- **Domain impersonation**: Registering similar domains (e.g., @micros0ft.com vs. @microsoft.com)

Example

A global construction company lost over $70 million after an attacker posed as a legitimate vendor and requested a change in bank details for pending invoices.

Table 10.4 BEC scenarios and requests

Scenario	Impersonated party	Typical request
Vendor payment fraud	External supplier	Change of bank account for invoice payment
CEO fraud	Company executive	Urgent wire transfer for a confidential deal
Payroll diversion	HR or finance staff	Change in direct deposit details
Legal impersonation	Law firm or counsel	Request for settlement payments

The attacker had previously gained access to internal emails, allowing them to time the request perfectly and mimic the communication style of both parties.

Common BEC scenarios

Table 10.4 portrays the common BEC scenarios and allied requests.

10.7.5 Cloud and SaaS exploits

As more organizations transition to cloud-based environments and software-as-a-service (SaaS) platforms, the attack surface for social engineering widens significantly. These platforms, ranging from productivity suites like Microsoft 365 and Google Workspace to collaboration tools like Slack, Trello, and Zoom, become lucrative targets for cybercriminals seeking access to business operations, data, and communications.

How do attackers exploit cloud and SaaS?

- **Credential phishing**: Attackers send emails resembling legitimate login pages for Microsoft, Google, or Adobe services, often using OAuth (Open Authorization) scams to trick users into granting app permissions.
- **Third-party integrations**: Many SaaS platforms integrate with third-party apps. Attackers may exploit poorly secured plugins or extensions to gain access to cloud data.
- **Token hijacking**: Session tokens stored in cookies or Uniform Resource Locators (URLs) can be intercepted, giving attackers persistent access without needing passwords.
- **Insider threats**: Malicious or negligent insiders may abuse their access to cloud resources, especially in organizations lacking granular access controls.

Example

In 2020, attackers exploited a misconfigured Google Workspace add-on that had excessive privileges. Through phishing, they tricked users into authorizing the add-on, which then harvested email metadata and contact lists, feeding further spear-phishing campaigns.

10.7.6 Remote work vulnerabilities

The rapid and widespread adoption of remote work has created new avenues for social engineering attacks. While remote work offers flexibility and continuity, it also shifts a significant portion of organizational operations to less secure home environments, where traditional cybersecurity controls may be weaker or absent.

Key vulnerabilities introduced by remote work

- **Unsecured home networks**: Home Wi-Fi routers often lack enterprise-grade security settings and may not be updated regularly, making them susceptible to network intrusion.
- **Use of personal devices**: Employees may access corporate systems using personal laptops or mobile phones that lack proper endpoint protection, anti-virus software, or data encryption.
- **Shared workspaces**: Working in shared environments increases the risk of shoulder surfing, physical device access, or accidental information disclosure.
- **Informal communication tools**: Reliance on messaging apps like WhatsApp, Telegram, or personal email for professional communication creates unmonitored, insecure channels ripe for exploitation.

Social engineering in remote contexts

- **Fake meeting invites**: Attackers impersonate popular conferencing tools like Zoom or Microsoft Teams to send phishing links disguised as meeting requests or calendar updates.
- **IT support impersonation**: Employees working remotely are more likely to fall for fake IT helpdesk messages, especially when facing technical issues.
- **VPN and MFA fatigue exploits**: Attackers send fake VPN alerts or repeated MFA prompts, tricking users into approving illegitimate login requests.

Example

During the height of the COVID-19 pandemic, a major consulting firm experienced a breach when an employee clicked on a fake "mandatory Zoom security update" link. The phishing site harvested credentials, granting attackers access to internal documents shared over cloud platforms.

10.8 Detection and prevention techniques

Preventing and detecting social engineering attacks requires a comprehensive defense-in-depth approach that combines people, processes, and technology. No single solution can stop all attacks, but when multiple layers of defense are in place, the risk is significantly reduced. The sections below cover the different approaches that can help detect and prevent social engineering attacks.

10.8.1 User awareness and training

Humans are often the weakest link in cybersecurity, making training the most critical preventive measure.

- Regular awareness campaigns: Run periodic campaigns educating employees on phishing, baiting, and impersonation tactics.

- Simulated attacks: Use controlled phishing simulations to evaluate user response and reinforce training.
- Interactive learning modules: Provide video-based or gamified modules to improve retention.
- Role-specific training: Customize content for executives, HR, finance, and IT teams based on their risk exposure.

10.8.2 Organizational policies and procedures

- Verification protocols: Establish clear processes for verifying requests related to finance, HR, or sensitive data.
- Incident reporting mechanisms: Encourage a culture of early reporting without blame.
- Access management policies: Implement the principle of least privilege and enforce role-based access control.
- Document control: Prevent unauthorized sharing of sensitive documents or credentials.

10.8.3 Technical controls

- Multi-Factor Authentication (MFA): A critical safeguard that prevents unauthorized access even if credentials are compromised.
- Endpoint Detection and Response (EDR): Detects anomalous user behavior and system-level changes.
- Email gateways: Tools like Mimecast or Proofpoint can block phishing, spoofed domains, and malicious attachments.
- Secure Web Gateways (SWG): Prevent users from accessing dangerous websites or links.
- Browser isolation: Opens unknown URLs in sandbox environments, preventing malware installation.

10.8.4 Behavioral analytics and AI monitoring

- User and Entity Behavior Analytics (UEBA): Uses AI to establish user baselines and alert to deviations.
- SIEM (Security Information and Event Management) Integration: Tools like Splunk or IBM QRadar correlate logs and raise red flags in real time.
- Phishing detection engines: Modern tools can scan the tone, grammar, and structure of emails to detect impersonation.

10.8.5 Physical and environmental controls

- Badge and access control systems: Prevent unauthorized entry via tailgating or impersonation.
- Secure workstations: Use automatic screen locks and disable external ports.
- Awareness posters and reminders: Physical cues can reinforce digital training.

10.8.6 Metrics and continuous improvement

- Track metrics such as phishing click-through rates, incident response times, and training completion rates.
- Conduct periodic audits and red-team exercises to identify weak spots.
- Implement feedback loops from incidents to improve processes and systems.

10.9 Legal and ethical aspects

Social engineering may involve psychological manipulation, but the legal and ethical consequences are very tangible. It lies at the intersection of cybersecurity, privacy law, criminal fraud, and ethical behavior in both offensive and defensive practices. Organizations and individuals must understand not only how social engineering attacks occur but also the laws that govern them and the ethical boundaries when simulating or responding to such threats.

The sections below cover the legal implications of social engineering attacks. Social engineering can trigger a wide range of legal liabilities for both attackers and affected organizations. Depending on the jurisdiction, successful or even attempted attacks may violate several acts, resulting in fines, criminal prosecution, or reputational damage.

10.9.1 Data protection and privacy laws

Data protection laws mandate how personal and sensitive information should be collected, stored, and shared. When social engineering leads to unauthorized access or data disclosure, organizations may be held liable under these laws, even if the breach occurred through human error.

- General Data Protection Regulation (GDPR): The EU's flagship privacy law imposes heavy fines (up to 4% of annual global turnover) for breaches involving mishandling or exposure of personal data, regardless of intent.
- Health Insurance Portability and Accountability Act (HIPAA): In the US, healthcare entities must ensure protected health information (PHI) is secure. If a phishing attack results in unauthorized access, both civil and criminal penalties may apply.
- California Consumer Privacy Act (CCPA): Companies operating in California must protect consumer data. Even if an employee is manipulated into leaking data, the company may face legal claims unless strong preventive measures are in place.

10.9.2 Fraud and impersonation statutes

Social engineering is often used to impersonate someone in authority, extract sensitive data, or authorize financial transactions. These actions typically violate national anti-fraud and cybercrime laws.

- Computer Fraud and Abuse Act (US): Criminalizes unauthorized access to computer systems, which includes access gained via deceptive tactics.

- UK Fraud Act (2006): Covers false representation and failure to disclose information, both common in social engineering schemes.
- Indian IT Act (Sections 66C and 66D): Penalizes identity theft and impersonation using electronic means, carrying imprisonment and monetary penalties.

Laws are being expanded to include advanced techniques like voice cloning and phishing-as-a-service, which further criminalize even the tools used in these attacks.

10.9.3 Corporate liability and duty of care

Beyond the actions of external attackers, companies may be held responsible if it is found that they failed to provide adequate cybersecurity measures or awareness training. Courts and regulators increasingly expect businesses to anticipate social engineering risks and act proactively.

- Organizations must demonstrate they have implemented industry-standard controls and regularly trained staff on how to recognize and report threats.
- Failure to act or report incidents promptly may constitute negligence, attracting lawsuits from clients or customers whose data or funds were affected.
- Insurance policies may also deny claims if negligence can be demonstrated, compounding the financial loss.

Duty of care is not just a legal expectation; it is a corporate governance issue tied to brand trust and stakeholder confidence.

10.9.4 Red teaming and penetration testing

To prepare for real attacks, companies often engage ethical hackers or "red teams" to test their employees' susceptibility to deception tactics. These simulated social engineering engagements are valuable but must be conducted within clear ethical boundaries.

- Authorization: Every exercise must be approved by executive leadership or risk/legal teams to ensure legality.
- Scope limitation: The simulation must avoid areas like personal harassment, emotional triggers, or exposure of sensitive data.
- Documentation: The test plan, actions taken, and outcomes must be logged and reviewed to demonstrate compliance and ensure accountability.

Refer to Table 10.5 for the key ethical principles. Failure to follow these principles can turn a learning opportunity into a legal liability or PR (public relations) disaster.

Table 10.5 Key ethical principles and description

Principle	**Description**
Informed consent	Participants or leadership must be aware of or approve the test in advance.
Minimal harm	Tests should not cause humiliation, panic, or reputational damage.
Debriefing	Employees must receive constructive feedback and learning after the test.

10.9.5 Gray areas and emerging risks

As social engineering simulations evolve, new ethical and legal dilemmas emerge, especially with the use of technologies like AI and the application of social tactics in non-cyber contexts.

- Deepfake simulations: Some red teams now use AI-generated audio or video to impersonate CEOs or colleagues. Without explicit disclosure and control, this can cross into ethical misconduct or even violate consent laws.
- Social engineering in hiring processes: Using social engineering to test a candidate's "real-world awareness" during recruitment, without informed consent, is both deceptive and legally questionable. It may breach employment law or discrimination statutes.

Organizations must tread carefully when innovating security testing methods. The line between simulation and violation is thin, and staying on the right side of ethics and law is essential.

10.10 Tools and technologies for defense

While human vigilance is essential, defending against social engineering also requires a comprehensive technological foundation. Tools and technologies form the backbone of a layered security model, providing visibility, automation, and rapid response capabilities. These solutions work across various digital surfaces, email, cloud, devices, networks, and identities to detect, prevent, and respond to manipulation-based threats in real time.

This section explores the essential categories of security technologies, the role they play in thwarting social engineering, and examples of leading tools in each space.

10.10.1 User awareness and simulation platforms

Training employees to recognize and respond to social engineering attempts is the most critical defense layer. Awareness platforms educate users through real-world phishing simulations, interactive training, and behavioral analytics. These tools, as seen in Table 10.6, not only reinforce good security hygiene but also help organizations assess and improve their human firewall over time.

Table 10.6 Tools for defense simulation

Tool	Features
KnowBe4	Phishing simulations, interactive training modules, and risk scoring for users.
Cofense	Enterprise-level phishing awareness, user reporting plugin, and threat intelligence integration.
Hoxhunt	Gamified phishing simulation and response tracking customized by employee behavior.

Value: Reduces employee susceptibility to deceptive techniques and provides measurable awareness metrics.

10.10.2 Email security gateways and anti-phishing tools

Email remains the most frequently exploited vector in social engineering. Secure Email Gateways (SEGs) and phishing protection tools scan, block, and quarantine malicious content before it reaches end users. They defend against phishing, spoofing, domain impersonation, and business email compromise (BEC). Table 10.7 provides the list of such tools along with their capabilities.

10.10.3 Endpoint Detection and Response (EDR) tools

Endpoints are primary targets in social engineering schemes, especially when attacks succeed in delivering payloads like spyware or ransomware. EDR solutions continuously monitor endpoints for malicious behavior, anomalies, and suspicious file execution. They provide detection, isolation, and automated remediation features. Refer to Table 10.8.

10.10.4 Identity and Access Management (IAM) tools

IAM systems manage how users authenticate and what systems they can access. In the event of a credential theft via phishing, IAM tools, as listed in Table 10.9, enforce strong authentication policies such as multi-factor authentication (MFA),

Table 10.7 Email security gateways and tools

Tool	**Key capabilities**
Proofpoint	Threat intelligence, URL rewriting, spoof detection, and BEC protection.
Mimecast	Real-time link analysis, attachment sandboxing, and impersonation detection.
Microsoft Defender for Office 365	Safe Links/Safe Attachments, phishing AI, and policy-based alerts.

Value: Intercepts email-based threats at the gateway, preventing them from reaching user inboxes.

Table 10.8 Endpoint detection and response tools

Tool	**Key capabilities**
CrowdStrike Falcon	Behavioral analysis, real-time threat detection, quarantine, and remote investigation.
SentinelOne	Autonomous detection and rollback of malicious activity.
Tanium	Unified endpoint visibility and threat hunting across distributed systems.

Value: Detects malware and system compromise early, before an attacker can move laterally or escalate privileges.

Table 10.9 Identity and access management tools

Tool	Key capabilities
Okta	Single Sign-On (SSO), Multi-Factor Authentication (MFA), and identity governance.
Duo Security	Adaptive MFA, device trust, and secure login enforcement.
Ping Identity	Centralized identity control with AI-powered threat detection.

Value: Protects accounts from compromise even if credentials are exposed through social engineering.

Table 10.10 Cloud access security broker tools

Tool	Capabilities
Netskope	SaaS visibility, anomaly detection, and user behavior analytics.
Microsoft Defender for Cloud Apps	OAuth abuse monitoring, risky app blocking, and session control.
McAfee MVISION Cloud	Shadow IT discovery, DLP (Data Loss Prevention) enforcement, and cloud-native threat detection.

Value: Protects cloud data from compromise, especially when access is gained through social engineering tricks.

conditional access, and identity-based analytics to prevent unauthorized access to critical assets.

10.10.5 Cloud Access Security Brokers (CASBs)

With the rise of SaaS adoption, organizations need tools to monitor and secure user behavior in cloud applications. CASBs provide visibility into cloud usage, enforce data policies, detect anomalies, and prevent unauthorized file sharing. They are particularly effective when social engineering targets cloud platforms through phishing or app authorization. Refer to Table 10.10 for the tools and their capabilities.

10.10.6 Security Information and Event Management (SIEM) systems

SIEM systems gather logs from endpoints, networks, email, cloud, and applications, then correlate that data to detect patterns associated with social engineering attacks, such as unusual logins or unauthorized access attempts. SIEMs are the nerve center of incident detection and response. Refer to Table 10.11.

10.10.7 Browser and web security solutions

Phishing often involves redirecting users to malicious websites or forms. Browser isolation and Domain Name System (DNS)-based web filtering tools provide safe

Table 10.11 SIEM tools

Tool	Features
Splunk	Advanced analytics, UEBA integration, and custom dashboards.
IBM QRadar	Correlation rules for phishing, identity misuse, and access anomalies.
LogRhythm Tool	Real-time alerting, behavior analytics, and compliance reporting. Features

Value: Helps security teams detect and respond to manipulation-based attacks with speed and context.

Table 10.12 Browser and web security tools

Tool	Key capabilities
Menlo Security	Remote browser isolation to eliminate web-based threats.
Zscaler Internet Access	Cloud firewall, DNS security, and SSL inspection.
Cloudflare Gateway	Secure DNS, URL filtering, and browser-based access policies.

Value: Prevents malicious websites, fake login pages, and drive-by malware from executing on user systems.

Table 10.13 Threat detection and anomaly detection tools

Tool	Capabilities
Recorded Future	Real-time threat intelligence and domain/IP reputation scoring.
Darktrace	AI-driven behavior modeling to detect insider threats or account misuse.
Anomali	Threat feed aggregation and automated incident correlation.

Value: Enhances situational awareness and allows proactive threat hunting based on known attack patterns.

web experiences by either blocking suspicious domains or rendering potentially dangerous sites in isolated environments. Refer to Table 10.12 for the browser and web security tools.

10.10.8 Threat intelligence and anomaly detection

Threat intelligence platforms and anomaly detection tools, as seen from Table 10.13, help predict, detect, and contextualize social engineering attacks by analyzing threat actor behaviors, domain/IP reputation, and user activity deviations.

Key points to remember

- Social engineering attacks exploit human psychology, such as trust, urgency, fear, and authority, rather than technical vulnerabilities.

- These attacks follow a lifecycle: reconnaissance, engagement, exploitation, execution, and exit, each requiring different defense strategies.
- Common types of social engineering include phishing, vishing, smishing, baiting, pretexting, quid pro quo, and physical attacks like tailgating.
- Psychological triggers are central to manipulation; attackers frequently use authority, urgency, fear, reciprocity, curiosity, scarcity, and social proof.
- Real-world cases (e.g., Google/Facebook invoice fraud, RSA breach, Colonial Pipeline attack) highlight how even large organizations are vulnerable.
- Modern digital threats include deepfakes, AI-generated emails, and voice cloning, making attacks harder to detect and more convincing.
- Social media platforms are a rich source of intelligence for attackers, who use personal and professional data to craft realistic attack narratives.
- Multi-channel attacks (combining email, SMS, and phone) increase credibility and success rate by reinforcing the scam through different mediums.
- Business Email Compromise (BEC) is among the most financially damaging attack types, often bypassing technical controls through impersonation and timing.
- Remote work and increased SaaS/cloud usage have expanded the attack surface, making endpoint security and cloud governance critical.
- Prevention requires a multi-layered defense strategy combining user training, secure email gateways, endpoint protection, identity management, and real-time monitoring.
- Tools like KnowBe4, Proofpoint, CrowdStrike, Okta, Netskope, and Splunk play key roles in defending against various attack vectors.
- Ethical hacking (e.g., red teaming) must follow principles like informed consent, minimal harm, and proper debriefing to remain lawful and constructive.
- Legal frameworks like GDPR, HIPAA, CCPA, and various fraud statutes impose strict penalties for breaches and require proactive security measures.
- Building a cyber-resilient culture involves integrating technology with continuous employee education, behavior analytics, and zero-trust principles.
- As attacks become more automated and AI-enhanced, future defenses will rely heavily on biometrics, deepfake detection, behavioral modeling, and adaptive authentication.

Questions (try answering this yourself)

1. Define social engineering in the context of cybersecurity and explain why it is considered one of the most dangerous attack methods.
2. How do social engineering attacks differ from traditional cyberattacks targeting technical vulnerabilities?
3. Discuss the role of human psychology in enabling social engineering attacks. Provide three examples of common psychological triggers.
4. Explain why employee training is critical in reducing the risks of social engineering.

5. Describe the lifecycle of a social engineering attack and explain how defenders can intervene at each stage.
6. What are the major types of phishing attacks? Explain how they differ from each other.
7. Compare smishing and vishing, providing real-world examples of how attackers use them.
8. Explain the concept of baiting in social engineering. How do physical and online baiting differ?
9. What is pretexting, and why does it often succeed compared to phishing?
10. Define quid pro quo in the context of social engineering and give examples of how it can compromise organizations.
11. Differentiate between tailgating and piggybacking. Why are physical access attacks still effective today?
12. Using the 2020 Twitter Bitcoin scam, map each stage of the attack lifecycle to actions taken by the attackers.
13. Discuss the role of authority and urgency in successful social engineering campaigns. Give case examples.
14. How do fear and anxiety influence victims during phishing or vishing attempts?
15. What role does reciprocity play in social engineering? Provide an example scenario.
16. Evaluate how modern technologies like AI and deepfakes increase the effectiveness of social engineering attacks.
17. Explain how attackers use social media mining for reconnaissance. What preventive steps can organizations take?
18. Discuss the impact of remote work on the rise of social engineering attacks. Mention at least three vulnerabilities.
19. What is Business Email Compromise (BEC)? Provide examples of common BEC scenarios and their outcomes.
20. Outline the key legal, ethical, and technological measures that organizations must adopt to defend against social engineering attacks.

Objective questions

1. Social engineering primarily exploits:
   (a) Software bugs
   (b) Human psychology
   (c) Hardware flaws
   (d) Network latency

2. Which factor best distinguishes social engineering from traditional cyberattacks?
   (a) Use of zero-day exploits
   (b) Focus on human manipulation over technical flaws
   (c) Reliance on DDoS

   (d) Need for admin privileges

3. Which is not a phishing variant?
   (a) Spear phishing
   (b) Whaling
   (c) Clone phishing
   (d) Port scanning

4. Smishing refers to:
   (a) Phone-call impersonation
   (b) SMS-based phishing
   (c) USB bait drops
   (d) Social media scraping

5. Vishing attacks typically involve:
   (a) QR codes
   (b) Voice calls impersonating trusted entities
   (c) Hardware trojans
   (d) Drive-by downloads

6. Baiting relies most on which trigger?
   (a) Scarcity
   (b) Curiosity
   (c) Authority
   (d) Social proof

7. Pretexting differs from phishing mainly because it:
   (a) Uses urgency and fear
   (b) Builds a credible scenario/identity over time
   (c) Always uses SMS
   (d) Requires malware execution

8. Quid pro quo attacks generally offer:
   (a) Free VPNs with MFA
   (b) A benefit in exchange for access/info
   (c) System patches via vendors
   (d) Encrypted backups

9. Tailgating is best described as:
   (a) Email spoofing
   (b) Following an authorized person into a secure area
   (c) Browser hijacking
   (d) Credential stuffing

10. In the attack lifecycle, reconnaissance most likely includes:
   (a) Exfiltrating data
   (b) Deleting logs
   (c) Mining LinkedIn and corporate sites
   (d) Launching ransomware

11. The 2020 Twitter Bitcoin scam prominently involved:
    (a) Supply-chain malware
    (b) Insider manipulation and vishing
    (c) Bluetooth exploits
    (d) DNS poisoning
12. Which pair are common psychological triggers in social engineering?
    (a) Redundancy and parity
    (b) Authority and urgency
    (c) Hashing and salting
    (d) Elasticity and scalability
13. Deepfake-enabled attacks most directly enhance:
    (a) SQL injection
    (b) Identity impersonation via audio/video
    (c) Buffer overflows
    (d) ARP spoofing
14. Social media mining primarily supports which phase?
    (a) Engagement
    (b) Reconnaissance
    (c) Exit and cover-up
    (d) Exploitation
15. Multi-channel campaigns increase success by:
    (a) Using only encrypted email
    (b) Reinforcing the narrative across email/SMS/calls
    (c) Disabling MFA
    (d) Blocking SEGs
16. Business Email Compromise (BEC) commonly involves:
    (a) Random mass mailing
    (b) Vendor payment fraud and CEO impersonation
    (c) Browser zero-days
    (d) BIOS tampering
17. In cloud/SaaS-targeted social engineering, a frequent tactic is:
    (a) OAuth consent phishing to gain app permissions
    (b) Cold boot attacks
    (c) DMA memory reads
    (d) Rowhammer
18. A remote-work–specific risk is:
    (a) Spoofed GPS signals
    (b) Fake meeting invites and MFA fatigue prompts
    (c) Quantum key cracking
    (d) Fiber tap injection

19. Which control primarily reduces credential phishing risk?
    (a) Disabling TLS
    (b) Multi-Factor Authentication (MFA)
    (c) Port mirroring
    (d) UDP tunneling
20. A metric useful for continuous improvement against social engineering is:
    (a) Average disk IOPS
    (b) Phishing click-through rate
    (c) CPU cache misses
    (d) MTBF of UPS units

Answer keys for objective questions:

1. b
2. b
3. d
4. b
5. b
6. b
7. b
8. b
9. b
10. c
11. b
12. b
13. b
14. b
15. b
16. b
17. a
18. b
19. b
20. b

Further reading

[1] Hadnagy C. *Social Engineering: The Art of Human Hacking*. Hoboken, NJ: Wiley; 2010.
[2] Hadnagy C. *Social Engineering: The Science of Human Hacking*. 2nd ed. Hoboken, NJ: Wiley; 2018.
[3] Mitnick KD, and Simon WL. *The Art of Deception: Controlling the Human Element of Security*. Hoboken, NJ: Wiley; 2002.
[4] Hadnagy C. *Unmasking the Social Engineer: The Human Element of Security*. Hoboken, NJ: Wiley; 2014.

[5] Shapiro SJ. *Fancy Bear Goes Phishing*. New York: Farrar, Straus and Giroux; 2023.

[6] Karagiannopoulos V, Nurse JRC, and Li S. *Social Engineering in Cybersecurity: Threats and Defenses*. London: Routledge; 2023.

[7] Bhujade RK, and Bhattacharya S (eds.). *Effective Strategies for Combatting Social Engineering*. Hershey, PA: IGI Global; 2024.

[8] SANS Institute. *SEC467: Social Engineering for Security Professionals [Course]*. Bethesda, MD: SANS Institute; [cited 2025].

[9] Cybrary. *Social Engineering Course [Online course]*. Cybrary; [cited 2025].

[10] LinkedIn Learning. *Cybersecurity Awareness: Social Engineering [Online course]*. LinkedIn; [cited 2025].

[11] CQURE Academy. *Social Engineering and Phishing Mastery [Course]*. CQURE; [cited 2025].

[12] Udemy. *Cybersecurity Social Engineering Courses [Online course]*. Udemy; [cited 2025].

[13] Alhassan J, Karagiannopoulos V, and Nurse JRC. Social engineering in cybersecurity: a domain ontology and knowledge graph application. *Cybersecur*. Springer; 2023.

[14] Alotaibi A, Alhaidari FA, and Alshamrani A. A study on the psychology of social engineering-based cyberattacks. *Appl Sci*. Basel: MDPI; 2022.

[15] Chapagain D, Kshetri N, Aryal B, and Dhakal B. SEAtech: Deception techniques in social engineering attacks. *arXiv preprint*. arXiv:2408.02092, 2024.

[16] Schmitt M, and Flechais I. Digital deception: generative artificial intelligence in social engineering and phishing. *Artif Intell Rev*. 2024;57:324.

[17] Falade PV. Decoding the threat landscape: ChatGPT, FraudGPT, and WormGPT in social engineering attacks. *Journal of Scientific Research in Computer Science, Engineering and Information Technology*. 2023;9(5): 185–198.

Chapter 11

Social media attacks

Learning objectives

After completing this chapter, readers will be able to

(a) Define and understand the concept of social media attacks and their growing relevance in cybersecurity.
(b) Identify the major types of social media-based attacks and their impact on individuals, businesses, and the banking sector.
(c) Analyze common scams and phishing techniques used across popular platforms such as Facebook, Instagram, LinkedIn, and X (formerly Twitter).
(d) Recognize how social media channels are exploited to execute digital payment fraud and data theft.
(e) Understand the role of fake handles and impersonation campaigns in identity theft and misinformation.
(f) Apply best practices to safeguard personal and institutional data on social platforms.
(g) Correlate real-world case studies to evaluate mitigation and response strategies.
(h) Explore further learning resources, regulatory guidelines, and emerging trends in social media cybersecurity.

11.1 Introduction

Social media has undergone a dramatic transformation in the past two decades. What began as simple online networking spaces designed to connect friends and colleagues has now grown into a **vast global ecosystem** that influences commerce, communication, culture, and even geopolitics. Platforms such as Facebook, Instagram, LinkedIn, YouTube, and X (formerly Twitter) collectively host **billions of active users**, exchanging content, financial transactions, and personal data at unprecedented volumes and speeds. This interconnectedness makes social media one of the most powerful tools of the digital age, yet it simultaneously creates one of the **largest and fastest-growing attack surfaces for cybercriminals**.

The digital economy increasingly depends on social platforms for advertising, e-commerce, recruitment, customer engagement, and payments. At the same time, **cybercriminals follow the data and money**, exploiting the trust inherent in online interactions. Unlike corporate systems that are typically hardened with firewalls, strict authentication, and layered defenses, social media is built on principles of **openness and user engagement**. This design philosophy, while fueling global communication, introduces vulnerabilities that attackers manipulate with ease.

11.1.1 The shift from technical exploits to human-centric attacks

Traditional cyberattacks often relied on technical flaws such as unpatched software, weak encryption, or unsecured networks. Social media, however, presents a different paradigm. Threats on these platforms primarily **exploit human psychology, trust, curiosity, greed, and urgency, rather than technical loopholes.**

For example, phishing scams on email typically require crafting a convincing domain or spoofing an email address. On social media, attackers bypass this hurdle by simply creating a fake profile that appears to belong to a legitimate individual, brand, or institution. Since users inherently trust content that comes from a "friend" or familiar account, they are far more likely to click on malicious links or disclose sensitive information.

The **virality of social media** amplifies this risk. A single malicious link or fake investment post can spread across thousands of accounts in minutes, weaponizing the platform's sharing mechanism. In this sense, users themselves often become **both targets and unwitting accomplices**, distributing the very attacks that compromise their peers.

11.1.2 Common cyber threats on social media

1. **Identity theft and profile cloning**
   Attackers clone the identity of a real user, often copying photos, bio information, and friend lists. Once established, these fake accounts trick victims into sharing private information or sending money. Identity theft can also be leveraged to damage reputations or impersonate executives (a tactic known as *CEO fraud*).
2. **Phishing and impersonation scams**
   Fraudulent messages or posts appear to originate from legitimate institutions, such as banks, tech companies, or government agencies. For example, a fake "account verification" message from a social platform may trick users into entering their login details on a counterfeit site, granting attackers direct account access.
3. **Social engineering manipulation**
   Cybercriminals use social media as a goldmine of personal data, birthdays, employment history, and family connections that can be exploited to manipulate targets. Attackers craft convincing narratives to persuade users to reveal sensitive data, such as credit card numbers or one-time passwords.
4. **Digital payment and investment frauds**
   The rise of integrated payment systems and social commerce (Instagram shops, Facebook Marketplace, and YouTube live shopping) has opened new channels

for fraud. Criminals post fake offers, run investment scams promising high returns, or send fraudulent fund requests that prey on victims' trust.

5. **Misinformation and malware distribution**
   Beyond financial fraud, social media is also used to spread malware through disguised downloads or malicious advertisements. In some cases, misinformation campaigns themselves are weaponized to destabilize organizations, economies, or political systems.

11.1.3 Why are social media threats unique?

What sets social media threats apart from conventional cyberattacks is their **emotional and psychological foundation**. Whereas traditional cybercrime may rely on brute force or malware, social media exploits rely on:

- **Trust:** People assume that messages from friends, followers, or verified-looking accounts are legitimate.
- **Emotions:** Attackers use urgency ("Your account will be deleted!"), greed ("Win a free iPhone"), or fear ("Your bank account has been compromised") to manipulate decision-making.
- **Virality:** Content designed to spread quickly (clickbait, sensational headlines) doubles as a delivery mechanism for attacks.
- **Blended roles of users:** On social media, individuals are not just consumers but also **distributors of content**. Once compromised, they amplify the attack by unintentionally spreading malicious links within their own trusted networks.

These factors make social media an **ideal hunting ground for cybercriminals**, combining low barriers to entry with high reward potential.

11.1.4 The expanding scope of threats

The risks associated with social media extend far beyond individual users. Corporations face brand impersonation attacks, where fraudsters create fake company pages to scam customers. Banks and financial institutions are increasingly targeted with phishing campaigns that mimic customer service interactions. Even governments are vulnerable, as disinformation campaigns have demonstrated their ability to sway public opinion and disrupt democratic processes.

Moreover, the rise of artificial intelligence-generated content (deepfakes, AI-written posts) adds another layer of complexity. Attackers can now generate realistic audio, video, or text to impersonate executives, spread disinformation, or manipulate markets. For example, a deepfake video of a CEO announcing false financial results could cause real-world stock market fluctuations.

Social media has evolved into a **double-edged sword**: while it empowers communication, commerce, and global connectivity, it simultaneously creates fertile ground for cybercriminals. Platforms like Facebook, Instagram, LinkedIn, YouTube, and X host billions of interactions daily, each one a potential opportunity for exploitation. Unlike traditional cyberattacks, which often exploit technical

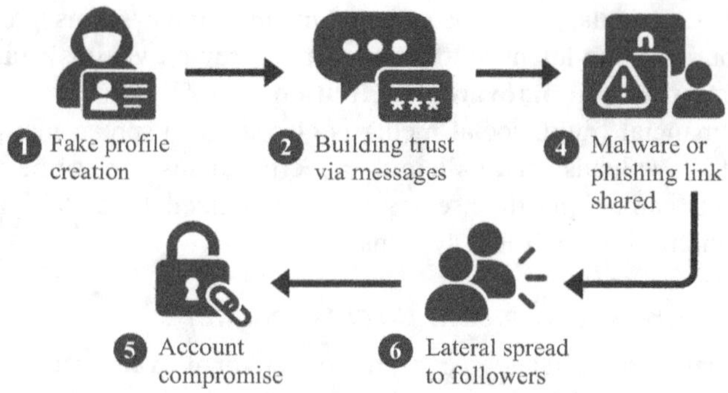

Figure 11.1 Anatomy of a social media attack

flaws, social media threats exploit **trust, emotions, and virality**, making them deeply human in nature.

In this landscape, awareness and proactive defenses are critical. Both individual users and organizations must recognize that social media is not just a communication tool but also a **critical vector in modern cyber warfare and fraud ecosystems**. The challenge for the future lies in striking a balance between openness and security, ensuring that social media continues to be a force for connection without becoming a persistent channel for exploitation.

Figure 11.1 illustrates the anatomy of a social media attack, tracing the process from fake profile creation to lateral spread among followers.

11.1.5 Example 1: the "Help Me Urgently" scam

One of the most emotionally manipulative scams on social media is the so-called "Help Me Urgently" scam, which thrives on exploiting trust and panic. In this scheme, a cybercriminal creates a fake account that perfectly mimics a victim's close friend, family member, or colleague. They often copy the profile photo, name, and even mutual connections, making the impersonation appear authentic.

The attacker then sends a message along the lines of

"Hey, I'm stuck abroad. Can you send ₹5,000 quickly via UPI?"

The urgency of the message is deliberate; it triggers a strong emotional response where the victim focuses on helping rather than questioning authenticity. Because the request comes from a seemingly trusted profile, victims often bypass verification steps and immediately transfer money. Only later do they discover that the handle was fake, the funds are unrecoverable, and the real friend never made such a request.

This type of scam demonstrates the psychological engineering power of social media attacks. Unlike phishing emails, where poor grammar or suspicious domains can raise red flags, here, the trust is embedded in the identity itself. It also shows how criminals leverage instant payment systems (like UPI or PayPal) to collect funds quickly before detection.

Lesson learned: Always verify urgent financial requests through a second channel, such as a phone call, before transferring funds. Social media, no matter how convincing, should never be the sole basis for financial transactions.

11.1.6 Example 2: LinkedIn job offer scam

The professional networking platform LinkedIn has become a hunting ground for fraudsters seeking to exploit job seekers' aspirations. One of the most widespread schemes is the "fake job offer" scam.

In this case, attackers create a professional-looking recruiter profile, often claiming to represent well-known multinational companies. They send connection requests to potential candidates, followed by attractive job offers, sometimes promising roles in established firms or lucrative work-from-home opportunities.

The message typically contains a link to an "application portal." On clicking, the victim is either:

1. Redirected to a malicious website that mimics an official company page, where they are asked to enter personal details, login credentials, or even passport and PAN information, or
2. Tricked into downloading malware disguised as an application form or HR document.

In many cases, the stolen credentials are later used for identity theft, unauthorized access to corporate systems, or financial fraud. Some variants of the scam even demand an "advance processing fee," exploiting desperate job seekers financially as well as digitally.

This attack highlights how cybercriminals target not only money but also valuable identity data, which can be sold on the dark web or used to penetrate corporate networks. As hiring increasingly shifts to online platforms, such scams undermine trust in digital recruitment.

Lesson learned: Candidates should verify recruiter identities, cross-check job postings on official company websites, and avoid downloading files or sharing sensitive details outside verified portals. Companies, in turn, must actively monitor LinkedIn and other platforms for fraudulent accounts impersonating their brand.

11.2 Scenarios and typical examples

Social media attacks can be categorized based on intent, target, and technique, as depicted in Table 11.1.

11.2.1 Real-world scenario: Twitter Bitcoin scam (2020)

In July 2020, hackers gained access to high-profile Twitter accounts (including those of global figures and companies). They posted cryptocurrency donation requests promising double returns.

Table 11.1 Social media attacks summary

Attack type	Platform	Method	Example	Impact
Phishing links	Facebook, Instagram	Malicious URLs in messages	"Click to verify your account"	Credential theft
Fake giveaways	X (Twitter), YouTube	Scam promotions	"Win an iPhone - send ₹499 for verification"	Monetary loss
Fake job offers	LinkedIn	Impersonating recruiters	"You're shortlisted - pay ₹1,000 for registration"	Financial + identity loss
Catfishing	Instagram, Dating Apps	Emotional manipulation	Fake romantic interest	Psychological + data exposure
Malware sharing	WhatsApp, Telegram	Forwarded attachments	"Festival wishes video" carrying a Trojan	Device compromise

Figure 11.2 Types of social media threats

Within hours, they collected **over $100,000 in Bitcoin**, showcasing how powerful social media manipulation can be when backed by verified accounts.

One can have a look at Figure 11.2 to understand the types of social media threats.

11.3 Scams

Social media scams have evolved from simple chain messages into **multi-layered, AI-assisted deception ecosystems**. These scams exploit human psychology, greed, urgency, empathy, and curiosity.

11.3.1 Giveaway and lottery scams

Users are told they have won prizes or vouchers. The scam demands a **"processing fee"** or card details to claim the reward. *Example:* Fake "Amazon Gift Voucher" campaigns spread through Facebook and WhatsApp.

11.3.2 Investment and crypto scams

Fraudsters impersonate investment advisers or influencers promoting high-return crypto projects. They use doctored screenshots of "profit statements" to build credibility.

11.3.2.1 Case study

In 2023, Indian authorities arrested scammers behind fake Telegram crypto groups that duped investors of ₹150 crore through false portfolio dashboards.

11.3.3 Romance and emotional manipulation scams

Often known as *catfishing*, attackers build emotional relationships and request financial help. Victims hesitate to report due to embarrassment.

11.3.4 Charity and disaster-relief scams

During crises (e.g., earthquakes, floods, or pandemics), fake charity accounts solicit donations.

Example: Several fake COVID-19 relief pages collected funds without any traceable NGO (Non-Governmental Organization) registration.

11.3.5 Brand impersonation

Attackers clone verified company pages to offer "customer support" links that redirect to phishing pages.

Example: "Your account has been suspended - click here to appeal" links often mimic Facebook or Paytm interfaces.

One can refer to Figure 11.3 to visualize the psychological triggers used in social media scams.

11.4 Digital payment frauds

Social media is increasingly used to initiate or disguise financial frauds, particularly via UPI and wallet-based systems.

11.4.1 Fake storefronts

Fraudsters create "shops" on Instagram or Facebook, selling electronics or apparel at deep discounts. Payments are collected in advance via UPI; the products never arrive.

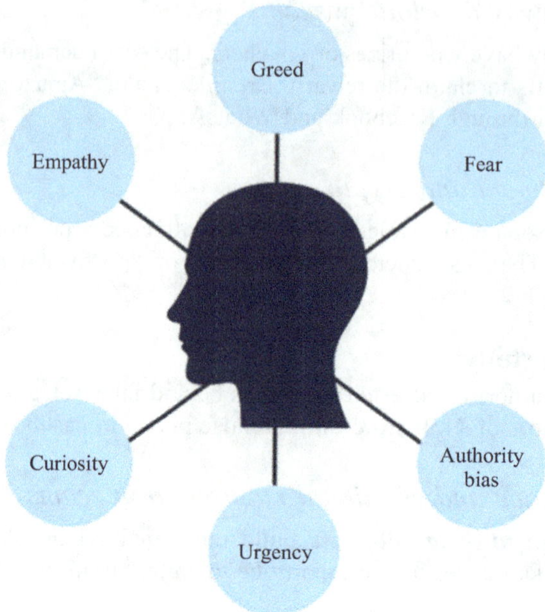

Figure 11.3 Psychological triggers used in social media scams

11.4.2 UPI QR code manipulation

Scammers send fake QR codes asking victims to "receive" money, but in reality, scanning initiates payment from the victim's account.

11.4.3 Phishing via payment apps

Attackers send messages with fake "refund" or "reward" links. The link mimics trusted platforms like Paytm or Google Pay, leading to credential capture.

11.4.4 Business email and social media compromise

Corporate social accounts are hacked to post false vendor payment updates or fake promotions.

One can refer to Table 11.2 to understand the common social media payment fraud patterns.

11.4.5 Example: the Paytm refund scam

A user receives a call claiming to be from Paytm ("Pay Through Mobile") support. The caller requests screen-sharing "to help process a refund." Once connected, the scammer remotely accesses the app and transfers funds. Such incidents underline that social engineering trumps technology when users are unaware.

Table 11.2 Common social media payment fraud patterns

Fraud type	**Description**	**Real example**	**Preventive tip**
Fake product sellers	Instagram "flash sale" pages	₹2,500 lost via UPI	Verify seller reputation before payment
QR code reversal	"Receive payment" trap	Victims unknowingly pay	Never scan a QR code to receive funds
Refund phishing	Fake "refund due" messages	Payment app spoof	Use only official app links
Influencer investment	Fake crypto/ investment ads	"Guaranteed double returns"	Cross-check with official brand sites

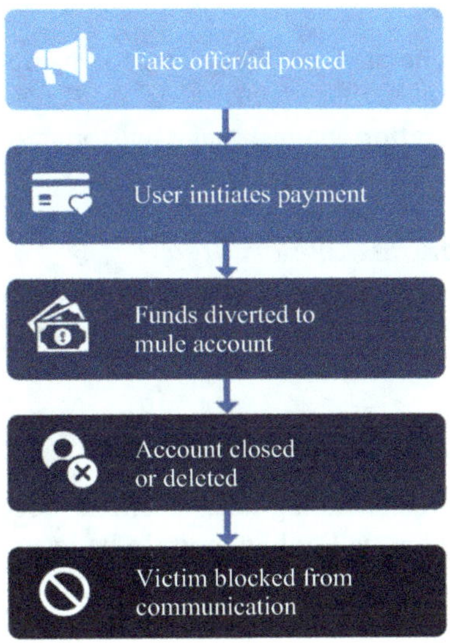

Figure 11.4 Flow of digital payment fraud via social media

One can have a look at Figure 11.4 to understand the flow of digital payment fraud via social media.

11.5 Fake handles in social media

Fake accounts, also known as **cloned, impersonated, or bot-generated handles**, have become one of the largest threats to both individuals and brands.

Table 11.3 Indicators of fake handles

Parameter	Authentic account	Fake account
Verification	Blue tick (officially verified)	Often missing or misused
Engagement	Organic, consistent	Sudden spikes, repeated posts
Language	Professional, error-free	Spelling/grammar issues
Links	Redirect to official sites	Redirect to unknown domains
Profile Creation	Long-standing history	Recently created

11.5.1 Types of fake handles

- **Identity clones:** Duplicate real users using stolen photos and bios.
- **Influencer impersonators:** Fake profiles posing as celebrities or experts for scams.
- **Bot accounts:** AI-generated profiles used to manipulate trends or amplify scams.
- **Corporate impersonation pages:** Fake customer care accounts soliciting personal info.

11.5.2 How fake handles are created

Attackers harvest public data (names, images, followers) and automate account generation using **bot farms** or **AI-generated profile pictures**. They engage with real users to build trust.

11.5.3 The verification trap

Many victims are lured into contacting fake "verified" accounts because scammers use lookalike usernames (e.g., @BankSupport_India vs. @Bank_SupportIndia).

11.5.4 Case study: the fake RBI Twitter account (India, 2022)

A handle mimicking the Reserve Bank of India posted messages offering "easy personal loans." Over 2,000 users were duped before Twitter suspended the account.

Table 11.3 presents the indicators of the fake handles.

11.6 Best practices to ensure security

11.6.1 For individuals

- Verify before trusting. Check profile authenticity before sharing personal or payment details.

- Use 2FA (Two-Factor Authentication) on all social accounts.
- Be skeptical of offers that sound too good to be true.
- Avoid sharing OTPs or screenshots of payment apps.
- Keep accounts private and restrict who can message or tag you.
- Educate family members, especially senior citizens and teenagers.

11.6.2 For businesses

- Implement official social media verification for all channels.
- Use AI-based social media monitoring tools to detect brand impersonation.
- Train employees on social engineering defense and incident response.
- Coordinate with law enforcement for fake account takedowns.

11.6.3 For financial institutions

- Integrate AI-driven anomaly detection on social handles.
- Establish official hashtags and channels for customer queries.
- Run awareness campaigns like *"Bank Never Asks"* or *"RBI Kehta Hai."*

One can have a look at Figure 11.5 to understand the social media safety matrix.

Social media is a double-edged sword, a tool for connection and a channel for exploitation. From phishing links to fake handles, attackers leverage trust and virality to deceive users.

The rise of UPI and instant payments has blurred the line between social interaction and financial transaction, creating new vulnerabilities. Ultimately, the first line of defense is **awareness**, followed by responsible digital behavior and verified engagement.

Cybersecurity is no longer limited to passwords and firewalls; it now extends to **likes, shares, and messages** that shape our digital identity.

Individuals	Businesses	Banks
Enable privacy settings	Verify accounts	Monitor mentions
Watch for suspicious links	Moderate content/posts	Educate customers
Be wary of fund requests	Limit personal data shared	Respond to threats
Use strong, unique passwords	Train employees	Deploy secure messaging
Report fake profiles	Implement MFA	Detect payment fraud

Figure 11.5 Social media safety matrix

Key points to remember

- Social media has become a major cyberattack surface, where criminals exploit trust, emotions, and online behavior to steal data, money, and identity. Users often underestimate these risks, making awareness critical.
- Phishing and impersonation remain the most common threats; attackers disguise themselves as friends, banks, or officials to trick users into revealing credentials or clicking on malicious links.
- Scammers exploit human psychology, using triggers such as urgency, greed, and empathy to bypass rational decision-making, especially during emotional or crisis situations.
- Fake handles and cloned profiles are used to spread misinformation, manipulate trends, and impersonate brands or individuals, eroding public confidence and privacy.
- Digital payment fraud on social platforms has surged, leveraging UPI, wallets, and fake QR codes to redirect funds instantly to mule accounts.
- Cybercriminals increasingly use AI-generated content and deepfakes to make scams appear authentic; voice cloning, fake videos, and synthetic profile images are growing threats.
- Corporate social media accounts are prime targets since a single compromised handle can mislead thousands of customers or damage brand reputation overnight.
- Malware and spyware often spread through shared links, attachments, or “fun” videos, especially on WhatsApp, Telegram, and Facebook Messenger, exploiting curiosity.
- Romance and relationship-based scams blend social engineering with emotional dependency, often leading to both financial and psychological harm for victims.
- Fake job offers and recruitment scams on LinkedIn lure professionals with high-pay promises, harvesting resumes, bank details, and application fees under false pretenses.
- Giveaway and lottery frauds are designed to appear legitimate through fake celebrity endorsements or sponsored ads, leading victims to share sensitive payment information.
- Charity and disaster-relief scams emerge after major events; fake NGO pages and crowdfunding links collect donations that never reach intended beneficiaries.
- Data shared publicly, birthdays, phone numbers, travel plans, fuels targeted attacks, enabling social engineering with a personal touch that feels authentic.
- AI-driven monitoring and content-verification tools now help detect impersonation and scam patterns, but human vigilance is still indispensable.
- Organizations must establish verified handles and reporting protocols to prevent fake pages from misleading customers or damaging institutional credibility.
- Two-factor authentication (2FA) and privacy controls are fundamental; they add friction for attackers and protect accounts even if credentials are leaked.

- Government and regulatory initiatives, such as RBI's "RBI Kehta Hai" and India's cybercrime helpline 1930, empower citizens to report and recover from social frauds.
- Education and awareness programs across schools, workplaces, and communities can significantly reduce vulnerability by turning end users into the first line of defense.
- Cyber hygiene on social media is as vital as technical security, requiring regular password updates, cautious sharing, and avoidance of unverified links or pages.
- Ultimately, social media safety depends on informed behavior, cross-platform cooperation, and prompt reporting, ensuring that technology serves as a tool for connection, not exploitation.

Questions (Try answering them yourself)

Q1. What is the most common factor exploited in social media attacks?
- A) Software bugs
- B) Human psychology and trust
- C) Hardware malfunctions
- D) Network congestion

Q2. Which of the following best defines a "fake handle"?
- A) An account created for marketing
- B) A duplicate or impersonated account used for deception
- C) A secure corporate account
- D) A temporary guest login

Q3. The 2020 global Twitter Bitcoin scam involved:
- A) Stealing user photos
- B) Posting fraudulent crypto donation messages from verified accounts
- C) Spreading ransomware via links
- D) Manipulating Twitter search algorithms

Q4. What is a common psychological trigger used in social media scams?
- A) Logic
- B) Curiosity and urgency
- C) Patience
- D) Discipline

Q5. Which platform is most associated with fake job recruitment scams?
- A) LinkedIn
- B) Instagram
- C) YouTube
- D) Snapchat

Q6. Which of the following is a clear indicator of a fake handle?
- A) Consistent engagement and grammar
- B) Verified blue tick

C) Recently created account with suspicious links
D) Official URL in bio

Q7. What is "catfishing"?
A) Spamming users with promotional messages
B) Creating fake romantic identities to deceive people
C) Installing spyware through attachments
D) Sharing malicious QR codes

Q8. Which type of scam typically appears after disasters or pandemics?
A) Investment scam
B) Charity and relief fund scam
C) Lottery scam
D) Job offer scam

Q9. How do criminals use QR codes in digital payment fraud?
A) To verify identity
B) To redirect payments from victim accounts
C) To transfer cashback rewards
D) To store transaction history

Q10. What is the safest practice before responding to a social media offer?
A) Share it with friends
B) Verify its authenticity and source
C) Click immediately to claim
D) Ignore all alerts

Q11. Which government helpline assists Indian citizens in reporting cyber frauds?
A) 1020
B) 1930
C) 1122
D) 1919

Q12. What is the best method to secure your social media accounts?
A) Weak password with personal details
B) Using the same password across platforms
C) Two-Factor Authentication (2FA)
D) Saving passwords in browsers

Q13. Which of the following is NOT a common sign of a fake account?
A) Repeated content
B) New profile picture every day
C) Consistent professional tone and verified status
D) Sudden follower spikes

Q14. The main reason digital payment fraud thrives on social media is:
A) Poor app performance
B) Instant payment systems and a lack of verification

C) Server downtime
D) Unused wallets

Q15. Fake "brand support" pages usually try to:
A) Offer genuine customer support
B) Collect user credentials or payment details
C) Promote verified campaigns
D) Send technical updates

Q16. "Smishing" refers to:
A) Phishing through SMS
B) Malware in social posts
C) Voice-based phishing
D) Image manipulation in scams

Q17. What should you do if you find a fake handle impersonating your business?
A) Ignore it
B) Engage with the account
C) Report and request takedown via the platform's official process
D) Post about it without reporting

Q18. Which of the following scams most commonly uses emotional manipulation?
A) Crypto investment
B) Romantic relationship scam
C) Data harvesting
D) Credential stuffing

Q19. What is the key defense against malware links shared via WhatsApp or Telegram?
A) Download all attachments to check
B) Click to inspect source
C) Never open unknown links or files
D) Install multiple random apps

Q20. Why are verified badges (blue ticks) not foolproof indicators of authenticity?
A) They disappear after some time
B) Hackers can still compromise verified accounts
C) Verification is always fake
D) They are only for celebrities

Q. No. Answer key

1. B
2. B
3. B
4. B
5. A
6. C
7. B

8. B
9. B
10. B
11. B
12. C
13. C
14. B
15. B
16. A
17. C
18. B
19. C
20. B

Further reading

[1] Buhari A, and Sulaiman ZI. Social media and cybersecurity: Protecting against online threats and attacks. *ResGate Preprint*. 2023.

[2] Frauenstein ED. Susceptibility to phishing on social network sites. *PLoS One*. 2020;15(6): e0235121.

[3] Goyal B, Gupta H, and Aggarwal N. Securing social spaces: Machine learning techniques for fake account detection. *SN Soc Sci*. 2024;4: 299.

[4] Bacha Shaheen A. Fake profiles in online social networks: Implications for privacy and cybersecurity in a globalized world. *ResGate Preprint*. 2024.

[5] Revathi V. Intelligent detection of fake profiles on social media using machine learning. *PhilArchive Preprint*. 2025.

[6] Al-Rafidain Journal of Engineering. Cybersecurity in social media. *Al-Rafidain J Eng*. 2023;30(4): 45–53.

[7] Zhang J, Zhang R, Yan G, *et al.* The rise of social botnets: Attacks and countermeasures. *arXiv Preprint*. 2016.

[8] Bordbar J, Mohammadrezaie M, Ardalan S, and Shiri ME. Detecting fake accounts through generative adversarial networks in online social media. *arXiv Preprint*. 2022.

[9] Paul Khandpur R, Ji T, Jan S, Wang G, Lu CT, and Ramakrishnan N. Crowdsourcing cybersecurity: Cyberattack detection using social media. *arXiv Preprint*. 2017.

[10] Sharevski F, Treebridge P, Jachim P, Li A, Babin A, and Westbrook J. Malware-induced misperception attacks on polarized Facebook discourse. *arXiv Preprint*. 2020.

[11] Anonymous. Cybersecurity practices for social media users: A systematic review. *MDPI J Cybersec*. 2021;2(1): 1–12.

[12] Anonymous. Impact of cybersecurity breaches on social media: A case study on awareness. *J Inf Secur*. 2025;18(2): 70–82.

[13] Anonymous. Scams and frauds in the digital age: ML-based detection. *ACM Digital Library*. 2025;34(1): 14–22.
[14] Deloitte. Global insights on social media fraud. *Deloitte Insights Report*. 2025.
[15] Kaspersky Lab. Evolution of social media scams: A decade review. *Kaspersky Cybercrime Report*. 2024.
[16] IBM Security. Protecting brand integrity on social platforms. *IBM White Paper*. 2024.
[17] Europol. *Internet Organised Crime Threat Assessment (IOCTA)*. The Hague: Europol; 2024.
[18] Reserve Bank of India. *Digital Payment Security Guidelines*. Mumbai: RBI; 2023.
[19] CERT-In. *Cybersecurity Guidelines for Social Media Users*. New Delhi: Ministry of Electronics and IT; 2024.
[20] Ministry of Home Affairs (India). *Cybercrime Reporting and Prevention Manual*. New Delhi: Government of India; 2024.
[21] OECD. *Responsible AI Use in Social Media Governance*. Paris: OECD Publishing; 2024.
[22] Transparency International. *Global Corruption Barometer 2024*. Berlin: Transparency International; 2024.
[23] PwC India. *Social Media Risk and Compliance Survey*. New Delhi: PricewaterhouseCoopers; 2025.
[24] Prodaft Intelligence. *The Cybersecurity Pitfalls of Social Media*. Zurich: Prodaft; 2023.
[25] University of Portsmouth. *Fake Social Media Accounts as Cybersecurity Risks*. Portsmouth: University Press; 2025.
[26] Revathi S, and Manikandan R. Social engineering threats on social platforms: Detection and defense models. *Int J Inf Technol Secur*. 2024;12(3): 115–128.
[27] Mahajan S, and Deshmukh A. Cyber frauds through social networking sites in India: Trends and countermeasures. *Indian J Criminology*. 2023;51(2): 84–95.
[28] F-Secure Labs. *Fake Handle Detection and Response Strategies*. Helsinki: F-Secure Research Report; 2024.
[29] NortonLifeLock. *Social Media Identity Theft and Digital Payment Fraud*. California: NortonLifeLock Report; 2024.
[30] UNODC. *Global Cybercrime and Online Scam Trends Report*. Vienna: United Nations Office on Drugs and Crime; 2024.

Chapter 12

Enlightening customers on cybersecurity and safety

Learning objectives

After reading through the chapter, the reader will gain a clear understanding of

- The importance of customer awareness as the first line of defense against cyber threats.
- Analyze effective communication strategies for educating customers in simple, accessible, and engaging ways.
- Recognize safe digital behaviors through the concept of "KYC – Know Your Click" to avoid phishing, malicious links, and scams.
- Apply basic cybersecurity practices at a personal level, such as password hygiene, Multi-Factor Authentication (MFA), and mobile safety.
- Identify and respond to suspicious online activities by using proper reporting channels and escalation mechanisms.
- Evaluate real-world case studies of cyber fraud and prevention campaigns to understand practical applications.
- Develop a customer-centric cybersecurity mindset that balances technology with awareness, vigilance, and responsibility.

12.1 Introduction

In today's hyper-connected world, the customer has become the primary target of cybercriminals. No matter how advanced firewalls, intrusion detection systems, or encryption technologies are, attackers have learned that it is often easier and more effective to exploit human behavior than to bypass hardened security systems. This makes customer awareness the first line of defense in modern cybersecurity.

12.1.1 Why is customer awareness the first line of defense?

Most cyberattacks succeed not because of sophisticated hacking but because of simple human mistakes, like clicking a malicious link, downloading an infected attachment, or sharing credentials unknowingly. Phishing, smishing (SMS phishing), vishing (voice phishing), and social engineering are carefully designed to trick end-users.

- A single careless click can lead to credential theft, fraudulent transactions, or identity compromise.
- Customers are the gatekeepers of their personal devices, which are often outside the corporate security perimeter.
- Proactive awareness empowers customers to identify red flags and act before damage occurs.

Thus, an aware customer acts as a human firewall, reducing the success rate of attacks dramatically.

12.1.2 Statistics on cybercrime targeting end-users

Recent data reinforces the urgency of customer education.

- According to the 2024 IBM Cost of a Data Breach Report, over 82% of breaches involved a human element, such as phishing or stolen credentials.
- The Reserve Bank of India (RBI) reported that in FY 2023–2024, over ₹1,250 crore was lost to digital banking frauds, with phishing and Unified Payments Interface (UPI) scams topping the list.
- The FBI Internet Crime Complaint Center (IC3) recorded 880,418 complaints in 2023, with reported losses of over $12.5 billion, most linked to social engineering and fraud.
- Telecom operators worldwide have noted a surge in SIM swap fraud, where customers unknowingly share One-Time Passcodes (OTPs) with attackers.

These figures highlight that end-users are now the softest targets, and criminals exploit this weakness at scale.

12.1.3 Role of banks, e-commerce, and telecom in educating customers

Enterprises that handle sensitive data and financial transactions cannot treat security as purely a technology problem; it is also a customer education problem.

- Banks and fintech: RBI mandates awareness campaigns like *"RBI Kehta Hai"* to warn users against sharing OTPs, PINs, and passwords. Banks frequently push SMS alerts, website banners, and in-app notifications.
- E-commerce platforms: Companies such as Amazon and Flipkart run "Safe Shopping" campaigns educating users on identifying fake offers, counterfeit sellers, and secure payment practices.
- Telecom providers: Operators play a vital role in alerting users to fraudulent calls or SMS campaigns. TRAI (Telecom Regulatory Authority of India) and telecom companies in India, for instance, launched the Digital Intelligence Unit (DIU) to detect and block suspicious communication.

When these sectors actively train and inform customers, fraud rates decrease substantially.

12.1.4 Concept of the "shared responsibility model" for security

Traditionally associated with cloud computing, the shared responsibility model is equally relevant in customer cybersecurity. Security is a joint responsibility:

- Organizations must provide secure platforms, encrypted transactions, fraud detection, and awareness campaigns.
- Customers must remain vigilant by never sharing credentials, verifying communication sources, and reporting suspicious activities promptly.

For example, even if a bank deploys multi-factor authentication, the model fails if a customer discloses the OTP over a phishing call. Similarly, e-commerce companies can enforce secure payments, but customers must avoid transacting on fake websites.

This partnership creates a resilient ecosystem where both technology and human awareness combine to reduce risks.

12.2 Communication strategy

Cybersecurity education for customers is only effective when it is delivered clearly, consistently, and in a format that customers can understand and act upon. The success of such initiatives depends not only on *what* is communicated but also on *how* it is communicated.

12.2.1 Importance of clear, jargon-free messaging

Most customers are not technology experts. Technical jargon like "multi-factor authentication bypass" or "phishing payload injection" only confuses and alienates them.

- **Simplicity first**: Instead of "Do not disclose credentials over an unencrypted channel," banks should say, "Never share your PIN or OTP with anyone."
- **Action-oriented advice**: Customers respond better when instructions are direct: "Click only on links sent by your bank's official website or app."
- **Trust through clarity**: Straightforward language reduces skepticism. When customers understand the message, they are more likely to follow it.

Lesson: Security awareness is not about showcasing technical depth; it is about ensuring even the least tech-savvy customer understands and acts safely.

12.2.2 Awareness campaigns (SMS, email, app notifications, in-branch posters)

Organizations must reach customers through multiple channels because no single medium is sufficient.

1. **SMS alerts**
   - Widely used in India for reminders like "Do not share OTPs with anyone, even if they claim to be bank staff."
   - SMS is short and can gain immediate attention, but should avoid overuse to prevent customers from ignoring it.
2. **Email campaigns**
   - Useful for detailed advice with visuals.
   - Example: E-commerce companies send monthly newsletters with "5 tips for safe shopping."
   - Challenge: Phishing emails themselves confuse users, so genuine emails must be clearly branded.
3. **App notifications**
   - In-app banners and push notifications are effective since they reach users *while they are banking/shopping.*
   - Example: Payment apps like Google Pay warn customers about suspicious requests in real time.
4. **In-branch posters and Automated Teller Machines (ATMs)**
   - For customers who rely on physical branches, posters and screen alerts serve as constant reminders.
   - Example: At ATMs, RBI depicts warnings like "Your bank never asks for PIN or OTP."

A **multi-channel campaign ensures inclusivity**, as customers vary in digital literacy, device ownership, and preferred communication style.

12.2.3 Multi-language and accessibility for diverse customers

India and many other nations are linguistically diverse. A one-size-fits-all English campaign fails to reach rural or regional customers.

- **Language inclusivity**: RBI's campaigns use Hindi, Tamil, Bengali, and other regional languages to reach rural populations.
- **Accessibility**: Messages should consider visually impaired or elderly customers, such as audio alerts, voice-enabled assistants, or large-font printouts.
- **Cultural sensitivity**: Examples should resonate with local practices. For instance, explaining digital wallets in rural areas through analogies like "just like keeping money in your pocket, but digital."

Such efforts broaden reach and reduce the gap between digital literacy and digital safety.

12.2.4 Real-life case study: RBI's "RBI Kehta Hai" campaign

Launched in 2020, *"RBI Kehta Hai"* (RBI Says) is a national multimedia campaign aimed at educating citizens about safe banking.

- **Mediums used**: TV commercials, radio jingles, SMS alerts, posters, and social media.
- **Core messages**: "RBI never asks for your PIN, password, or OTP." / "Always check for the RBI logo and secure payment gateway."
- **Impact**: The campaign gained high visibility across urban and rural India, leading to greater awareness of digital banking fraud.
- **Key takeaway**: A regulator-led, repeated message across multiple platforms builds trust and improves customer vigilance.

This campaign is a benchmark example of how storytelling + repetition + simplicity = effective customer cybersecurity communication.

12.2.5 Best practices for communication

One can have a look at the layers of customer communication presented in Figure 12.1.

1. **Periodic training**
   - Continuous reminders are more effective than one-time campaigns.
   - Example: Quarterly SMS reminders or festive-season fraud alerts (when scams spike).
2. **Story-based awareness**
   - Stories resonate better than instructions.
   - Example: A short animated video showing a scammer tricking someone with a fake lottery link is more memorable than plain text warnings.
3. **Gamification**
   - Interactive quizzes, mobile app challenges, or reward-based learning improve engagement.
   - Example: A bank app could show a fake vs. real SMS and reward customers for spotting the fake.

Figure 12.1 Layers of customer communication

4. **Consistency across channels**
   - The same core message in every medium: "Never share OTP" must be reinforced on SMS, app, ATM screen, and poster.
5. **Measurement and feedback**
   - Campaign effectiveness should be tracked (fraud rates before vs. after, customer surveys).
   - Example: RBI measured increased awareness levels post such programs as "RBI Kehta Hai."
6. **Leverage trust figures**
   - Campaigns featuring trusted faces (e.g., celebrities, brand mascots) gain closer attention.
7. **Emotional appeal**
   - Customers respond when communication connects to family safety or personal loss ("Don't let fraudsters steal your hard-earned money").

12.3 KYC—Know Your Click

The term KYC—Know Your Customer—is a well-established principle in banking and financial services, requiring businesses to verify the identity of clients before offering services. Extending this analogy, in cybersecurity, a new form of KYC has emerged: "Know Your Click." Just as financial institutions must validate their customers, customers must validate every click they make online. Whether opening an email, scanning a QR code, or visiting a website, each action carries potential risks.

Analogy to Know Your Customer (KYC)

- In banking, KYC prevents fraud by ensuring the authenticity of a client.
- In digital life, "Know Your Click" prevents fraud by ensuring the authenticity of a link or action.
- Both rely on verification before trust.
  - Bank: "Is this person genuine?"
  - Customer: "Is this link genuine?"
- Just as regulators penalize banks for KYC failures, individuals pay a heavy price for not verifying their clicks, loss of money, identity theft, or data exposure.

12.3.1 Explaining safe clicking habits

12.3.1.1 Phishing links

Phishing remains the most common form of digital fraud. Attackers send links designed to mimic genuine portals (banks, government sites, e-commerce).

- Example: A fake email pretending to be from SBI Net Banking asks the customer to "verify account details" through a malicious link.
- Safe Habit: Always type the bank's URL manually or use a bookmarked link.

12.3.1.2 Shortened URLs

Services like bit.ly or tinyurl hide the true destination. Attackers exploit this to trick customers.

- Safe habit: Use URL expanders (many browsers or security apps preview the full URL).

12.3.1.3 QR codes

QR phishing, or quishing, is rising, where fake QR codes lead to malicious sites or auto-install apps.

- Example: In Bengaluru (2023), scammers pasted fake QR codes on parking machines, redirecting payments to fraudulent accounts.
- Safe habit: Verify QR codes from official sources; avoid random street posters or emails with QR images.

12.3.2 Red flags customers must watch

By recognizing these red flags, customers train themselves to pause before clicking.

1. Spelling errors and poor grammar
   - Example: "Your accaount is bloced, clik here."
   - Genuine institutions rarely make such mistakes.
2. Urgency messages
   - "Your account will be suspended in 2 hours unless you act now."
   - Scammers pressure customers into hasty actions.
3. Fake domains
   - Subtle alterations like paytm-secure.in instead of paytm.com.
   - Rule of thumb: Always double-check the domain spelling.
4. Unusual sender address
   - Official banks will never email from @gmail.com accounts.
5. Attachments from unknown sources
   - Especially executable files (.exe), zip files, or macro-enabled Word documents.

12.3.3 Tools and methods to support safe clicking

1. URL previews
   - Hovering over links (desktop) or long-pressing (mobile) to preview the true destination.
2. Anti-phishing browser plugins
   - Extensions like Netcraft, Norton Safe Web, or built-in Google Safe Browsing warn about unsafe websites.
3. DNS filtering services
   - Public DNS providers like Quad9 or Cloudflare block known phishing domains automatically.
4. Banking security apps
   - Some banks (e.g., ICICI iSafe) offer secure browsing within their apps, restricting fraudulent redirects.
5. AI-driven fraud detection
   - Modern browsers and banking apps now employ machine learning to detect suspicious clicks in real time.

12.3.4 Case examples of phishing scams

India

- UPI Phishing (2022–2023): Fraudsters sent fake "KYC update" links, asking customers to enter UPI PINs, draining bank accounts. Losses crossed ₹500 crore nationwide.
- Fake Income Tax Refund Emails: Customers were lured with fake refund portals during tax season. CERT-In flagged multiple such campaigns.

Global

- COVID-19 Vaccine Scams (2021): The World Health Organization (WHO) reported phishing sites posing as vaccine registration portals, stealing millions of records.
- PayPal and Netflix fake emails: Customers received emails claiming "payment failed" with links to credential-harvesting sites.
- British Airways data breach (2018): Customers were redirected to a fraudulent payment page due to malicious script injection, leading to a £183 million fine under GDPR.

These incidents underline the global scale of unsafe clicking and the critical role of awareness. The simple steps every customer should follow before clicking any link or scanning a QR code are given in Figure 12.2.

As shown in Figure 12.2, customers can follow a simple checklist to verify the safety of any link or QR code before acting.

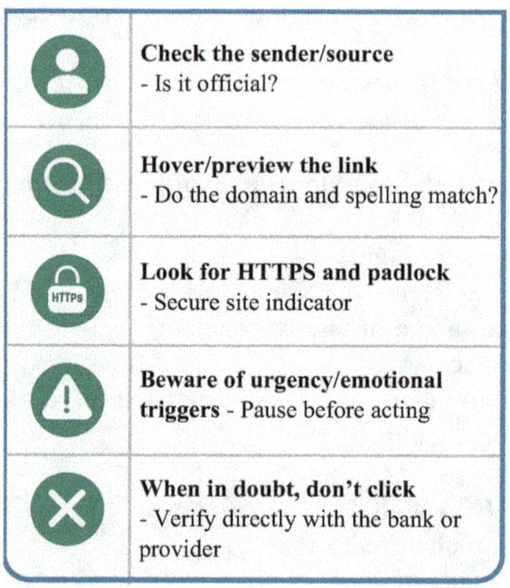

Figure 12.2 Safe click checklist

12.4 Cybersecurity at your fingertips

In the digital economy, most interactions, banking, shopping, communication, and even healthcare, happen at our fingertips, primarily via smartphones. While this convenience is unmatched, it also means that a single careless action on a mobile device can expose sensitive information, financial assets, or even personal identity. Cybersecurity, therefore, must be viewed not as a technical concept but as a daily habit every customer can practice at their fingertips.

12.4.1 Everyday actions customers can take

1. ***Strong passwords***
   - Use unique, complex passwords for each account.
   - Combine uppercase, lowercase, numbers, and special characters.
   - Avoid predictable patterns like birthdays or "12345."
   - Example: "Shr1Ram!2025#" is stronger than "shriram123."
   - Password managers can help manage multiple accounts safely.
2. ***Multi-Factor Authentication (MFA)***
   - Adds an extra layer beyond passwords (OTP, biometrics, app confirmation).
   - Even if credentials are stolen, attackers cannot access the account without the second factor.
   - Many banks in India mandate OTP-based MFA for UPI and card transactions.
3. ***Updating apps and operating systems***
   - Hackers exploit outdated apps.
   - Regular updates patch vulnerabilities and strengthen defenses.
   - Example:WhatsApp frequently releases updates to fix security flaws; customers who delay updates risk exposure.
4. ***Secure Wi-Fi practices***
   - Avoid using public Wi-Fi for banking or payments.
   - If unavoidable, use a VPN.
5. ***Data backups***
   - Regular backups protect against ransomware or accidental data loss.
   - Cloud services or encrypted local drives can be used.

12.4.2 Mobile-first protection

Smartphones are the primary devices for most digital interactions. Mobile-first protection is therefore critical.

1. ***App store safety***
   - Download apps only from official stores (Google Play, Apple App Store).
   - Avoid sideloading Android Package Kits (APKs) from unknown websites.

   - Fraudulent loan apps in India (2022) exploited sideloading to steal data and money.

2. ***Permissions awareness***
   - Grant apps only the necessary permissions.
   - A calculator app does not need access to your camera or contacts.
   - Regularly review and revoke unused permissions.

3. ***Device security***
   - Enable biometric locks (fingerprint, face ID).
   - Avoid rooting/jailbreaking, as it bypasses built-in protections.
   - Use device-locating features (Find My iPhone, Google Find My Device).

12.4.3 Social media hygiene: oversharing risks

Social media is often exploited by fraudsters for social engineering.

- Oversharing personal details (birthdays, pet names, schools) helps hackers guess passwords or answer security questions.
- Fake job offers and investment scams are spread via social media ads and DMs (Direct Messages).
- Example: In 2023, LinkedIn was used for fake work-from-home job scams that tricked thousands into transferring money.
- Safe Practices:
  - Restrict profile visibility.
  - Avoid sharing sensitive updates like “Got my new debit card today.”
  - Be cautious when clicking unknown friend requests or links in DMs.

12.4.4 Role of banks in providing fingertip security

Banks and financial institutions have a dual role: providing technology-driven safeguards and educating customers.

1. One-Time Passwords (OTPs)
   - Widely used as a secure step for online transactions.
   - Limitation: Customers must never share OTPs over calls or SMS.

2. App locks and biometric authentication
   - Many banks provide in-app fingerprint or face recognition features.
   - Reduces reliance on PINs, which are often reused or shared.

3. AI fraud detection
   - Banks increasingly rely on machine learning to detect unusual transaction patterns.
   - Example: Sudden overseas transactions or high-value UPI transfers trigger alerts.

4. Awareness campaigns
   - Push notifications and SMS alerts remind customers of safe practices.
   - Example: “Never click links asking for KYC update. Visit the branch or official app only.”

12.4.5 Case example: UPI fraud prevention awareness

Unified Payments Interface (UPI) revolutionized digital payments in India but also has become a magnet for fraudsters.

- Scam pattern: Fraudsters pretend to be buyers on OLX or social media marketplaces, sending fake "payment request" links.
- Victim response: Customers, thinking they are receiving money, enter their UPI PIN, unknowingly authorizing debit transactions.
- Preventive measures:
  - NPCI (National Payments Corporation of India) launched safety awareness campaigns like "UPI Chalega" to educate customers.
  - Banks integrated alerts within apps, e.g., "Do not enter UPI PIN to receive money."

This case illustrates that cybersecurity at your fingertips is not just about technology but about training customers to recognize fraud tactics.

The simple fingertip practices to help customers stay safe in their everyday digital activities are provided in Figure 12.3.

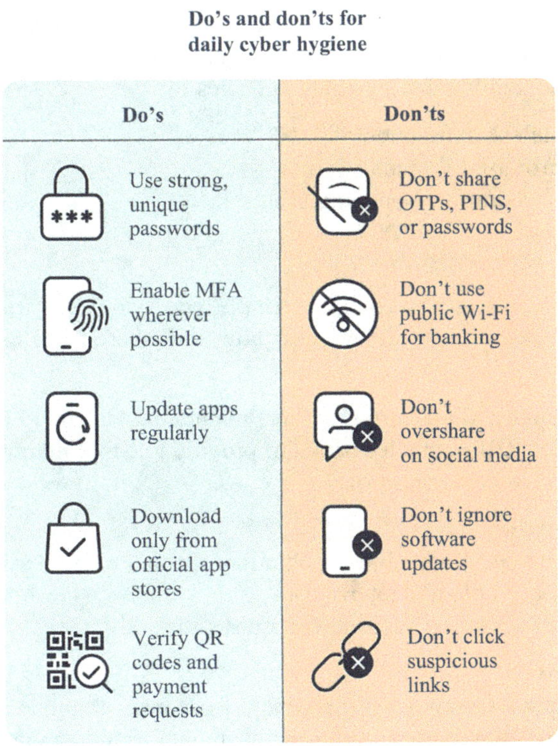

Figure 12.3 Do's and don'ts for daily cyber hygiene

Following such simple do's and don'ts helps customers maintain strong daily cyber hygiene.

12.5 Suspicious activity reporting

Cybersecurity is not just about preventing attacks but also about detecting and responding quickly when something suspicious occurs. Customers play a pivotal role in this process: their vigilance and timely reporting can prevent fraud from escalating into severe financial or identity loss.

12.5.1 Importance of customer vigilance

Even with the most advanced monitoring systems, organizations cannot always detect fraudulent activities immediately. Customers are often the **first to notice unusual activity**, such as

- Unauthorized debit card transactions.
- Unexpected login alerts from unknown devices.
- Emails or calls requesting confidential information.
- Fake apps mimicking banking or government services.

Customer vigilance is therefore a critical defense mechanism, helping institutions take corrective actions before major damage occurs. Quick reporting allows banks, regulators, and law enforcement agencies to:

- Freeze fraudulent transactions.
- Block compromised accounts.
- Alert other customers of ongoing scams.

12.5.2 Easy reporting channels

For reporting to be effective, it must be simple, accessible, and trusted. Customers are more likely to report when they know how and where to do it.

1. **Helplines**
    - Most banks and telecom providers maintain 24×7 fraud helplines.
    - Example: RBI mandates banks to provide toll-free numbers for reporting unauthorized transactions.
2. **In-app reporting**
    - Digital payment apps like Google Pay, PhonePe, and Paytm have built-in "Report a Problem" features.
    - Customers can flag suspicious requests instantly.
3. **CERT-In portal**
    - The Indian Computer Emergency Response Team (CERT-In) allows individuals to report phishing, malware, and fraud attempts online.
    - Website: www.cert-in.org.in

4. **Police and cybercrime portals**
   - The Government of India operates the **National Cyber Crime Reporting Portal** (cybercrime.gov.in), specifically for financial fraud and cyber harassment cases.
5. **SMS and email alerts**
   - Many institutions encourage customers to forward suspicious SMS or emails to dedicated addresses (e.g., the 1930 helpline for digital frauds in India).

12.5.3 Real-world timeline: how quick reporting saves losses

The **speed of reporting** often determines the outcome:

- **Case 1: UPI fraud**
  - The customer unknowingly approves a UPI payment request.
  - If reported within **30 minutes**, the bank can freeze the transfer and recover funds.
  - If delayed beyond a few hours, the money is usually siphoned into multiple mule accounts, making recovery nearly impossible.
- **Case 2: Card skimming in Mumbai (2022)**
  - Victims who noticed unauthorized ATM withdrawals and reported them immediately had their cards blocked and losses reversed.
  - Those who delayed reporting by even 24 hours faced greater financial exposure.

Lesson: **The first 1–2 hours are critical.** Quick reporting increases the chances of recovery and prevents attackers from exploiting further.

12.5.4 Obstacles customers face in reporting

Despite the importance, many incidents go unreported due to barriers such as

1. **Fear of blame**
   - Customers hesitate, thinking they will be blamed for carelessness.
2. **Shame and embarrassment**
   - Victims often feel ashamed about "falling for a scam," leading to silence.
3. **Lack of awareness**
   - Many customers simply do not know the helpline numbers or reporting portals.
4. **Complex processes**
   - Lengthy forms or unclear instructions discourage quick reporting.
5. **Mistrust**
   - Some customers doubt whether reporting will actually result in recovery.

Addressing these obstacles requires customer-friendly, empathetic, and fast response systems.

12.5.5 Global and Indian frameworks for consumer reporting

1. India
   - RBI Guidelines: Banks must reverse fraudulent electronic transactions if reported within a stipulated timeline (usually 3 days).
   - 1930 helpline: A centralized phone line for digital payment fraud.
   - CERT-In and Cybercrime Portal: Centralized mechanisms for citizens to escalate cases.
2. United States
   - FBI Internet Crime Complaint Center (IC3) records consumer complaints and coordinates investigations.
   - FTC (Federal Trade Commission) provides reporting and guidance for identity theft and online fraud.
3. European Union
   - Strong frameworks under GDPR ensure consumers can report breaches, and companies are obligated to act within strict timelines.
4. Global collaboration
   - Interpol and Europol coordinate large-scale cybercrime responses, relying on timely reporting from local agencies.

These frameworks reflect a **shared responsibility** between institutions, regulators, and customers to build trust and safety in the digital ecosystem.

12.5.6 Infographic suggestion: Report → Verify → Act → Protect Cycle

A **4-step circular flow diagram** with arrows:

1. Report: Customer flags suspicious activity via helpline/app/portal.
2. Verify: Bank or authority validates the complaint.
3. Act: Immediate response: block cards, freeze funds, alert systems.
4. Protect: Prevent recurrence through awareness and improved security.

Such a cycle, as shown in Figure 12.4, ensures the timely handling of suspicious activities and safeguards customers from further losses. It also provides a structured approach for customers and institutions to manage suspicious activities effectively.

Key points to remember

1. Customer awareness is the first line of defense: **Most cyberattacks succeed due to human error; informed customers act as human firewalls**.

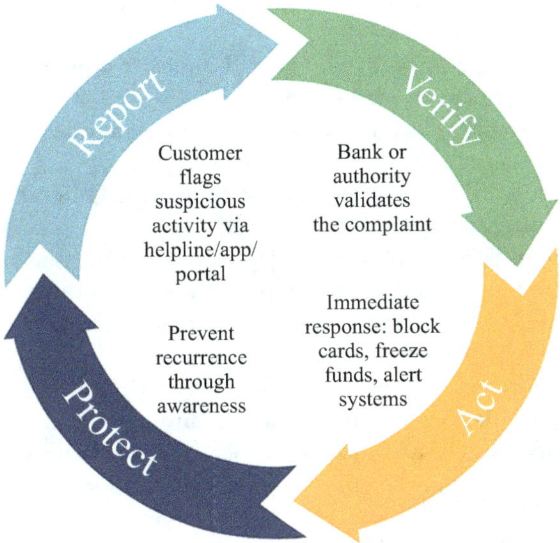

Figure 12.4 *Report → Verify → Act → Protect Cycle*

2. Simple, jargon-free messaging works best: **Security advice should be clear and actionable, not technical or overwhelming.**
3. Multi-channel communication is essential: **SMS, email, app notifications, posters, and media together ensure wide coverage.**
4. Consistency builds trust: **The same message, repeated across channels, reinforces safe practices in customer behavior**.
5. Local language campaigns increase reach: **Regional and accessible formats help bridge digital literacy gaps.**
6. Stories and real cases resonate: **Customers remember warnings better when linked to relatable fraud examples.**
7. KYC = Know Your Click: **Just as banks verify customers, customers must verify links before clicking.**
8. Safe clicking saves money: **Checking URLs, previewing links, and avoiding suspicious QR codes prevent phishing losses.**
9. Red flags should never be ignored: **Spelling errors, urgency, fake domains, and odd sender IDs are danger signals.**
10. Use tools for protection: **URL previews, browser plugins, and fraud-detection apps provide an extra shield.**
11. Cyber hygiene starts with basics: **Strong passwords, MFA, and regular updates are everyday essentials.**
12. Mobile safety is critical: **Download apps only from trusted stores and restrict unnecessary permissions.**

13. Social media is a goldmine for fraudsters: **Oversharing personal details can enable scams and identity theft.**
14. Banks support fingertip security: **OTPs, biometric app locks, and AI-driven fraud detection protect customers.**
15. UPI fraud awareness is vital: **Customers must remember that UPI PINs are only for sending money, never for receiving it.**
16. Suspicious activity must be reported immediately: **Quick action within the first hours often prevents bigger losses.**
17. Multiple reporting channels exist: **Helplines, in-app reports, CERT-In, and the National Cyber Crime Portal are accessible options.**
18. Overcoming shame and fear is important: **Reporting scams helps prevent others from falling victim too.**
19. Frameworks protect customers globally: **From RBI in India to FTC in the US, strong regulatory systems back vigilant customers.**
20. Cybersecurity is a shared responsibility: **Organizations provide secure systems, but customers must stay alert and cautious.**

Questions (try answering them yourself)

1. Explain why customer awareness is often called the "first line of defense" in cybersecurity. Support your answer with examples.
2. Discuss the role of communication strategy in creating effective cybersecurity awareness campaigns for customers.
3. Compare the effectiveness of SMS alerts, email notifications, and in-app messages in spreading cybersecurity awareness. Which do you think is most impactful, and why?
4. Evaluate the significance of using multiple languages and accessible formats in customer awareness campaigns. Provide real-life examples.
5. Describe the RBI's "RBI Kehta Hai" campaign. What lessons can other sectors learn from this initiative?
6. Explain the concept of "KYC – Know Your Click." How does it parallel the traditional KYC process in banking?
7. Identify and elaborate on at least five red flags that customers should check before clicking on a link or scanning a QR code.
8. Discuss the importance of anti-phishing tools and URL preview techniques in ensuring safe browsing practices.
9. Present two real-world phishing case studies (one from India and one global). Analyze the mistakes victims made and suggest preventive steps.
10. Describe everyday actions customers should take to maintain cyber hygiene. Why are these small actions critical?
11. Explain how mobile-first protection strategies (like app store safety and permission awareness) can prevent fraud.
12. Discuss the risks of oversharing on social media and its impact on cybersecurity. Support your answer with examples.

13. Analyze the role of banks in providing fingertip security through OTPs, biometric authentication, and AI-driven fraud detection.
14. Illustrate with an example how awareness campaigns helped to reduce UPI fraud in India.
15. Why is quick reporting of suspicious activity essential in cybersecurity? Explain using a real or hypothetical timeline.
16. What obstacles do customers face when reporting suspicious activity? Suggest measures to overcome these barriers.
17. Compare the suspicious activity reporting mechanisms in India with those in the United States or the European Union.
18. Describe the Report → Verify → Act → Protect cycle. How does it ensure customer safety?
19. Discuss how regulators, organizations, and customers share responsibilities in ensuring cybersecurity. Provide practical examples.
20. If you were tasked with designing a new customer awareness campaign for your local bank, what strategies and tools would you use? Justify your choices.

Objective questions

1) The phrase "Know Your Click" is primarily aimed at preventing:
   a) Social engineering
   b) Unsafe online transactions
   c) Clicking on malicious links
   d) Data backups

2) Which of the following is the most jargon-free message for customers?
   a) "Do not disclose credentials over an unencrypted channel."
   b) "Never share your OTP with anyone."
   c) "Protect your PII from phishing payload injection."
   d) "Encrypt data during digital interactions."

3) Which campaign was launched by the RBI to spread banking awareness?
   a) Safe Banking Always
   b) RBI Kehta Hai
   c) Cyber Dost
   d) UPI Chalega

4) Which is a red flag of a phishing attempt?
   a) HTTPS-enabled website
   b) Domain mismatch or spelling errors
   c) Official bank email address
   d) In-app notifications

5) Which of these is NOT a safe cyber hygiene practice?
   a) Using strong passwords
   b) Updating apps regularly

c) Sharing OTPs with trusted friends
d) Enabling MFA

6) In India, which number can customers dial to report digital payment frauds?
   a) 100
   b) 1930
   c) 112
   d) 1551

7) Which one of these is an obstacle to suspicious activity reporting?
   a) Awareness campaigns
   b) Customer embarrassment
   c) In-app reporting options
   d) Helpline availability

8) Which of the following is NOT part of the Report → Verify → Act → Protect cycle?
   a) Report
   b) Encrypt
   c) Act
   d) Protect

9) UPI PIN should be entered only when:
   a) Receiving money
   b) Sending money
   c) Checking balance
   d) Installing apps

10) Which global agency runs the Internet Crime Complaint Center (IC3)?
    a) Europol
    b) Interpol
    c) FBI
    d) CERT-In

True or false

11) Customer awareness campaigns are only effective if delivered in English.
12) Shortened URLs can hide malicious destinations.
13) Multi-factor authentication reduces risks even if passwords are compromised.
14) Oversharing on social media can help attackers guess passwords.
15) CERT-In is India's official body for handling cybersecurity incidents.

Fill in the blanks

16) The RBI campaign _______ emphasized, "Never share your PIN, password, or OTP."
17) The helpline number for reporting digital fraud in India is _______.

18) _______ fraud involves criminals pasting fake QR codes to redirect payments.
19) The phrase "customers act as a human firewall" highlights the importance of _______.
20) The global regulation _______ in the EU mandates strict breach reporting timelines.

Answer key

MCQs

1. c) Clicking on malicious links
2. b) "Never share your OTP with anyone."
3. b) RBI Kehta Hai
4. b) Domain mismatch or spelling errors
5. c) Sharing OTPs with trusted friends
6. b) 1930
7. b) Customer embarrassment
8. b) Encrypt
9. b) Sending money
10. c) FBI

True/false

11. False
12. True
13. True
14. True
15. True

Fill in the blanks

16. RBI Kehta Hai
17. 1930
18. QR (Quishing)
19. Customer awareness/vigilance
20. GDPR

Further reading

[1] IBM Security. *Cost of a Data Breach Report 2024*. IBM and Ponemon Institute; 2024.

[2] IBM Security. *Cost of a Data Breach Report 2025*. IBM; 2025.

[3] Zscaler. *7 Key Takeaways from IBM's Cost of a Data Breach Report 2024*. Zscaler Blog; 2024.

[4] Reserve Bank of India. *RBI Kehta Hai*. Reserve Bank of India; 2020.

[5] Government of India. *National Cyber Crime Reporting Portal*. Ministry of Home Affairs; 2019.

[6] Government of India. *Indian Cybercrime Coordination Centre (I4C)*. Ministry of Home Affairs; 2020.

[7] BreachRx. *India's CERT-In Directive – Regulatory & Reporting Requirements*. BreachRx; 2023.
[8] UpGuard. *India's 6-Hour Data Breach Reporting Rule*. UpGuard; 2023.
[9] CSO Online. What is the cost of a data breach? *CSO* Online; 2025.
[10] UpGuard. What is the cost of a data breach in 2024? *UpGuard*; 2024.
[11] Government of India. *Cyber | Open Government Data (OGD) Platform India*. Government of India; 2022.
[12] Government of India. *Report Financial Fraud through the National Cyber Crime Reporting Portal*. Government of India; 2022.
[13] Securityium. *CERT-In Cyber Incident Reporting Guidelines: A Complete Guide*. Securityium; 2024.
[14] American Express India. *RBI Kehta Hai Campaign*. American Express India; 2021.
[15] Times of India. *Beware of E-challan Scam*. The Times of India; 2025.
[16] Indian Computer Emergency Response Team. Wikipedia, The Free Encyclopedia; 2025.
[17] National Centre for Financial Education. *Stakeholders' Initiatives – RBI Kehta Hai*. NCFE; 2021.
[18] Government of India. *National Cybercrime Reporting Portal Launch*. Government of India; 2023.
[19] IBM Security. *Cost of a Data Breach Report 2024: Financial Industry*. IBM; 2024.
[20] Government of India. *Indian Cybercrime Coordination Centre (I4C) – Information Page*. Ministry of Home Affairs; 2024.

Chapter 13

Notable real-world case studies (lessons learned)

Learning objectives

After reading this chapter, the reader will gain a clear understanding of

- The significance of real-world case studies in identifying how cyber incidents unfold and why studying those helps prevent recurrence.
- Analyzing major banking and financial sector frauds (e.g., Bangladesh Bank heist, Punjab National Bank (PNB) scam, Cosmos Bank attack) to extract lessons on security gaps and customer awareness.
- Examining e-commerce and consumer fraud cases to understand the role of platform responsibility, seller verification, and customer vigilance.
- Evaluating telecom and digital payment frauds such as SIM swap and Unified Payments Interface (UPI) scams to recognize the need for robust Know Your Customer (KYC) and in-app awareness mechanisms.
- Investigating global cyber incidents like Equifax, Target, and WannaCry to learn about patching, vendor risk, ransomware defense, and data protection.
- Assessing Indian public sector cases (Aadhaar leaks, Indian Railway Catering and Tourism Corporation (IRCTC) phishing) to highlight the importance of securing large citizen databases and critical services.
- Developing a holistic understanding of lessons learned from diverse case studies to strengthen the shared responsibility model between organizations, regulators, and customers.

13.1 Introduction

Cybersecurity is often understood in terms of concepts, frameworks, and best practices, but the real test of its effectiveness comes from how organizations and customers respond when incidents actually occur. While technical standards and regulations provide the foundation, it is the study of real-world cases that reveals the practical gaps, human factors, and overlooked vulnerabilities that enable cybercriminals to succeed.

13.1.1 Importance of studying real incidents

Examining real incidents provides a window into reality that theory alone cannot capture. Each case exposes flaws, whether in technology, processes, or behavior, that serve as valuable lessons for the future.

- Learning from mistakes: When a large-scale breach occurs, analyzing what went wrong helps organizations prevent similar scenarios.
- Raising awareness: Customers become more alert when they hear about actual fraud rather than abstract warnings.
- Driving policy changes: Regulators and governments often refine guidelines after major incidents, such as the RBI (Reserve Bank of India) mandating fraud helplines in India after rising UPI scams.
- Building resilience: Businesses and customers alike become better prepared when they understand the patterns of real fraud attempts.

13.1.2 How case studies help bridge theory and practice

Cybersecurity education often focuses on principles such as "never share your password" or "keep systems updated." However, case studies demonstrate how these principles fail in practice when ignored.

- For example, the Bangladesh Bank heist (2016) showed how weak internal controls in SWIFT (Society for Worldwide Interbank Financial Telecommunication) messaging systems could result in losses of millions.
- The Target breach (2013) highlighted the risks of neglecting vendor security.
- The Cosmos Bank hack (2018) in India demonstrated how malware in ATM servers can compromise entire payment networks.

By linking theoretical safeguards with practical failures, case studies transform cybersecurity from abstract rules into lived realities.

13.1.3 Common threads across case studies

Though each incident may differ in scale, geography, or sector, certain recurring themes emerge:

1. Human error
    - The weakest link is often human behavior; employees clicking on phishing emails, customers falling for fake links, or staff overlooking security warnings.
2. Communication gaps
    - Customers and even employees are sometimes unaware of protocols. Many victims later admit they did not know how to report fraud or recognize suspicious activity.
3. Lack of vigilance
    - Attackers exploit complacency. Simple steps such as updating systems, monitoring transactions, or verifying domains could prevent several high-profile frauds.

These threads emphasize that cybersecurity is not just about technology but about people, processes, and culture.

13.2 Looking ahead

This chapter presents a series of notable real-world case studies from banking, e-commerce, telecom, digital payments, and global cyber incidents. Each case not only highlights how the fraud or breach occurred but also extracts "lessons learned" that customers, businesses, and regulators must apply. By studying them, readers will see how theory translates into practice and how awareness, vigilance, and shared responsibility can turn lessons from past failures into stronger defenses for the future. Most breaches share underlying issues of human error, poor communication, and lack of vigilance, as depicted in Figure 13.1.

13.2.1 Case study 1: the Bangladesh Bank heist (2016)

In February 2016, one of the most audacious cyberattacks in history targeted the Bangladesh Bank, the central bank of Bangladesh. Hackers infiltrated the bank's systems and sent fraudulent SWIFT messages to transfer nearly $951 million from its account at the Federal Reserve Bank of New York.

- Out of this, $81 million was successfully stolen and laundered through casinos in the Philippines.
- The attackers exploited weak internal security, including the absence of firewalls and outdated systems.
- A spelling error ("fandation" instead of "foundation") in one of the transfer requests alerted Deutsche Bank, stopping a portion of the fraud.

Lesson learned

- Insider vigilance is critical: employees must be trained to spot anomalies in transactions.
- Layered authentication and monitoring are essential when dealing with high-value financial transfers.
- Even central banks are not immune; trust in systems must be supported by continuous audits.

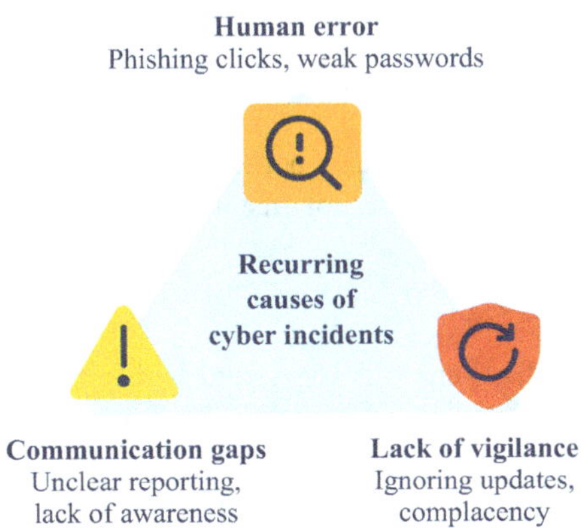

Figure 13.1 Common threads in cybersecurity incidents

Lesson learned

- Out of this, $81 million was successfully stolen and laundered through casinos in the Philippines.
- The attackers exploited weak internal security, including the absence of firewalls and outdated systems.
- A spelling error ("fandation" instead of "foundation") in one of the transfer requests alerted Deutsche Bank, stopping a portion of the fraud.

13.2.2 Case study 2: Punjab National Bank (PNB) scam (India, 2018)

In early 2018, India witnessed one of its largest-ever banking frauds involving Punjab National Bank (PNB). The scam, valued at nearly ₹11,400 crore (approx. $1.8 billion), was carried out by diamond merchants Nirav Modi and Mehul Choksi.

- Internal controls are nonnegotiable: Frauds of this scale usually involve insiders exploiting loopholes.
- Regulatory oversight must be proactive: Periodic audits could have flagged unusual patterns.
- Trust cannot be blind; systems need verification at every step.

Lesson learned

- They fraudulently obtained Letters of Undertaking (LoUs) from PNB officials without proper collateral.
- The fraud went undetected for several years due to collusion with insiders and weak regulatory oversight.
- Other Indian banks honored the fake LoUs, amplifying the loss.

13.2.3 Case study 3: Cosmos Bank cyber attack (India, 2018)

In August 2018, Cosmos Cooperative Bank in Pune, one of India's oldest cooperative banks, suffered a cyberattack that resulted in losses of nearly ₹94 crore (approx. $13.5 million).

- Real-time monitoring of payment systems is crucial. Malware can remain undetected unless strong detection mechanisms are in place.
- Global coordination is required, as cyber fraud often spans multiple geographies.
- Cooperative and smaller banks, not just large commercial ones, are equally vulnerable.

Lesson learned

- Attackers infiltrated the bank's ATM switch system using malware.
- Fraudulent transactions were executed in 28 countries simultaneously, using cloned debit cards.
- Additionally, funds were siphoned via SWIFT transfers to a bank in Hong Kong.

13.2.4 Case study 4: Yes Bank phishing case (India, 2020)

In 2020, customers of Yes Bank became targets of a phishing campaign. Fraudsters sent emails and SMS messages pretending to be official bank communication.

- Customer communication clarity is essential: banks must proactively warn customers against such fraud.
- Two-way awareness: while banks secure their platforms, customers must also verify the authenticity of communications.
- Continuous anti-phishing education and in-app alerts help prevent such incidents.

Lesson learned

- Customers were told that their accounts would be blocked unless they updated their Know Your Customer (KYC) details through a link.
- The link led to fake websites designed to steal login credentials, card numbers, and OTPs.
- Several customers fell victim, resulting in financial losses and reputational damage to the bank.

13.2.5 Synthesis of lessons from banking case studies

Across these incidents, the following insights emerge:

1. Technology alone cannot stop fraud; insider vigilance and customer awareness are equally important.
2. Internal controls and regulatory oversight must be enforced strictly to prevent long-running fraud.
3. Global and cross-industry collaboration is essential since cybercriminals operate without borders.
4. Customer-facing awareness campaigns (like "Never click on links for KYC updates") reduce phishing success rates.

13.3 E-commerce and consumer fraud case studies

E-commerce platforms have transformed global retail, offering speed, convenience, and wide accessibility. However, the very features that attract customers—digital payments, online listings, and remote transactions—are also exploited by fraudsters. This section highlights three notable consumer fraud cases and the lessons that organizations and customers must learn.

13.3.1 Case study 1: Amazon gift card scam (global, 2020–2021)

Between 2020 and 2021, Amazon customers worldwide were targeted by fraudsters posing as Amazon representatives. Victims typically received a phone call or email claiming:

- A problem with their Amazon order, Prime subscription, or payment.
- A request to resolve the issue by purchasing Amazon gift cards and sharing the codes as "verification."
- Fraudsters then redeemed or resold the gift cards for profit.

The US Federal Trade Commission (FTC) reported that in 2021 alone, consumers lost $148 million to gift card scams, with Amazon being the most commonly mentioned brand. Elderly customers were disproportionately targeted due to their trust in phone-based instructions.

Lesson learned

- Customers must be educated that legitimate companies never ask for payment via gift cards.
- Awareness campaigns should specifically warn about fake support calls and refund scams.
- Platforms like Amazon should integrate stronger fraud detection alerts and customer verification mechanisms to prevent exploitation.

13.3.2 Case study 2: Flipkart Big Billion Sale fraud (India, 2019)

During the Flipkart Big Billion Days sale in 2019, multiple customers reported being defrauded by fraudulent sellers.

- Some listings advertised heavily discounted products (such as smartphones or electronics) that were never delivered.
- In other cases, customers received counterfeit or substandard products.
- Fraudsters exploited the surge in festive-season shopping, knowing customers were attracted by limited-time deals.

The incidents created social media uproar, forcing Flipkart to suspend several seller accounts and issue refunds to affected customers.

Lesson learned

- Stronger seller verification is critical during high-volume sales. Platforms must screen merchants for legitimacy.
- Customer trust depends on swift refunds and grievance redressal mechanisms.
- Seasonal spikes in shopping must be accompanied by enhanced fraud monitoring.

13.3.3 Case study 3: eBay phishing scams (global, ongoing)

Since its early days, eBay has been a target of phishing scams where fraudsters exploit its auction-based model.

- Attackers send fake emails to customers, claiming issues with their bids, payments, or shipping.
- These emails redirect victims to spoofed websites that closely resemble eBay's official site.

- Customers, believing the sites to be genuine, enter their login credentials or payment details, which are then stolen.

In many cases, scammers also trick customers into completing payments outside eBay's secure system (through wire transfers or PayPal requests), bypassing eBay's buyer protection program.

Lesson learned

- Platforms must strengthen secure payment gateways and discourage off-platform transactions.
- Customers should be trained to recognize official eBay communications and verify URLs.
- Continuous anti-phishing campaigns are necessary to reduce long-term fraud risks.

13.3.4 Synthesis of lessons from e-commerce case studies

Across these consumer frauds, certain lessons are clear

1. **Education is the first shield**: Customers must be reminded that no genuine company asks for gift cards or sensitive data.
2. **Seller and listing verification**: Platforms must implement robust mechanisms to verify sellers, especially during peak sales.
3. **Payment security**: Secure, on-platform payment systems should always be promoted; off-platform payments should be discouraged.
4. **Quick redressal builds trust**: Refunds, account suspensions, and visible corrective action reassure customers and preserve brand credibility.

The comparative overview in Figure 13.2 presents a compact summary of four major fraud incidents, their methods, losses, and key lessons for banks and customers. These cases reveal recurring patterns in methods, financial impact, and lessons on vigilance, controls, and customer communication.

Case	Method	Loss	Lesson learned
Bangladesh bank heist	Fraudulent swift	$81 m stolen	Insider vigilance
PNB scam	Fake LoUs	₹11,400 crore scam	Internal controls
Cosmos bank cyber	ATM switch malware	₹94 crore stolen	Payment monitoring
Yes bank phishing	Phishing KYC emails	Customer losses	Clear communication

Figure 13.2 Banking and financial sector case studies

13.4 Telecom and digital payments case studies

The telecom and digital payments ecosystem has expanded rapidly over the past decade, enabling faster communication and seamless financial transactions. However, these very conveniences have also opened new avenues for fraudsters. Telecom identity theft and digital payment scams are some of the fastest-growing forms of consumer fraud. Below are three notable cases and the lessons they provide.

13.4.1 Case study 1: Jio and Airtel SIM swap fraud (India, 2019)

In 2019, several incidents of **SIM swap fraud** were reported across India, targeting customers of major telecom providers like Jio and Airtel.
Modus operandi

- Fraudsters acquired customer details (name, phone number, ID proofs) through phishing, data leaks, or social engineering.
- Using fake IDs, they convinced telecom service providers to issue duplicate SIM cards.
- Once the original SIM was deactivated, all OTPs for online banking, UPI, or card transactions were routed to the fraudsters.
- Victims often realized too late, when their phones lost connectivity, and their bank accounts had already been drained.

Lesson learned

- Stronger telecom KYC and SIM issuance processes are critical to prevent fraudulent duplications.
- Customers must be alerted immediately via multiple channels (email, SMS to alternate number) before SIM swaps are activated.
- Telecom operators need to coordinate with banks to flag sudden SIM reactivations followed by large transactions.

13.4.2 Case study 2: UPI fraud in OLX transactions (India, 2022)

Unified Payments Interface (UPI) has revolutionized digital payments in India, but fraudsters have exploited its widespread adoption. A common fraud pattern in 2022 emerged on **online marketplaces like OLX**.
Modus operandi

- Fraudsters posed as buyers interested in products listed on OLX.
- They sent victims a "payment request" link, claiming it was to transfer money for the purchase.
- Unaware that entering a UPI PIN is only required for sending, not receiving money, victims entered their PIN.
- Instead of receiving funds, their bank accounts were debited.

Lesson learned

- Apps must display clearer in-app warnings, e.g., "Do not enter UPI PIN to receive money."
- Awareness campaigns like National Payments Corporation of India's (NPCI) *"UPI Chalega"* are essential to educate users about correct UPI practices.
- Customers should double-check requests before approving transactions.

13.4.3 Case study 3: PayPal phishing campaigns (global, ongoing)

PayPal, one of the world's largest online payment platforms, has been a long-time target for **phishing attacks**.

Modus operandi

- Fraudsters send emails imitating PayPal's official communication, often claiming:
  - "Your account has been suspended."
  - "We detected suspicious activity. Verify now."
- The links lead to spoofed websites designed to steal login credentials and credit card details.
- Victims who entered their credentials often had their accounts compromised and linked cards misused.

Lesson learned

- Multi-layer customer awareness is crucial: customers must learn to verify sender addresses, check URLs, and avoid acting on urgency-driven messages.
- Platforms like PayPal must invest in advanced email authentication (DMARC—Domain-based Message Authentication, Reporting, and Conformance; SPF—Sender Policy Framework; DKIM—DomainKeys Identified Mail) to reduce spoofing.
- Anti-phishing training, coupled with browser and app warnings, reduces the success rates of such attacks.

13.4.4 Synthesis of lessons from telecom and payment case studies

From these incidents, several insights emerge:

1. Telecom security is linked to financial security; SIM swaps directly enable banking fraud.
2. Clarity in customer communication saves money; simple warnings in UPI apps could have prevented many scams.
3. Phishing is persistent and global; platforms must continuously update their fraud detection and awareness measures.
4. Collaboration between telecom operators, banks, and regulators is essential for reducing cross-industry fraud.

Telecom and digital payments case studies–comparative overview

Case	Scam method	Victim impact	Lesson learned
Jio and airtel SIM swap	Fake IDs used to obtain SIM duplicates	Loss of banking access	Stronger telecom KYC
OLX UPI fraud	Fake UPI 'payment requests'	Unauthorized debits	Clearer in-app warnings
PayPal phishing	Phishing emails imitating PayPal	Credentials stolen, payment misuse	Multi-layer customer awareness

Figure 13.3 Telecom and digital payments case studies

The comparative overview provides the scam methods, victim impacts, and lessons learned from SIM swap, UPI fraud, and PayPal phishing incidents. As shown in Figure 13.3, telecom and digital payment frauds like SIM swap, UPI scams, and PayPal phishing reveal critical lessons on KYC, in-app warnings, and layered customer awareness.

13.5 Global cyber incidents

While national case studies highlight localized vulnerabilities, global cyber incidents reveal the scale and cross-border impact of cyberattacks. From massive data breaches to ransomware disrupting critical services, these events have reshaped cybersecurity policies worldwide. Below are five notable global incidents that provide lasting lessons.

13.5.1 Case study 1: Equifax data breach (USA, 2017)

In September 2017, Equifax, one of the largest credit reporting agencies in the US, disclosed a data breach that exposed the personal information of 147 million people.

Details

- Attackers exploited an unpatched vulnerability in Apache Struts, a widely used web application framework.
- The compromised data included names, Social Security numbers, birth dates, addresses, and driver's license numbers.
- Equifax faced lawsuits, reputational damage, and a $700 million settlement with US regulators.

Lesson learned

- Timely patching is critical; delays in addressing known vulnerabilities can lead to catastrophic breaches.
- Transparent and prompt disclosure of breaches builds trust, whereas delays amplify reputational harm.
- Large organizations must maintain continuous vulnerability scanning and patch management.

13.5.2 Case study 2: British Airways breach (UK, 2018)

In 2018, British Airways (BA) experienced a cyberattack that compromised 500,000 customer records.

Details

- Hackers injected malicious code into BA's website and mobile app, redirecting customers to a fraudulent payment page.
- Payment details, including credit card numbers, CVV codes, and travel booking information, were stolen.
- The UK Information Commissioner's Office (ICO) fined BA £20 million under GDPR regulations.

Lesson learned

- Website script monitoring is essential, as attackers often insert malicious code into third-party scripts.
- Real-time detection tools (e.g., Content Security Policy violation reports) help identify unauthorized modifications.
- Regulatory compliance (e.g., GDPR) requires organizations to secure customer data proactively.

13.5.3 Case study 3: Target data breach (USA, 2013)

In late 2013, US retailer Target suffered a major data breach affecting 40 million credit and debit card records and 70 million personal records.

Details

- Attackers infiltrated Target's systems through a third-party HVAC (Heating, Ventilation, and Air Conditioning) vendor, which had weak security controls.
- Malware was installed on Target's point-of-sale (POS) systems, enabling attackers to steal card data during transactions.
- The breach cost Target over $200 million in settlements and upgrades.

Lesson learned

- Third-party/vendor risk management is critical. Even small vendors can serve as gateways for large breaches.
- Organizations must monitor vendor access, enforce least-privilege principles, and implement supply chain security audits.

- Segmentation of networks can prevent vendor access from reaching sensitive systems.

13.5.4 Case study 4: Colonial Pipeline ransomware attack (USA, 2021)

In May 2021, **Colonial Pipeline**, the largest fuel pipeline operator in the US, was hit by a ransomware attack.
Details

- The DarkSide ransomware group gained access through a compromised VPN account without multi-factor authentication.
- Operations were shut down, leading to fuel shortages across the US East Coast.
- Colonial paid a ransom of $4.4 million, part of which was later recovered by US authorities.

Lesson learned

- Critical infrastructure resilience must be prioritized, as cyberattacks on utilities can disrupt national economies.
- Stronger authentication (e.g., MFA) could have prevented the breach.
- Incident response and disaster recovery plans must be tested regularly.

13.5.5 Case study 5: WannaCry ransomware attack (global, 2017)

In May 2017, the WannaCry ransomware attack spread rapidly across the globe, infecting more than 200,000 computers in 150 countries.
Details

- The malware exploited a Windows vulnerability known as EternalBlue, allegedly developed by the NSA (National Security Agency) and leaked by hackers.
- Victims included hospitals (e.g., the UK's National Health Service), transport systems, and businesses.
- Hospitals were forced to cancel appointments and operations due to locked systems.

Lesson learned

- Regular updates and backups are essential to minimize ransomware damage.
- Outdated systems (like old Windows machines in hospitals) create systemic risks.
- Global cooperation is needed, as ransomware campaigns ignore geographic boundaries.

13.5.6 Synthesis of lessons from global incidents

These global incidents underline critical points

1. Patching and updates must be treated as high-priority operations.
2. Third-party and vendor risks can no longer be overlooked.

Year	Organization/ Incident	Impact	Lesson learned
2013	Target	40M card details, 70M personal records stolen	Third-party/ vendor risk management
2017	Equifax data breach	147 million records exposed	Timely patching and disclosure
2017	WannaCry	Hospitals and businesses affected	Importance of regular updates and backups
2018	British airways	400,000 payment details compromised	Website script monitoring
2021	Colonial pipeline ransomware	Pipeline operations shut down	Critical infrastructure resilience

Figure 13.4 Global cyber incidents—comparative overview

3. Monitoring digital assets in real time (websites, payment systems, apps) is essential.
4. Critical infrastructure needs stronger resilience, especially energy, healthcare, and transport.
5. Backups and recovery plans are as important as prevention strategies.

The key takeaways from major international breaches and ransomware attacks between 2013 and 2021 are illustrated in Figure 13.4, where the global cyber incidents highlight recurring lessons on patching, vendor risk, monitoring, resilience, and backups.

13.6 Indian context—government and public sector case studies

India's push toward digitization has created a vast ecosystem of government-led digital services, from Aadhaar-based identity systems to Indian Railway Catering and Tourism Corporation's (IRCTC) online ticketing. While these initiatives offer efficiency and convenience, they also attract cybercriminals looking to exploit large databases and citizen-facing platforms. The following cases highlight the risks and lessons in the public sector.

13.6.1 Case study 1: Aadhaar data leaks (India, multiple instances)

The Aadhaar system, managed by the Unique Identification Authority of India (UIDAI), is the world's largest biometric identity program, covering over 1.3 billion residents. However, multiple instances of data leaks have raised concerns over privacy and security.

Details

- In 2018, reports indicated that Aadhaar numbers and demographic details of millions were accessible online through poorly secured government portals and third-party websites.
- Journalists from *The Tribune* revealed that Aadhaar data was allegedly being sold for as little as ₹500 by unauthorized agents.
- While UIDAI denied large-scale breaches, several cases of unregulated access and storage vulnerabilities were documented.

Impact

- Exposure of Aadhaar-linked details (names, addresses, bank account numbers) heightened risks of identity theft and financial fraud.
- Citizens lost trust in government data handling, prompting debates around data protection laws.

Lesson learned

- Secure storage and regulated access to sensitive citizen data are paramount.
- Government agencies must enforce strict access controls, encryption, and audit trails.
- Stronger data protection legislation is necessary to safeguard citizens' identities.

13.6.2 Case study 2: Indian railways e-ticketing phishing (2019)

The IRCTC, which handles millions of online bookings daily, became a target of phishing attacks in 2019.

Details

- Fraudsters created fake websites resembling IRCTC's official portal and circulated their links via SMS and email.
- Unsuspecting passengers entered login credentials, personal information, and even payment card details into these spoofed sites.
- Several passengers reported financial losses, and IRCTC had to issue public warnings.

Impact

- Compromised user accounts were exploited for ticket fraud and financial theft.

- The phishing campaigns tarnished IRCTC's reputation, forcing it to strengthen customer awareness initiatives.

Lesson learned

- Stronger domain protection is essential to prevent spoofing and phishing.
- Official portals must adopt measures like EV SSL certificates, DNS security, and DMARC policies.
- Regular customer advisories should warn passengers to use only the official IRCTC website or mobile app.

13.6.3 Synthesis of lessons from Indian public sector cases

1. Public trust depends on secure data handling; government databases must adopt the same or higher standards as private enterprises.
2. Citizen-facing platforms are high-value phishing targets; domain protection and customer education are crucial.
3. Regulatory and legislative safeguards (such as a comprehensive Data Protection Act) are vital to ensure accountability.

Aadhaar data leaks and IRCTC phishing scams highlight the need for secure storage, regulated access, and stronger domain protection, as illustrated in Figure 13.5.

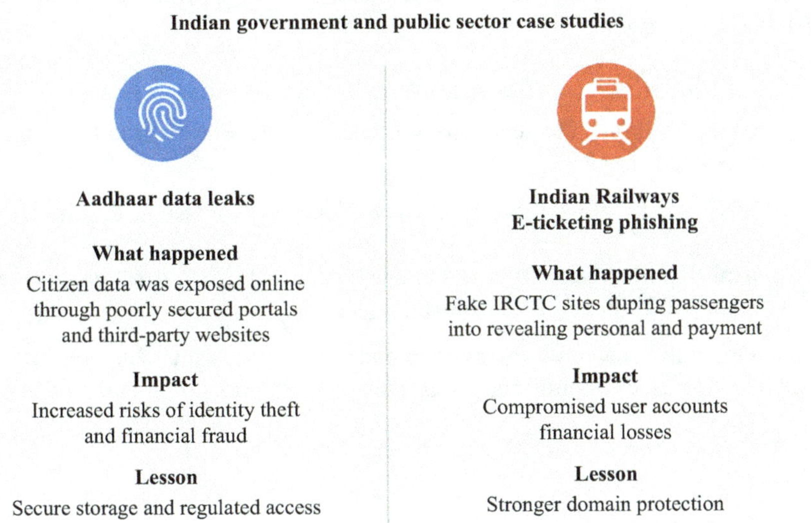

Figure 13.5 Indian government and public sector case studies

13.7 Lessons learned

The review of banking, e-commerce, telecom, digital payments, global cyber incidents, and Indian public sector case studies highlights several common themes that cut across geographies and industries. While the methods and scale of attacks differ, the lessons remain consistent and universally relevant.

13.7.1 Human error is the biggest vulnerability

Despite advancements in encryption, firewalls, and AI-driven fraud detection, the weakest link remains human behavior.

- Employees overlooking suspicious transactions (Bangladesh Bank heist).
- Customers entering UPI PINs while "receiving" money (OLX fraud).
- Passengers trusting spoofed websites (IRCTC phishing).

Lesson: Building a "human firewall" through training, awareness campaigns, and habit-building is as important as deploying cutting-edge technology.

13.7.2 Communication gaps increase fraud success

Fraudsters exploit unclear or inconsistent communication between organizations and their customers.

- Yes Bank phishing exploited vague KYC awareness.
- Amazon gift card scams succeeded because customers did not know that gift cards are never legitimate payment requests.

Lesson: Clear, jargon-free, and repetitive messaging across SMS, apps, and media channels helps customers instantly recognize fraud.

13.7.3 Vigilance + technology = effective defense

Neither vigilance alone nor technology alone can prevent all fraud. A balanced combination is essential.

- The PNB scam showed that internal vigilance was missing, despite banking controls.
- Colonial Pipeline ransomware demonstrated that MFA (technology) could have stopped an attack if enforced.

Lesson: Organizations must integrate human vigilance with technological safeguards like AI-based monitoring, patch management, and strong authentication.

13.7.4 The shared responsibility model is critical

Cybersecurity is not the sole responsibility of banks, telecom providers, or governments; it is shared.

- Organizations must secure platforms, monitor vendors, and communicate clearly.

- Customers must practice safe habits and report suspicious activity quickly.
- Regulators must enforce accountability and provide robust reporting mechanisms.

Lesson: When all three stakeholders—organizations, regulators, and customers—work in tandem, fraud rates decline significantly.

13.7.5 Customer empowerment through awareness reduces losses

Ultimately, customers form the first line of defense. In nearly every case study, losses could have been reduced or prevented had customers been more aware.

- UPI awareness campaigns ("UPI Chalega") cut down transaction fraud.
- RBI's "RBI Kehta Hai" improved banking vigilance.
- FTC warnings on gift card scams reduced victimization rates.

Lesson: Awareness is not a one-time event but a continuous process. Empowered customers make informed decisions and reduce overall systemic risk.

Human error, communication gaps, vigilance with technology, shared responsibility, and customer awareness form the foundation of effective cybersecurity defense as portrayed in Figure 13.6.

13.8 Closing thoughts

The lessons from real-world cyber incidents reinforce a simple truth: cybersecurity is not only about protecting systems, but it is also about protecting people. While technology evolves, fraudsters will always seek to exploit human psychology, communication gaps, and complacency. The future of safer digital ecosystems lies in embedding awareness, responsibility, and vigilance into everyday practices.

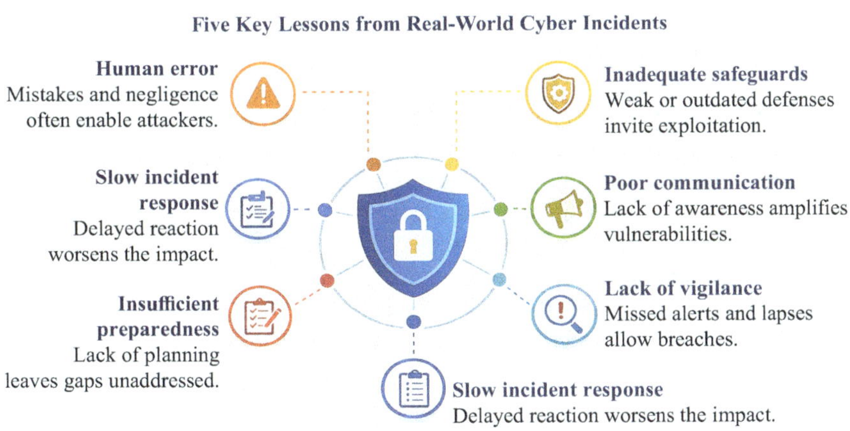

Figure 13.6 Five key lessons from real-world cyber incidents

Key points to remember

- **Case studies bridge theory and practice**: they show how real-world failures happen when principles like patching, vigilance, or communication are ignored.
- **The Bangladesh Bank heist (2016)** demonstrated how weak internal controls and a lack of layered authentication can lead to multimillion-dollar frauds.
- **The PNB scam (2018)** highlighted that insider collusion and poor regulatory oversight can sustain large frauds for years.
- **The Cosmos Bank attack (2018)** proved that even cooperative banks are vulnerable when ATM and SWIFT systems lack real-time monitoring.
- **The Yes Bank phishing case (2020)** showed how vague customer communication creates room for social engineering fraud.
- **Amazon gift card scams (2020–21)** revealed that customers must be educated that no legitimate firm ever demands payment via gift cards.
- **Flipkart's Big Billion Sale fraud (2019)** emphasized the need for stronger seller verification and robust refund mechanisms.
- **eBay phishing scams** underscored the importance of secure on-platform payments and discouraging off-platform transactions.
- **SIM swap fraud in India (2019)** showed the direct link between telecom identity theft and financial fraud.
- **UPI fraud on OLX (2022)** highlighted the importance of clear in-app warnings ("Do not enter UPI PIN to receive money").
- **PayPal phishing campaigns** illustrated how global platforms must combine email authentication, awareness, and browser warnings to reduce risks.
- **The Equifax breach (2017)** proved that delays in patching known vulnerabilities can expose millions of personal records.
- **The British Airways breach (2018)** emphasized the need for script monitoring and compliance under GDPR.
- **The Target breach (2013)** revealed how third-party vendors can serve as weak links in otherwise strong organizations.
- **The Colonial Pipeline ransomware (2021)** demonstrated the national-level risks of compromised critical infrastructure.
- **The WannaCry ransomware (2017)** showed that outdated systems without backups can cripple hospitals and businesses globally.
- **Aadhaar data leaks** reinforced the need for secure storage, encryption, and regulated access to sensitive citizen data.
- **IRCTC phishing (2019)** proved that government-facing platforms are high-value phishing targets requiring stronger domain protection.
- **Human error remains the top vulnerability**: from clicking fake links to overlooking red flags, people are the weakest link.
- **Shared responsibility is nonnegotiable**: regulators, organizations, and customers must work together, as vigilance plus technology is the only sustainable defense.

Questions (Try answering them yourself)

1. Why is studying real-world cyber incidents essential for bridging the gap between theory and practice in cybersecurity?
2. Analyze the Bangladesh Bank heist (2016). What key failures allowed the fraud to succeed, and what lessons can central banks learn?
3. Discuss how insider collusion contributed to the PNB scam (2018). What measures could have detected it earlier?
4. Evaluate the Cosmos Bank cyberattack (2018). How did the attackers exploit system vulnerabilities, and what controls could have stopped them?
5. Explain how phishing emails in the Yes Bank case (2020) highlight the importance of customer communication clarity.
6. Examine the Amazon gift card scam (2020–2021). Why were elderly customers particularly vulnerable?
7. Assess Flipkart's Big Billion Sale fraud (2019). What role does seller verification play in maintaining e-commerce trust?
8. Describe how eBay phishing scams exploit auction-based systems. What safeguards can platforms adopt to prevent them?
9. What does the SIM swap fraud (2019) reveal about the link between telecom security and financial fraud?
10. Using the OLX UPI fraud (2022), explain why app-based warnings are vital for preventing payment scams.
11. How do PayPal phishing campaigns demonstrate the need for multi-layered customer awareness?
12. Discuss the Equifax data breach (2017). How did patching delays escalate their impact?
13. Analyze the British Airways breach (2018). What role did third-party scripts play in compromising customer data?
14. Using the Target breach (2013), explain how vendor risk management is a critical part of a cybersecurity strategy.
15. Assess the Colonial Pipeline ransomware attack (2021). How did it impact critical infrastructure, and what lessons apply to India?
16. Explain how the WannaCry ransomware attack (2017) revealed systemic risks of outdated operating systems.
17. What do Aadhaar data leak cases reveal about challenges in securing large-scale citizen databases?
18. Discuss the IRCTC phishing case (2019). How does domain protection strengthen consumer trust in government services?
19. Across all case studies, identify three common threads (human error, communication gaps, lack of vigilance). Which do you consider the most critical, and why?
20. Suggest a framework combining vigilance, technology, and customer empowerment that could reduce the recurrence of such incidents in the future.

Objective questions

1. In the Bangladesh Bank heist (2016), how much money was successfully stolen?
   (a) $951 million
   (b) $500 million
   (c) $81 million
   (d) $1 billion
2. The Punjab National Bank scam (2018) primarily involved fraudulent:
   (a) ATM withdrawals
   (b) Letters of Undertaking (LoUs)
   (c) UPI transactions
   (d) Credit card cloning
3. The Cosmos Bank attack (2018) was executed using:
   (a) Malware in ATM switch system
   (b) Insider collusion
   (c) Phishing emails
   (d) Loan fraud
4. Which bank's customers were targeted in a KYC phishing campaign in 2020?
   (a) HDFC Bank
   (b) Yes Bank
   (c) ICICI Bank
   (d) Axis Bank
5. In the Amazon gift card scam (2020–2021), fraudsters typically asked victims to:
   (a) Share debit card details
   (b) Purchase gift cards and share codes
   (c) Update bank KYC online
   (d) Transfer funds via UPI
6. Flipkart's Big Billion Sale fraud (2019) was caused by:
   (a) Fake seller listings
   (b) Credit card cloning
   (c) Delivery agents stealing goods
   (d) Mobile app malware
7. eBay phishing scams often trick customers into:
   (a) Paying outside the platform
   (b) Downloading malicious apps
   (c) Buying counterfeit goods
   (d) Entering OTPs in fake SMS

8. SIM swap fraud enables attackers to:
   (a) Gain OTPs for online transactions
   (b) Clone debit cards
   (c) Hack payment gateways
   (d) Compromise Wi-Fi networks

9. In OLX UPI fraud (2022), customers lost money because they:
   (a) Shared their OTPs
   (b) Entered UPI PIN while "receiving" money
   (c) Clicked on shortened URLs
   (d) Downloaded fake apps

10. PayPal phishing campaigns often send:
   (a) SMS alerts
   (b) Fake refund or account suspension emails
   (c) OTP request calls
   (d) Push notifications in apps

11. The Equifax breach (2017) was caused by:
   (a) Weak passwords
   (b) Phishing attack
   (c) Unpatched Apache Struts vulnerability
   (d) SIM swap

12. The British Airways breach (2018) was traced to:
   (a) Fake IRCTC websites
   (b) Malicious code injection in website scripts
   (c) Rogue employees
   (d) Compromised ATMs

13. The Target breach (2013) originated from:
   (a) Malware in payment apps
   (b) Third-party HVAC vendor compromise
   (c) Customers oversharing online
   (d) Gift card scams

14. Colonial Pipeline (2021) was disrupted by:
   (a) Phishing attack
   (b) Ransomware through VPN access
   (c) Insider fraud
   (d) POS malware

15. WannaCry ransomware (2017) spread by exploiting:
   (a) Outdated Windows vulnerability (EternalBlue)
   (b) Cloud misconfiguration
   (c) SIM card duplication
   (d) DNS hijacking

16. Aadhaar data leaks mainly exposed:
    (a) Bank transaction details
    (b) Biometric and demographic records
    (c) Passwords and PINs
    (d) ATM PIN codes
17. IRCTC phishing scams tricked passengers into:
    (a) Downloading fake apps
    (b) Entering details on spoofed ticketing websites
    (c) Using public Wi-Fi for booking
    (d) Sharing OTPs over calls
18. Which of the following is a common thread across most incidents?
    (a) Vendor risk only
    (b) Human error, communication gaps, vigilance issues
    (c) Outdated hardware alone
    (d) Lack of cloud storage
19. Which regulatory framework fined British Airways £20 million?
    (a) RBI Act
    (b) GDPR
    (c) PCI DSS
    (d) CCPA
20. Which phrase best summarizes the collective lesson from these case studies?
    (a) Prevention is impossible
    (b) Shared responsibility is critical
    (c) Customers are solely responsible
    (d) Technology is enough

Answer key

1. c
2. b
3. a
4. b
5. b
6. a
7. a
8. a
9. b
10. b
11. c
12. b
13. b
14. b
15. a

16. b
17. b
18. b
19. b
20. b

Further reading

[1] BBC News. *Bangladesh Bank Hit by $81m Hack*. BBC; 2016.

[2] Federal Reserve Bank of New York. *Statement on Bangladesh Bank Cyber Incident*. FRBNY; 2016.

[3] Reserve Bank of India. *Report on Punjab National Bank Fraud*. RBI; 2018.

[4] Central Bureau of Investigation. *Investigation into Nirav Modi and Mehul Choksi Case*. CBI; 2018.

[5] Cosmos Bank. *Press Release on Cyberattack*. Pune: Cosmos Cooperative Bank; 2018.

[6] National Payments Corporation of India. *Annual Report on Fraud Trends*. NPCI; 2019.

[7] CERT-In. *Public Advisory on Phishing Attacks Against Yes Bank Customers*. CERT-In; 2020.

[8] Federal Trade Commission. *Consumer Sentinel Network Data Book*. FTC; 2021.

[9] Amazon. *Security Advisory on Gift Card Scams*. Amazon; 2021.

[10] Flipkart. *Statement on Fraudulent Seller Activities during Big Billion Days sale*. Flipkart; 2019.

[11] eBay. *Trust and Safety Report on Phishing Activities*. eBay; 2020.

[12] Telecom Regulatory Authority of India. *Advisory on SIM Swap Frauds*. TRAI; 2019.

[13] National Payments Corporation of India. *UPI Safety Awareness Campaign Report*. NPCI; 2022.

[14] PayPal. *Annual Risk and Compliance Report*. PayPal; 2020.

[15] Equifax. *Settlement Press Release on 2017 Data Breach*. Equifax; 2019.

[16] Information Commissioner's Office (UK). *Penalty Notice to British Airways under GDPR*. ICO; 2020.

[17] Target Corporation. *Breach Disclosure Statement*. Target; 2014.

[18] US Department of Justice. *Colonial Pipeline Ransomware Investigation Report*. DOJ; 2021.

[19] Europol. *Global Impact Assessment of WannaCry Ransomware*. Europol; 2017.

[20] Unique Identification Authority of India. *Clarification on Aadhaar Data Leak Reports*. UIDAI; 2018.

Chapter 14
Conclusion

Learning objectives

After reading through the chapter, the reader will gain a clear understanding of

(a) The summary of key lessons learned across all chapters of the book on cybersecurity in banking and finance.
(b) Identifying common themes and recurring vulnerabilities such as human error, communication gaps, and governance lapses.
(c) The open questions that remain unanswered in the current cybersecurity landscape.
(d) Evaluating future research directions in areas like AI, blockchain, RegTech, and quantum-safe cryptography.
(e) Understanding the importance of shared responsibility among regulators, organizations, and customers in fraud prevention.
(f) Connecting theory with real-world practices by linking conceptual knowledge to case studies and examples discussed in earlier chapters.
(g) Exploring further learning resources, including regulatory guidelines, industry reports, and academic courses for continued study.

14.1 Introduction

The journey through this book has highlighted the evolving landscape of cybersecurity in the banking and financial services sector. Starting from the fundamentals of cybersecurity and data protection, to specific domains like internet and mobile banking, and further into complex challenges such as cyber fraud, card fraud, money laundering, social engineering, and social media attacks, the chapters have painted a comprehensive picture of threats, vulnerabilities, and countermeasures. Alongside these challenges, we also explored the transformative role of technologies like artificial intelligence, machine learning, and blockchain in safeguarding banking operations. Real-world case studies reinforced the importance of awareness and vigilance, both at the organizational and customer level, while the focus on customer empowerment demonstrated that security is not only about technology but also about trust, awareness, and resilience.

14.2 Key points to remember

- Cybersecurity in banking is a holistic discipline; it involves technology, processes, regulations, and human behavior.
- Human error remains the most exploited vulnerability, reinforcing the need for awareness at every level.
- Data security measures such as firewalls, authentication, and secure networks form the backbone of digital safety.
- Mobile and internet banking demand specialized attention due to their massive adoption and exposure to phishing, malware, and credential theft.
- Cyber fraud is constantly evolving, requiring proactive fraud risk management, detection, and customer/employee training.
- Debit and credit card frauds exploit social media, phishing, and SIM swap vulnerabilities, making multi-layered defenses critical.
- Money laundering poses systemic risks, requiring integration of anti-money laundering (AML) and cybersecurity practices.
- AI and ML are double-edged; they can both empower fraudsters and help institutions detect and prevent fraud through predictive analytics.
- Blockchain technology offers immutability and transparency, strengthening transaction security in banking ecosystems.
- Social engineering and social media attacks prove that awareness is as important as technology in fraud prevention.
- Customer empowerment campaigns such as India's "RBI Kehta Hai" highlight the importance of simple, accessible communication.
- Case studies show that lessons are best learned from real-world failures, where governance lapses, communication gaps, and a lack of vigilance enabled major frauds.

14.3 Remaining open questions

- Despite significant advancements in cybersecurity frameworks, regulatory compliance, and technological innovations, several pressing questions remain unanswered. These open issues define the direction of upcoming research and policy evolution in banking cybersecurity.
- Balancing security and convenience: How can banks deliver seamless customer experiences without compromising authentication strength or increasing friction?
- AI governance and transparency: As artificial intelligence drives fraud detection and threat analytics, how can we ensure fairness, interpretability, and accountability in automated decisions?
- Data privacy vs. surveillance: What ethical and legal boundaries should exist between proactive monitoring for threats and respecting user privacy?

- Blockchain integration challenges: While blockchain ensures immutability, how can legacy banking systems integrate it without introducing new vulnerabilities?
- Quantum threat preparedness: With quantum computing on the horizon, how can financial institutions transition toward quantum-safe cryptography before current encryption becomes obsolete?
- Human-centric security design: Can cybersecurity awareness training evolve beyond compliance checklists to become behaviorally embedded within employees and customers?
- Cost and accessibility: How can smaller banks and rural financial institutions adopt advanced cybersecurity tools affordably and effectively?
- These questions emphasize that cybersecurity is not merely a technical pursuit; it is a multidisciplinary challenge that spans ethics, economics, psychology, and governance.

14.4 Future research directions

The future of cybersecurity in banking and financial services will be shaped by the convergence of **emerging technologies, evolving threats, and adaptive governance**. Key research and development directions include:

1. **AI and machine learning for adaptive defense:** Development of self-learning algorithms capable of autonomously identifying new attack patterns and reducing false positives in fraud detection.
2. **Quantum-safe cryptography:** Exploration of post-quantum algorithms such as lattice-based, hash-based, and multivariate encryption to secure future financial transactions.
3. **Explainable and ethical AI:** Creating transparent AI models that satisfy regulatory audits while maintaining decision integrity and privacy.
4. **Behavioral biometrics:** Advancing research in keystroke dynamics, gait analysis, and voice recognition to enhance identity verification beyond traditional passwords and PINs.
5. **Cyber resilience frameworks:** Moving beyond prevention to resilience, developing models that ensure quick recovery and continuity after cyber incidents.
6. **Integration of blockchain and RegTech:** Combining distributed ledger technology with regulatory technology for real-time compliance monitoring and anomaly detection.
7. **Cross-border collaboration:** Studying frameworks for international cooperation between financial regulators, fintech firms, and cybersecurity agencies to address global threats like money laundering and cross-border fraud.

Together, these research directions form the foundation for a **next-generation banking security ecosystem**, one that is intelligent, resilient, and transparent.

14.5 Further learning

For readers seeking to deepen their understanding, the following resources provide valuable knowledge across academic, regulatory, and practical domains:

Regulatory and policy frameworks

- Reserve Bank of India (RBI): Cyber Security Framework for Banks (2023 Update)
- Financial Action Task Force (FATF): Guidance on Digital Identity and AML
- Basel Committee on Banking Supervision: Operational Risk and Cyber Resilience Guidelines
- European Union GDPR: Data Protection and Compliance Frameworks

Industry reports and insights

- IBM Security: *Cost of a Data Breach Report (2024)*
- Accenture: *Banking Technology Vision*
- Deloitte: *Future of Cyber in Financial Services*
- Verizon: *Data Breach Investigations Report (DBIR)*

Academic and learning resources

- NPTEL Course: *Introduction to Cyber Security*
- Coursera: *AI for Cybersecurity Specialization*
- edX: *Blockchain for Financial Services*
- MIT Open Courseware: *Cybersecurity for Critical Infrastructure*

Professional certifications

- Certified Ethical Hacker (CEH)
- Certified Information Systems Security Professional (CISSP)
- Certified Anti-Money Laundering Specialist (CAMS)
- CompTIA (Computing Technology Industry Association) Security+

These resources will guide learners, professionals, and researchers toward continuous upskilling and staying relevant in an ever-changing cybersecurity landscape.

14.6 Summary

This concluding chapter emphasizes that cybersecurity in banking is not a destination but a continuous journey of adaptation and learning. From phishing scams to blockchain security, from social engineering to quantum-safe cryptography, the field demands vigilance, innovation, and collaboration. The lessons drawn from this book serve as a roadmap for secure, resilient, and trustworthy digital banking ecosystems of the future.

Index

www.ingramcontent.com/pod-product-compliance
Lightning Source LLC
LaVergne TN
LVHW011849200926
848484LV00002B/426